FALLING

THROUGH

CLOUDS

A

STORY

OF

SURVIVAL,

LOVE,

AND

LIABILITY

FALLING THROUGH CLOUDS

DAMIAN FOWLER

ST. MARTIN'S PRESS ⚏ NEW YORK

FALLING THROUGH CLOUDS. Copyright © 2014 by Damian Fowler. All rights reserved. Printed in the United States of America. For information, address St. Martin's Press, 175 Fifth Avenue, New York, N.Y. 10010.

www.stmartins.com

Designed by Anna Gorovoy

Library of Congress Cataloging-in-Publication Data

Fowler, Damian.
    Falling through clouds : a story of survival, love, and liability / by Damian Fowler. — First edition.
        pages cm
    Includes bibliographical references.
    ISBN 978-1-250-02622-4 (hardcover)
    ISBN 978-1-250-02623-1 (e-book)
    1. Pearson, Toby.   2. Pearson, Toby—Family.   3. Aircraft accidents—Minnesota—Grand Marais Region.   4. Aircraft accident victims—Minnesota—Biography.   5. Aircraft accident victims' families—Minnesota—Biography.   6. Children—Wounds and injuries—Treatment—Minnesota.   7. Fathers and daughters—Minnesota.   8. Pearson, Toby—Trials, litigation, etc.   9. Aviation insurance—Law and legislation—Minnesota—Case studies.   I. Title.
    TL553.525.M6F69 2014
    363.12'4092—dc23
    [B]

                                                        2013046592

St. Martin's Press books may be purchased for educational, business, or promotional use. For information on bulk purchases, please contact Macmillan Corporate and Premium Sales Department at 1-800-221-7945, extension 5442, or write specialmarkets@macmillan.com.

First Edition: May 2014

10 9 8 7 6 5 4 3 2 1

For my mum and dad, Judith and Norman

CONTENTS

Aviation in itself is not inherently dangerous. But to an even greater degree than the sea, it is terribly unforgiving of any carelessness, incapacity or neglect.

—CAPTAIN A. G. LAMPLUGH,
BRITISH AVIATION INSURANCE GROUP

The two children were so fond of each other that they always held each other by the hand when they went out together, and when Snow-white said, "We will not leave each other," Rose-red answered, "Never so long as we live."

—JACOB AND WILHELM GRIMM,
"SNOW-WHITE AND ROSE-RED,"
HOUSEHOLD TALES

FALLING THROUGH CLOUDS

WE FELL OUT OF THE SKY

On August 28, 2003, the fog rolled in and enveloped the little harbor town of Grand Marais, Minnesota, on the North Shore of Lake Superior. There was nothing particularly unusual about the changeable weather. Lake Superior—the biggest freshwater lake in the United States—is a vast inland sea that creates a maritime climate for the towns spread along its shoreline. Locals are used to the cooler summers, milder winters, and often foggy conditions.

Still, Carolyn Wall felt nervous as she drove down Gunflint Trail toward the airport in Grand Marais. Through the windshield of her car, she could see the heavy clouds all the way to the horizon, a thick, white blanket draped over the treetops of the surrounding Superior National Forest. It wasn't a good morning to fly, but Carolyn hoped that there'd be a break in the weather closer to the airport, where she was to meet her husband, Charlie Erickson, who was flying his own six-seater plane in from Duluth, a city one hundred miles to the southwest but a short thirty-minute hop by air. Charlie was carrying Carolyn's younger sister, Kathryn, and Kathryn's little girls, four-year-old Grace and three-year-old Lily.

The day before, the weather had been picture-perfect. Carolyn had sat on the porch at the family cabin on Saganaga Lake, sipping wine with her father, Jack, whose approaching seventy-second birthday was the occasion for the family gathering. The two of them had gazed in amazement at the orange-red light of Mars reflecting on the dark water of the lake. It was an extraordinary event. That day, the red planet was closer to Earth than it had been in sixty thousand years. To Carolyn, it looked almost as big as the moon, and she wished her sister were there already so she could see this wondrous Martian glimmer. Carolyn would later have cause to think otherwise, but at the time the romance of the distant light on the lake seemed like a blessing.

The cabin on the lake had been in the Wall family for years, and they'd spent many hours stargazing or watching the northern lights. Carolyn and Kathryn's grandfather, Otis John Wall, affectionately known as Gumpy, had built the place in 1934 along with a group of dentists from Saint Paul; they'd nicknamed it Shady Rest on Tooth Acres. Situated on Saganaga Lake, which traverses the Minnesota-Ontario boundary, the cabin was set in the midst of a glorious wilderness of forest and water. Its electrical power came from an outdoor generator, while running water was drawn from the pristine lake. With neither phone lines nor cell-phone reception, it had become a magical escape from daily life for the Wall family.

Growing up, Carolyn, Kathryn, and their brother John spent long summer weekends on the lake. In July or August, the family would load up the station wagon with food, drink, and bed linens and drive up the North Shore, then along the fifty-seven-mile Gunflint Trail to the head of the trail, where fingers of water break up the land mass. From here a boat ride would take them into the international boundary waters—technically no longer the United States—and eventually to their secluded cabin.

Summers on the lake were mostly idyllic. Blue dragonflies zipped busily over the water as swimmers splashed around, occasionally slapping away the biting black flies that pestered them. Sometimes the Walls went hiking through the forest trails, their dogs bounding ahead, excitedly catching the scent of wild animals. Bears, moose, lynx, and wolves all populated the forest. Every now and then, the high, haunting wail of a loon in search of another would punctuate the peace and quiet.

At Saganaga Lake, the wilderness was always on the doorstep. Carolyn was reminded of that when she woke up the day after she had watched Mars shine on the water. The weather had taken a dramatic turn for the worse. Thunderstorms had moved into the area overnight, agitating branches and rippling the water. Over breakfast with her father, she listened to the forecast on the radio, wondering if Charlie had been able to set off that morning.

Carolyn and Charlie had met twelve years before and eventually married—she a pretty thirty-year-old restaurant manager (and aspiring nurse), and he a self-made entrepreneur in his early forties with his own company, UltiMed, which manufactured specialist instruments for the health-care industry. They settled down together in Minneapolis. Although Charlie had older kids from a first marriage, he and Carolyn had no children. As an aunt, Carolyn lavished a lot of love on Grace and Lily, and was especially excited now that her nieces, and her sister, would get to fly in Charlie's plane for the very first time.

When the rain and thunder let up, Carolyn and her dad jumped into their little aluminum fishing boat and chugged across the choppy water—a forty-five-minute trip—to the trailhead where Carolyn had parked her car. Her dad headed back to the cabin to await his birthday guests as Carolyn sped off down Gunflint Trail toward Grand Marais Airport, an hour's drive away.

By the time she arrived it was noon and a thick fog had descended on the airport. It seemed unlikely that anyone could have landed in these conditions, and she could see no sign of Charlie's Beechcraft Baron on the tarmac. Carolyn went inside the modest terminal building to find out if there was any news about the delayed flight. It was empty, but she eventually found Rodney Roy, the airport manager who ran pretty much everything, including air traffic control.

"Have you heard anything from Charlie Erickson?" Carolyn asked.

"We had a radio call asking for clearance to approach, but I haven't heard anything since," replied Roy.

Roy explained that earlier he'd heard a plane fly over the airport, but he could barely see it as it was obscured by the clouds. When he lost contact, Roy had assumed that the pilot had flown either back to Duluth or to another local airport where conditions might have been more favorable for landing. Typically, in such a scenario, a pilot would have informed the air traffic controller (in this case Roy) that he was following a missed approach procedure—a published set of parameters unique to every airport that a pilot must follow after having missed a landing—but Roy had heard nothing after the first approach.

"I heard a plane fly over in the clouds, but I think he left the area," said Roy.

When she heard this, Carolyn turned pale.

"Are you okay?" asked Roy.

"What options would he have had?"

"He probably went back to Duluth."

"Oh, God," said Carolyn. "I don't think he did."

"Why not?" asked Roy.

"He wouldn't have gone back without filing a flight plan," said Carolyn, her mind flooding with panic. Roy was surprised by Carolyn's definitive comment and her startled reaction.

"Well, there's no way he can get in today," he said.

Carolyn rushed into the ladies' room, feeling as if she was going to be sick. She took some deep breaths and then called her mother, Marilyn, in Duluth. Divorced from Jack since the mid-eighties, Marilyn had not planned to visit the lake that weekend. Carolyn called her, wondering if she'd heard any news about the flight. In her heart she hoped they were still on the ground in Duluth, waiting for the weather to clear. But Marilyn said she'd called the airport and they'd left.

"Mom, call a friend," she said. "I don't want to alarm you, but I think you should be with someone."

With that, Carolyn jumped back in the car and drove the fifty-seven miles back along Gunflint Trail. Her mind was racing. She'd have to collect her things, pick up her dad and Kalli, her springer spaniel, and then shut the cabin up. The sky was slate gray. It was still raining. Her dad met her at the trailhead, surprised to find his daughter alone.

"Where is everyone?"

"They can't find the plane."

"What do you mean?"

"We have to go back."

As she and her dad made the boat ride back to the cabin, Carolyn looked down at the lead-colored lake and thought, I want to dive into that water rather than face what I'm going to have to face.

Back in Duluth, Toby Pearson was in his office hurrying to finish up a report. A lawyer by training, Toby was a thirty-six-year-old organizer and policy analyst for the National

Catholic Rural Life Conference (NCRLC), an advocacy group that aimed to empower rural communities and to support family farms and local businesses. His work had taken him all over the country, and especially across the Midwest, where he listened patiently to the problems of small farmers, helping them organize locally before taking their concerns back to Washington. The NCRLC had been founded in 1923 to address the needs of underserved Catholic communities in rural areas, but its role and mission had expanded during the Depression, when it started to attend to the economic plight of suffering farmers. Since then, it had grown into a powerful force for promoting just and sustainable agriculture policies on state and national levels. The job suited Toby very well, bringing together issues of economic justice, faith, and the law. In turn, the farmers trusted Toby—a sincere, handsome family man from Minnesota who clearly found meaning in his work.

That morning, Toby had made Kathryn and his daughters their favorite breakfast, bacon and French toast. Grace and Lily were excited about their very first plane ride together, especially because Uncle Charlie was going to be flying them and their mom up to the cabin on the lake.

Toby had met Kathryn in 1988 in Duluth. She was then working as a waitress at a local restaurant over the summer break while she attended the University of Minnesota, studying international politics. He'd been immediately taken with her natural beauty—dark eyes, dirty blond hair, and an infectious smile that dimpled her cheeks. She was gentle, unpretentious, and had a playful sense of humor. Even then, Toby knew she was the one he would marry. Three years later, he made good on his vow. Kathryn, following in the footsteps of her mother, began working as a nurse. When Grace and Lily were born, the young family settled down in a house on London Road in Duluth, close to Lake Superior.

Toby and Kathryn had decided that a "short, little flight," less than an hour up the North Shore, would be a good way to get the girls comfortable with flying. They'd discussed taking the girls to Chicago to see the world's biggest T. rex at the Field Museum, so this flight would be good practice for the longer trip. Toby wanted to travel with his family, but the report deadline kept him tied to his desk. Instead, he would drive up to Saganaga Lake later the next day—a five-hour car trip—to join everyone for Grandpa Jack's birthday party over the Labor Day weekend.

The girls left in a flurry of bags and excitement. Kathryn made sure she had the wine for the weekend, Grace her silky security blankets she called her "menkies," while Lily's main concern was her doll Pinky, which she stashed in her backpack. Toby buckled Grace and Lily into the car, kissed his wife, and said, "I love you. Have a safe flight." He could see their happy faces through the window of the Ford Explorer as it backed out of the driveway and headed down London Road. Lingering on the porch of the family's house, Toby noticed that the gently shifting water of Lake Superior was speckled with rain, a legacy of last night's storm, which had now moved north.

He made the short walk up the road to the local Catholic grade school, where he kept his office. He worked until around noon, when the school principal knocked on his door and handed him a message while he was on a conference call: "Call your mother-in-law right now." He wanted to put it off, but the principal insisted that it was urgent. When he reached Marilyn Wall, she was frantic.

"The plane is missing," she said. "The clouds were too low and they couldn't land."

"What?"

"They lost the plane that Charlie was flying. He hasn't landed."

Toby's mind was racing. The thunderstorms that had passed through Duluth and up the North Shore now seemed more ominous. Perhaps, he thought, Charlie had waited for the storm to move on and delayed his departure, not wanting to fly into bad weather. Toby needed answers. He began calling the airports, trying to find out if the plane had set off late, or if Charlie had changed his flight plan. How much gas did he have? How long could he stay in the air if the weather wouldn't let him land? He called Grand Marais airport and spoke to an operator, who by this time had more information. Yes, she told him, they'd received an ELT signal—emergency locator transmitter—that usually triggers automatically when a crash has occurred, but a rough landing could also have set it off. She said the airport was having problems triangulating the transmission because one of the signals was coming from a "ways out" in Lake Superior and another one from the land.

"I hope you're focusing on the land," said Toby, "because if they're in the lake they're dead."

The largest, coldest, and deepest of the Great Lakes, Lake Superior has frigid water even in the summer months. It was unlikely anyone could survive long in the chilly waters before hypothermia set in.

"There's only so much I can tell you," said the operator.

"Well, I'm the husband and father of those passengers, so I hope you can tell me more than you think you can."

A local pilot, Dan Anderson, watched the sky all morning, feeling anxious about a flying lesson he was due to give at 1:00 P.M. Maybe the weather would break, but if it didn't he decided that he'd run some ground instruction with his student instead. Now forty, Anderson had been flying since he was in high school—his nickname was Sky Dan—and he was quite used to the fickle weather of the North Shore. His was a familiar face around the little Grand Marais airport where he kept his small Cessna. As well as flying lessons, Anderson offered scenic flights over the surrounding forest, guaranteeing his passengers that within minutes of takeoff they would see a moose. Once, when he was coming in to land, he'd seen a family of wolves walking on the runway. Anderson was experienced enough to know that the best times to fly were early morning or late afternoon, when the winds were lighter. But today, it was unlikely he'd get off the ground. The cloud ceiling was clearly below the minimum descent altitude, the point at which a pilot must be able to see the runway in order to complete the approach and land. (This varies depending on the airport, but in the case of Grand Marais, that minimum is 544 feet above ground level; the airport sits ten miles above the town, up a mountain road, and is surrounded by the tall trees—pine, fir, aspen, spruce, and birch—of the Superior National Forest.)

While he waited for his student, Anderson encountered the airport manager, Rod Roy, who told him what he knew: a twin-engine plane, a Beechcraft Baron 58P, had flown over and then disappeared from radio contact. Roy was using his handheld radio to tune in to the ELT signal but said it wasn't easy to determine location. A reconnaissance aircraft of the Minnesota Wing Civil Air Patrol—a volunteer civilian auxiliary to the U.S. Air Force—had taken off from Duluth and was also involved in the search but had found nothing. Anderson watched Roy jump in his car and drive off in an attempt to home in on the signal.

Anderson feared the worst. The surrounding area was not only densely forested, but was rife with endless river valleys and high rocky hills, so any signal would bounce around the terrain like a Ping-Pong ball, making a search-and-rescue operation a major challenge. Alarmed by the thought of another pilot in distress, Anderson was determined to go up for some aerial reconnaissance. Perhaps he could spot the plane from the air. But that couldn't happen until the weather had cleared, so he was forced to wait.

A break in the sky—"a blue hole," Anderson called it—afforded him the opportunity he'd hoped for, and he took off in his Cessna around three P.M., some four hours after the plane was reported missing. Once he was up in the air, Anderson began tracing an east-west grid in the narrow band between the fog and the treetops. He tried to home in on the distress signal, but the peaks and valleys of the land kept skewing it. Nervous about the fog, he was fully prepared to fly above it and head south to Duluth if it got any worse. As it was, he kept a steady air speed of about sixty-five knots, flying two hundred feet above the forest. It was a dangerous maneuver even for an experienced pilot like Anderson, because at a slow speed like that he risked stalling the plane. Several aircraft had gone down in the surrounding wilderness over the years, including one flight that had crashed in 1971. This one in particular was on Anderson's mind. He'd been present twelve years later when the aircraft wreckage, along with traces of bone and hair fragments and a couple of forlorn shoes, was finally found. He had no doubt—going down in Superior National's ocean of trees was just as bad as disappearing in the middle of the Atlantic.

He picked up the emergency signal again; his hope flared, and he prayed the signal wouldn't vanish again. Looking down, he could see emergency vehicles traveling up Gunflint Trail. Flying parallel to the road, Anderson was so close he could signal to the vehicles from his cockpit window, pointing in the general direction of the beacon to get them closer. The forest immediately below him consisted of dense, old-growth trees that were used for timber, one small area of the three-million-acre Superior National Forest. How the hell am I going to get those guys in there? he thought.

It was then that he saw the bright white tail cone of the plane and pieces of debris on the edge of a freshly cut clearing. Anderson made another pass and could see the burned wreckage of the aircraft scattered like a jumbled jigsaw puzzle on the ground. Now he saw the burned-out fuselage and noticed that both the left and right wings had been ripped off the aircraft on impact. His heart sank. He radioed down to the search-and-rescue team: "There'll be no survivors. Just bring body bags."

Mark Falk, the thirty-seven-year-old chief deputy sheriff in Grand Marais, Deputy Sheriff Joe Zallar, and the Cook County Search and Rescue intercepted the grim news and raced toward the crash site. Falk had become the chief deputy sheriff in 1995 and had quickly become a well-respected figure in the area. He typically dealt with a range of issues—cabin break-ins, lost hikers, alcohol-related offenses, domestic disputes—but now he was dealing with a plane crash for the first time.

The only access to the site was down a local logging trail, so the rescuers had to make their approach on ATVs and then on foot. As they navigated through the thick trees, they came upon the clearing and saw a column of smoke curling up into the clouds.

Falk turned to Zallar and told him to start taking pictures to document the crash site. Up close, the scene was devastating. Pieces of the wreckage—the inverted torso of the cabin, a grotesquely twisted propeller, disemboweled pieces of rubber exhaust hose, dislocated wings—were strewn over three hundred square feet. He surmised that the plane must have been flying low in the clouds over the clearing before it hit a tree, then made impact with the ground before smashing into the wall of old-growth trees. Falk could see the deep, muddy slash in the forest floor where the plane plowed into the heavy trunks that must have halted its forward slide. It looked to Falk as if the cabin had flipped over before impact, though he didn't know for sure. He saw that one aircraft engine had broken from the airframe, slammed into the edge of a big tree, and charred the trunk charcoal black. Another engine had also been ripped off and evidently burned fiercely, the fire melting parts of the metal casing.

Falk approached what would have been the cockpit and saw the burned remains of two people. He did not know how many people were on this flight. The area around the cockpit was still intensely hot from the crash. Some of the big tree trunks were still smoldering, glowing red. Twenty yards to the right, Falk could see remnants of passenger seats that had been thrown clear of the cabin. Then he noticed what he thought was a little doll—a pale, impassive face in the midst of the carnage. Oh no, he thought, we've got kids in this crash. He approached the doll and saw what he thought was a fishnet stocking on a leg. As he got closer, he saw a head pop up and the alert blue eyes of a child. The girl, who looked to be about three years old, was conscious and lying on a seat that was completely reclined next to another little girl of similar age who was lying on her stomach, but also conscious. Both appeared to be calm.

"We've got survivors!" shouted Falk. He was astonished to find anyone alive in the midst of this destruction. Even though it had been more than five hours since the crash, the girls had remained near the debris, evidently far enough away from the hot flames that had consumed the other passengers. Falk could see now that the fishnet stocking was actually burned skin on one girl's leg. His team came running over to help lift the girls to safety. As he bent down to get closer, one of the girls said something that made him catch his breath.

"Mommy burned up."

———

Carolyn drove down Gunflint Trail for the second time that day, the dark trees now seeming to press in on either side of the winding road. At the trailhead store, she'd contacted the sheriff's office and been informed that plane wreckage had been spotted from the air, but there was no further information.

With that knowledge and without cell phone reception along the route, Carolyn made the anxious drive, her dad sitting next to her. They were already quite close to Grand Marais when Carolyn could finally make another call to the sheriff's office. Steeling herself, she pulled over and got out of the car to talk. That was when she learned the incomprehensible truth: Charlie and Kathryn were dead. Grace and Lily were still alive. Stunned, she got back into the car and told her dad what she knew. He slammed his hand down on the dashboard with a thud, a gesture that summed up the conflicting emotions surging through her body: an adrenaline shot of shock, anguish, and disbelief. Just then, an ambulance with its lights flashing sped by their car.

"That must be them," said Carolyn. She followed the ambulance to the Cook County North Shore Hospital in Grand Marais, a compact building with a small staff and just three beds in its emergency room. Still, it was well-enough equipped to diagnose and stabilize trauma victims before transferring them to a bigger facility. When Carolyn pulled up, she saw the paramedics carrying a little girl into the ER. It was Grace, who looked dazed and shocked.

She could see that Grace had twigs tangled in her hair, and she could smell the powerful odor of singed hair. She followed the paramedics into the ER as the girls were whisked there to receive urgent care. Then she saw Lily who, though badly injured, looked up at her aunt with big eyes.

"Hi, Lily," said Carolyn. "Are you hurting?"

"No," she said. "I just have to tinkle."

She didn't get to say much else because her traumatized body was swelling up fast, and so the doctors determined that they should insert a tube to assist breathing and prevent the possibility of suffocation.

As she waited in the brightly lit hospital, Carolyn found herself thinking, Why am I not collapsing on the floor wailing? She'd just lost her husband and her younger sister, but right then she felt them as a "calming presence," strengthening her for the ordeal ahead.

Deputy Sheriff Zallar, who'd been at the crash site, gingerly approached her and asked if they could talk privately. She sensed his nervousness and knew what was coming. It was his official duty to break the bad news to her about the deaths of Charlie and Kathryn. As he spoke, she realized he had some of his facts wrong; for example, he said that the plane had been an eight-seater. Carolyn said to herself, Maybe the whole thing is a big mistake and no one has really died.

In Duluth, Toby had been sitting by the phone, waiting for news. His close friends Patrice and Cynthia had come over to the house to wait with him. Toby had become friends with both women through his diocese in Duluth, where they'd worked together on social programs dealing with education and the homeless. Although their presence was a comfort, he was extremely anxious and jumped when the phone rang. It was an officer from the Cook County sheriff's department providing him with another update. The officer didn't use the word crash, preferring the less definitive heavy landing, though it was clear that something serious had happened to the plane. While they waited to find out more, Cynthia and Patrice did some tidying up, washing the breakfast dishes from that morning, and tried to stay positive.

But when Kathryn's brother, John, arrived at the house, they all sensed the worst. He looked at Cynthia and Patrice.

"Can I have a moment in private with Toby?" he said.

"It doesn't have to be private," said Toby.

"It's not all bad news," he said, reaching out to put his hand on Toby's shoulder. "The girls are okay. But Kathryn and Charlie are gone."

Toby started sobbing. Cynthia grabbed Patrice by the arm and they moved to the other room. Patrice could hear John speaking quietly to his brother-in-law.

"Toby, you were such a good husband to my sister. I am so grateful."

Toby collapsed on the counter and cried for fifteen minutes, thoughts of his wife flooding through him. Even then he couldn't linger in his grief. His daughters had survived and he didn't know much about their injuries. Should he make the drive up to Grand Marais to see them? Toby soon learned that the girls would be sent by ambulance to Duluth, where they'd receive emergency treatment at Saint Mary's Medical Center, which was better equipped to deal with burns. He spoke with his sister-in-law Carolyn, who would be traveling with Grace and Lily in the back of the ambulance. She explained that Grace was in better condition than Lily, who was more badly burned than her sister.

"What do you want me to tell them if they ask about Kathryn?" she asked.

"I don't know," Toby replied. "What do you tell a three- and a four-year-old who've just lost their mother?" He collected himself. "Tell Grace I'll see her at the hospital."

An agonizing two hours, the time it took for the ambulance

to travel down the highway to Duluth, followed. A series of frantic phone calls ensued, originating with Toby, who spoke to his mom and sister, barely believing the words coming out of his mouth. The extended Pearson family, from Colorado to Saint Cloud, dropped everything and started to converge on Duluth.

Toby arrived at Saint Mary's ahead of the ambulance. While he was waiting, he got a call from his friend Father Bill Graham, a priest in his early fifties who'd recently left the diocese to move to Chicago. Over the years, Toby, Kathryn, and Father Graham had grown close. Kathryn, who had been raised a Lutheran, had converted to Catholicism even as she'd challenged Graham with questions about faith, God, and the meaning of life. Father Graham had heard about the accident and reached out to his friend, but Toby was distracted.

"I can't talk now."

"You have eight minutes," said Father Graham.

A minute earlier, he'd called Toby's house on London Road; Patrice had picked up and told Father Graham the ambulance had just gone by. Since it was approximately eight minutes from the hospital, Father Graham knew he had a few moments to talk. Toby listened to the reassuring words of his friend from inside a fog of grief and hope.

There was commotion when the girls arrived at the hospital. Medics rolled Lily straight into the ICU to stabilize her. She was under sedation and breathing through a tube, but Grace was conscious and alert when she arrived. Toby ran over to his daughter, who started crying. They hugged each other and Toby told her how much he loved her. In the ambulance, according to Carolyn, she hadn't talked much about the crash, but she'd been worried about Lily's backpack and her doll Pinky. Still, she managed to give the adults some fragmentary clues about her experience.

"We fell out of the sky and we don't know where Mommy is," she said. "We were waiting for people to come, and I took care of Lily."

Grace had third-degree burns on her hands and legs but hadn't yet begun to feel the pain that would come. Lily, though she was conscious when she was rescued, was now in serious condition. When the doctors finally permitted Toby to see her, he was shocked. She looked like a marshmallow; her skin had turned pale white and was badly swollen, an early symptom of the third-degree burns she had on her arms, legs, and face. Toby found himself overwhelmed with helplessness. Grace fretted that Lily was "sleeping a lot." The doctors could offer little reassurance to Toby as to whether his youngest daughter would live. Toby learned that, in cases where more than 50 percent of the body sustains third-degree burns, the victim has a fifty-fifty chance of survival. All the doctors would say was "We'll know more tomorrow." They had no idea whether Lily could even breathe on her own.

That night, Toby and Kathryn's families gathered at the hospital: Carolyn, who'd been the first to learn the news, came along with her father, Jack. One by one, family members arrived, stunned, fearful, questioning. There was Kathryn and Carolyn's mom, Marilyn, in the waiting room, stricken by the impossible news of her daughter's sudden death. Toby's parents, Maureen and Tom, and his sister, Beth, soon joined them. Later, his brother Tony, an M.D. whose knowledge of internal medicine would help provide more insight into the girls' condition, arrived from Colorado, along with his wife, Anne. Toby's younger brother, Andy, made the journey from Saint Cloud. The focus now was on Grace and Lily, whose survival against all odds kept the shadow of grief at bay. There were hard questions to ask: How had the crash happened? Was Charlie to blame? Was it his bad judgment that cost him and Kathryn their lives? Would this tear the family apart? How would Toby cope? "It was a complicated grief situation," recalled Carolyn. For now, these questions would have to wait.

Carolyn went to her mother's house and took a shower, reflecting on the day that had taken her husband and sister from her. She let the hot water pour over her skin as grief overwhelmed her. After holding herself together all day long, she was now racked by sobs. Just twenty-four hours earlier, life had seemed blessed: on the porch, drinking wine with her dad, Kalli curled contentedly at her feet, waiting for the family to arrive. Then she remembered the shine of Mars on the lake, the red light from the planet named after the Roman god of war. "Since the accident," Carolyn would later say, "I will always consider Mars a portent of tragedy."

At Saint Mary's, the girls were moved into a big private room with Grace on one side of the room and Lily on the other. Toby and his mother kept a bedside vigil. At one point, Maureen went to comfort Grace, who started to tell her grandma some details about the crash. Toby wanted to know if there had been panic in the aircraft before the crash, but, according to Grace's description, they were flying along and suddenly they weren't. She talked about how she had to unbuckle Lily to move her away from the fire until it went down. "I protected her," Grace said. "We just waited and took a rest on the seat."

When Toby heard this for the first time, he was astounded. Not only had the girls survived the plane crash, but Grace had somehow known to stay near the wrecked aircraft even as it burned. Had the girls wandered off into the forest, they would have disappeared forever. No one, not even the doctors, had any medical explanation for their survival. It was shortly after this that Toby started hearing people use the word *miracle* in relation to the girls' survival. People could believe that if they wanted, Toby thought. Even if it was miraculous, it was still tainted with tragic loss.

2

TOBY AND KATHRYN

For Toby, it was love at first sight. In the summer of 1988, he and a couple of his oldest buddies, Greg McGee and Todd Richter, had headed over to Grandma's Saloon and Grill for a few beers. Situated on the banks of Lake Superior in Duluth, Grandma's housed a cornucopia of Americana—retro neon signs, classic ads for soda and cigarettes, antique stoves from the golden past—with conspicuously large hunting trophies of buffalo and moose heads overseeing the proceedings.

Nicknamed "the air-conditioned city" because of the cool air flowing off the lake, Duluth hardly had much in the way of nightlife, but Grandma's offered a lively scene, a good jukebox, and a pretty waitress who caught Toby's eye. With her short, blond new-wave hairstyle, she cut a fashionable, agile figure as she walked by this trio of young men in their early twenties, sitting out on the deck to watch a volleyball game.

Toby, who'd been noticing the waitress all evening, turned to his friends and declared that he'd have her number by the end of the night. "That's the woman I'm going to marry!" he declared. His friends both laughed at what they considered to be a typical beer-fueled boast, but for Toby it was as if he'd "been hit with a bolt of lightning" the very first time she walked by. But he didn't know her name. It took some further inquiries and another visit to Grandma's before he would discover it. This time Toby and his friend Todd did it right, sitting in her section and ordering a beer from her. She was Kathryn, a local young woman who was attending the University of Minnesota in Duluth. She was making ends meet by working at the restaurant over the summer. It was a thrill for Toby to speak to her.

After a little while, Toby went up to her to ask if she was "dateable." She smiled, shook her head, and said she had a boy-friend already. But then she added brightly, "I'd like to get to know you as a friend." She wrote down her number and handed it to him. With a big grin, Toby returned to his friend, Todd, having succeeded in his quest. Todd smiled, impressed by his friend's determination, before adding, "Too bad she has a boy-friend."

However, Toby never called because the last four digits of the number were 6666, and he assumed that the number was a fake. When, a few days later, he encountered Kathryn again at another volleyball game, she approached him and said, "You never called!" Toby explained that he didn't believe she'd given him a real number. "Well, I did," said Kathryn. A friendship developed, but despite his real attraction to her, Toby knew nothing would happen while Kathryn was going steady with her current boyfriend. They spent some time together on bike rides, running, and in-line skating around Duluth, a natural harbor set against a dramatic backdrop of steep hills. Kathryn loved showing off her hometown and enjoyed introducing Toby to different parts of Duluth. It was a special place, a Midwest port accessible to oceangoing vessels (known as "salties") from the Atlantic Ocean via the Great Lakes and the Saint Lawrence Seaway. High up on the ridge, Toby and Kathryn could watch the distant ships—some of them more than one thousand feet long—moving slowly across Lake Superior. At night, they could see the lights of Aerial Lift Bridge, which spans the ship canal and act as a gateway for the ships entering and leaving the harbor.

Disappointingly, Kathryn was considering a move to Minneapolis after the summer to be closer to her boyfriend, which didn't bode well for Toby's chance of a future relationship with her. Still, there was something about Kathryn; not only was she beautiful but she also had a rare intensity of purpose that struck a chord with Toby. It motivated him quietly to think about what he would do with his life. In the summer of 1988, he found himself living in a household of medical students in Duluth, along with his older brother, Tony, doing a series of summer jobs that meant little to him but a paycheck. Soon, he knew, he would have to get serious.

All his life Toby had been aware of how precious and precarious employment could be, how the American dream could take a turn for the worse. He had grown up in a middle-class neighborhood in Mankato, a small city in southern Minnesota whose name, according to local legend, dates back to the Dakota Indian word *mahkato*, meaning "blue earth." Toby was surrounded by the vast and fertile corn and soybean fields that roll across this part of the Midwest. Even as eleven- or twelve-year-olds, Toby and his friends would spend their summers sweating in the humid one-hundred-degree-plus conditions of these fields, detasseling the pollen-producing flowers from the tops of corn plants by hand. Other times, armed with a knife, they would go "bean walking" to uproot thorny weeds and rogue cornstalks in the bean fields. This was a common way for local kids to make money during the summer vacation, but it wasn't easy work. He and his friends Brion Hybertson and Greg McGee thought they had a smart way to avoid getting soaked by the wet leaves of the corn plants by wearing plastic bags, but it wasn't long before these makeshift shirts were slick with moisture and sweat.

On the face of it, the Pearson family had it good—a Victorian-style four-bedroom house built in the nineteenth century at the end of a quiet road, backing on to a small wooded area. It was well maintained thanks to the efforts of Toby's father, Tom, who'd painted the house in classic forest green. But the image of a middle-class house belied a deeper financial anxiety that all of the Pearsons felt. Tom Pearson started out running a shoe store, which gradually got nudged out of business by bigger stores. Another of Tom's business ventures, running a janitorial supply store for schools, also failed when it lost out to a bigger regional supplier. At some point, Toby and his brothers and sister—Tony, Beth, and Andy—were conscious of relying entirely on their mom, Maureen's, salary. She was the director of a nursing home in the area. Tom eventually went back to school and, in his midforties, graduated with a degree in psychology and social studies and began a new career as a teacher at a local high school. He found that career more gratifying than trying to launch another venture in a difficult economic climate, and it allowed him more time with his family.

For this reason Toby's parents put a great deal of faith in education, and they encouraged their children to see that their futures depended on doing well at school. Although Toby wasn't exactly an A student, he was diligent enough, preferring the humanities and social sciences to the math and science subjects at which his older brother, who had his sights set on a career in medicine, excelled. Toby was also a very good athlete, but since he was smaller than some of the other boys, it wasn't football or hockey where he made a mark, but gymnastics.

As a teenager, Toby had a mischievous streak and this

combined with his acrobatic ability landed him in some amusing situations. In what his close friend Greg McGee calls a "classic Toby instigation," the seventeen-year-old Toby decided it would be a goof to try out for the cheerleading squad, otherwise known as the Mankato West Scarlets. Part of the motivation was the pretty cheerleader Sheri Cox, who was already on the all-girl squad. So Toby and Greg signed up for the tryouts and, much to Greg's chagrin, actually impressed the head of athletics. When the joke looked like it was turning into a reality, Greg took Toby aside and urged him to turn down the offer. But when the athletic director confronted the two boys, she was annoyed and aggressive. "You're obviously not serious about doing this," she said sharply. Something in Toby objected to being so easily dismissed. "We absolutely are. We're in!" he blurted. Greg stared at his friend in disbelief, but it was too late. They became the first and possibly only male cheerleaders at Mankato West, a dubious privilege that meant having to wear white pants and red sweaters and to turn cartwheels at all high school sports events. One of Toby's specialties was the Greg-assisted backflip. His friend would launch him up in the air and with a yell of "Hubsabo," the lithe Toby would flip and come to land on his feet.

These were small-town thrills. In his teen years, much of the excitement outside of school depended on having a car. Once Toby passed his driving test, he would borrow his parents' Ford Pinto—which his friends nicknamed the "suicidemobile," because of allegations in the news that the model's gas tank could easily explode in the event of a collision—or better yet, his dad's van, which allowed Toby and his friends to stand up inside and "surf" the waves and dips of the local roads as the vehicle sped along. Inevitably, someone would end up flat on his face.

In 1984, Toby started his undergraduate life at Saint John's

University to study politics, with a minor in Spanish. Set in the rural Minnesota town of Collegeville, Saint John's was run by the Benedictine monks and offered a studious and reflective environment that wasn't as academically intense as an Ivy League school. This suited Toby. In the January term, he took a course that changed his thinking and, more important, introduced him to an important mentor in the figure of Father Rene McGraw, a priest in his fifties with a gentle manner and a brilliant intellectual pedigree, including a doctorate in philosophy from the University of Paris.

The class he taught, on the topic of nonviolent resistance, was based on the work of Gene Sharp, whose influential three-volume 1973 book, *The Politics of Nonviolent Action*, was the basic text for the semester. Sharp's practical methodology—inspired by the examples of Gandhi and Martin Luther King Jr.—offered up 198 methods of nonviolent action, from civil disobedience to noncooperation with government and business entities to "protest disrobings." Studying this strategic approach to resisting and subverting political power was very much in vogue on certain American campuses in the early eighties. The Vietnam War had ended only a decade earlier, and peace studies gradually started to appear at universities and colleges with a liberal tradition. Saint John's was no exception.

Father Rene noticed Toby's interest in the subject. He seemed very interested in the role of resiliency and personal characteristics of people who made it through difficult times. Toby and his friend Mike Peterson would stay up late at night to discuss world politics, such as the mounting opposition to apartheid in South Africa. The figure of Nelson Mandela—at this point in history still a political prisoner serving a twenty-seven-year sentence on Robben Island—fascinated Toby. Father Rene noted Toby and Mike's engagement with this field and asked them to liaise with the student body at Saint John's to build support for a proposed peace studies program. The process took a couple of years, with Toby and Mike reporting back to a committee of faculty members, and gradually a course developed as an outgrowth of government and political science. It allowed other students outside of the field to take the subject as a cross-curricular class because, as Toby thought then, there wasn't a whole lot you could do with a peace studies major on its own; social justice had to be considered within the context of economic and political systems. He received his bachelor's from Saint John's in 1988, with a major in government, a minor in Spanish, and a twentysomething's desire to do something significant with his life. It was around this time Toby moved to Duluth for the summer and, within a few days, had met and fallen in love with Kathryn Wall.

When Kathryn was still in elementary school, her family moved to a new house situated high on a rocky bluff in Duluth. Designed and built according to her parents' specifications, the house was notable for its unusual and idiosyncratic angles, but that was intentional. Once inside, almost every room afforded a tantalizing glimpse of Lake Superior. For Jack and Marilyn Wall, this was their dream house, with plenty of space for their three children—John, Carolyn, and their youngest, Kathryn—as well as spectacular views. The Walls were a well-regarded family in Duluth; Jack was an obstetrician-gynecologist in private practice and Marilyn was a nurse, though she had stopped working professionally to take care of her family.

For the children, this new home was a wonder because their rooms, on one side of the house on the ground floor, afforded them privacy away from the adults, who slept upstairs. The décor in Kathryn's bedroom reflected the aesthetic dreams of an

eight-year-old girl. It had white wallpaper featuring a pink ban-
danna design, white furniture, and a white carpet. Some of her
friends were a little jealous of this fairy-tale space, which looked
out through trees to water. Because Kathryn was five years
younger than Carolyn, she spent many childhood days with her
cousin, Rachel, who was a couple of years younger than Kathryn
and looked up to her as a wiser, older sister. The two bonded
forever after a life-changing incident at a local swimming pool
when the six-year-old Rachel enthusiastically launched herself
into the deep end of the pool, holding a ball. She promptly sank
like a stone. Kathryn, who was a strong swimmer, saw what had
happened. Instantly, she dove in and swam down to the bottom
of the pool, scooped up her cousin, and brought her to the surface, much to the relief of her hysterical aunt, who had observed
this ill-fated plunge and the rescue. From then on, Kathryn affectionately called her cousin by the nickname Rock.

For Kathryn and the other Wall children, swimming was a
central part of daily life. Not surprisingly in a state known as the
Land of Ten Thousand Lakes, there was a lot of activity focused
around the shoreline—from swimming to fishing to sailing.
In addition to their cabin on Saganaga Lake, the Wall family
owned a cabin on Pequaywan Lake, which provided a great retreat within easy reach of Duluth. On warm summer days, Kathryn and her friends loved to spend time at the cabin. Although
the cabin was small—with just one bedroom, a living room, and
a front porch—sometimes as many as fifteen girls would crowd
in there with sleeping bags. During the day they'd go swimming
or boating and then, in the evening, huddle around a campfire and
roast marshmallows, which they'd squish into s'mores. In her teen
years, Kathryn was at the cabin with a group of boys and girls,
including her close friend Teri and a visiting Italian exchange
student, Alessio. After a game of badminton, twilight fell and

the group returned to the cabin. They heard Alessio cry out in horror from the bedroom and came running in to see him gesture timidly toward a cluster of bats hanging inside the dresser drawers. The girls laughed. Bats were a part of life on the lake, too.

Her friends and family recognized that from an early age, Kathryn was bold beyond her years. When she was seven years old, the family took a rented motor home and drove south to Colorado for a vacation. Somewhere in Nebraska, Jack pulled the vehicle into a rest stop for refreshments. After the break, they pulled out again and headed off down the highway. Someone asked, "Where's Kathy?" Sure enough, they had driven off without her. Now, with a sense of rising anxiety, the family headed back to the rest stop and saw little Kathryn standing there calmly, waiting by the side of the road. She had not cried or panicked about her situation. Her mom said, "Kathy, what were you thinking you would do?" She responded, "I was just thinking that if I saw a car from Minnesota I would try to get a ride back and stay at Geva Lou's house." Geva Lou was a close family friend. Marilyn gathered her safely up in her arms, relieved and amazed by her daughter's poise in the face of danger.

Back at home, Kathryn was also an instigator of adventures. Late at night, she delighted in leading her friends down a steep, rocky path from the big family house onto the grounds of the exclusive Northland Country Club, which was situated at the foot of the bluff. Dr. and Mrs. Wall belonged to the members-only club, which boasted tennis courts, a beautifully maintained golf course, and an upscale restaurant. But what captivated the Wall children, and Kathryn in particular, was the alluring glow of the turquoise pool after dark. Once the club had closed for the day, Kathryn and her friends, including Rachel and Teri, would sneak over the fence to take a furtive swim under the stars. They called it the "Midnight Membership." The challenge was to avoid the security guard who would intermittently sweep his flashlight over the pool. Kathryn would order her friends to "get down," and they all took a deep breath and hid under the water, torchlight scanning the surface above. Once the girls got caught, and the guard gave chase as they ran back up the hill, abandoning their sandals and towels.

On another occasion, after an authorized afternoon swim, Kathryn took Rachel into the club restaurant and sat down at a table. "Let's eat," she said confidently, and proceeded to order expensive entrées from the bemused waiter, including a lobster dinner. Rachel was nervous about this and thought later that Kathryn's parents would surely be upset by the extra expense she'd racked up. Still, Jack and Marilyn were mostly delighted by their younger daughter's fearlessness. Even at the family dinner table, Kathryn would never just sit there and listen to other people holding forth, whether it was her older brother or her father, who was quite the raconteur. Once, during a conversation about God, Kathryn interjected, "Who says God is a he anyway? God could be a woman!" Even from an early age, Kathryn liked to challenge the official dogma of the church and, rather innocently, tended to ruffle feathers.

The Walls went to church every Sunday. They were part of the Lutheran congregation, the largest Protestant denomination in Minnesota, a state with a strong German and Scandinavian ethnic profile. After church, it was a family tradition to go to Bridgeman's Restaurant, famous all over Minnesota for its extravagant ice cream sundaes. But when Kathryn became a teenager, these reassuring family traditions soon ended. Her parents went through a protracted separation (and eventual divorce), an event that marked the end—in the words of Kathryn's cousin Rachel—of the "sense of safety, security, fun, and adventure" of childhood. Somehow Kathryn, though she was in the ninth grade, handled it. She remained strong for her mother, especially after her father moved out of the dream house on the hill. Once Kathryn found her mother curled up in her bedroom, inconsolable with tears. She went into the room, held her, and said, "Mother, I'd like you to sit and listen to me. Life is not fair but you're strong and you're going to make it." Even in her grief-stricken state, Marilyn was amazed at her daughter's openness and emotional maturity.

Throughout her high school years, with her brother and sister already away at college, Kathryn became "Marilyn's rock," as one of her friends put it. In the midst of the emotional upheavals that followed, Kathryn never outwardly blamed anyone for her parents' breakup, even as her friends were curious about the dissolution of the family and the doctor who was no longer with his wife. Because of the divorce, the house was put on the market and Marilyn herself went back to work as a nurse. The day that Kathryn had to leave the house was, according to her cousin, the day she left her childhood behind.

As Kathryn thought about life after high school, she made the decision to stay close to her mother and eventually attended the University of Minnesota, Duluth, where she studied business management. She had an easygoing ability to build friendships, and she had no qualms about walking up to someone and introducing herself. People quickly warmed to her. During her third year, she opted for a year's study abroad at the University of Birmingham in England. On August 7, before she left, Kathryn and friends old and new gathered at their friend Wendy's cabin in Canada for a "last hurrah" to celebrate the beginning of this European adventure. Someone snapped a picture of the group of young women, all but one wearing sunglasses on the sun-dappled lawn, with Kathryn in their midst flashing a peace sign.

By the beginning of 1989, Toby's desire to woo Kathryn had become reality: They were now a couple in love. Kathryn's previous relationship had eventually ended, although she had moved to Minneapolis to give it a chance. Then she had returned to Duluth to finish up her college degree and started spending many hours with Toby. Kathryn's friends gradually adjusted to this new man in her life, warming to Toby's boyish charm, his disarming movie-star smile, and his evident good nature. Beyond their obvious attraction to each other, Kathryn and Toby shared a deep philosophical underpinning. The two spent hours by the lake discussing religion, politics, spirituality, and issues of social justice. Sometimes, their twentysomething fervor would threaten a relaxed night out, as the two sparred intellectually while friends listened, somewhat awed by their ability to keep each other engaged. They were, according to Kathryn's close friend Teri Rogers, like two peas in a pod.

In the spring of 1989, Toby and Kathryn jumped at the opportunity to return to Europe when Kathryn's university organized an exchange trip to Berlin, which involved a rare chance to visit a family in East Berlin. When they arrived, Toby and Kathryn passed through Checkpoint Charlie and found themselves in the German Democratic Republic, Minnesotans in the heart of the Communist East. They were wide-eyed with amazement at what they initially saw. In stark contrast to the colorful capitalism of life in West Berlin, here they noticed the drab concrete buildings and the dark, immaculately clean streets.

After their short excursion to the GDR, Toby and Kathryn stayed in West Berlin with their German hosts, a college-aged man and his younger sister. A highlight was a family dinner in which the mother of the hosts was temporarily reunited with her sister, who lived in East Berlin. The two women had been separated when Berlin was divided in 1961 and now they could see each other only twice a year. Toby and Kathryn were full of questions about the Eastern bloc, curious about life in a walled city: What was it like having all of your basic needs met by the government? What did they have to live without? Was there a black market for goods? Why are you forced to stay in the East?

Although this was a family celebration, it was an emotional few hours, a reunion granted at the discretion of the GDR. The sisters explained to these curious Americans just how difficult it was to be separated. Someone mentioned President Reagan's 1987 speech at the Brandenburg Gate when he famously challenged Mikhail Gorbachev, the general secretary of the Soviet Communist Party: "Mr. Gorbachev, tear down this wall." Toby asked, "How long is this wall going to be here?" And the startling response: "It will be here for the rest of our lives." Even as late as the spring of 1989, there was no evidence this would change. East Berliners still tried to escape. In fact, in February of that year, a twenty-year-old man, Chris Gueffroy, was fatally shot by GDR border guards as he tried to cross the wall.

Just a few months later, Toby and Kathryn invited their new-found German friends to visit them in Duluth at the end of summer. Even then, they had no inkling that the wall would fall a few weeks later, on November 9, 1989. The trip to Berlin fed both Kathryn and Toby's curiosity about how to live a good life. For them, it surely wasn't one just based on luxury and acquisition. What they had seen in Eastern Europe had been stark and alienating; perhaps there was some middle ground. They were determined to do something that had social value, something that even had a global impact, after their trip to Europe.

Toby took a job as a youth minister at Saint Michael's Church, under the guidance and care of his friend and mentor, Father Bill Graham. Graham thought Toby did not have the best credentials for the position, but he was clearly the best candidate because of his empathy with the junior high school children he worked with. As Toby's trial period ended, the children pleaded with Father Graham, "Will you hire him, please?" It was Toby's first real job out of college, and he was responsible for the religious education of the kids who came to church, as well as for setting up social events. But Father Graham knew that Toby would go on to do more; religion was an engine that could drive social change, but Toby's burgeoning sense of spirituality was fired by a more pragmatic secularism as well.

On November 10, 1990, Toby and Kathryn got engaged, inadvertently, at the wedding of Jim Metry and Teri Rogers, their respective childhood friends. During the reception, Toby said matter-of-factly, "I really do think we should get married, too."

"Are you proposing to me right now?" Kathryn responded.

"Um. Yes," said Toby, realizing it was hardly the most elegant proposal.

Kathryn immediately ran off to tell her mother and her newly married friend, Teri, as word spread fast among the wedding guests. Then everyone raised a champagne toast to the married couple, who, in turn, shared the breaking news that Toby and Kathryn would follow suit. Toby, chagrined that he might be stealing the spotlight from Jim and Teri, was nonetheless thrilled. Later, he proposed in a more romantic manner, on a trip to Bluefin Bay, an upscale resort on Lake Superior, where he arranged to have wine and flowers in the room on arrival. At dinner, at a table overlooking the lake, Toby got down on one knee, produced the ring, and proposed. Of course, he already knew the answer.

Toby and Kathryn got married on a beautiful sunny day, August 10, 1991, at the Lutheran Church of the Good Shepherd in Duluth, which was the Wall family's local church. Toby's mentor, Father Rene McGraw from Saint John's University, co-celebrated the ceremony so there was a Roman Catholic element to the service. Toby and Kathryn had, as a matter of course, discussed the merits of both Lutheranism and Catholicism—with Kathryn still leaning toward her family's Lutheran tradition even as she began to appreciate the Catholic faith. In Toby's mind the Lutheran marriage wasn't going to be a deal breaker. There was, however, a precarious moment before the wedding. The couple had the photographs taken before the ceremony, so Toby slipped his ring on for the pictures. But when he tried to remove it, he found the ring was stuck fast on his finger. With frantic minutes to spare, he managed to remove it with the help of a bucket of ice and some dishwashing liquid. Apart from that, the ceremony went without a hitch. Kathryn—wearing her mother's wedding dress, which fit her perfectly—joined her beaming husband at the altar.

After the service, there was a reception dinner at a local restaurant. Then the wedding party trooped aboard the *Vista Queen*, one of the large tourist boats that cruised around the Duluth-Superior Harbor. Guests were served drinks, listened to music, and enjoyed panoramic views of the shore. As twilight faded to night, the newlyweds looked back on the city, with its steep backdrop of hills, as the lights started to punctuate the familiar landscape. On this evening, it was especially magical and poignant because Toby and Kathryn knew that within a couple of days they'd be heading off to Flagstaff, Arizona, where Toby would begin to study for his master's in political science, and Kathryn would study to become a nurse, like her mother before her. That was the plan.

———————

On August 10, 1992, Kathryn picked up a purple felt-tip pen and signed her name, the date, and an inscription on the opening page of her new diary: "To be, to dream, to become." The words encapsulated the idealism of the recently married couple, now a year into their new life in Arizona. Perhaps it was the grand scale of the landscape—they often went hiking, biking, and camping near the Grand Canyon—but both Kathryn and Toby were brimming with new ideas, a vision of their own future, and an altruistic desire to change the world. Toby, who was midway through his master's at Northern Arizona University, had discovered an exciting new field of study in liberation theology. He learned about its origins in Latin America in the 1950s and 1960s—a moral reaction to poverty caused by the massive social injustice in certain countries. The fusion of religious morality with political action stirred Toby deeply. One book in particular that fired his imagination was Paulo Freire's *Pedagogy of the Oppressed*. Written in Portuguese in 1968 and translated into English in 1970, the book outlined a philosophical methodology to show how oppressed people could achieve liberation from unjust economic and political environments. Freire argued that the first steps in this process of becoming a free human being were education and the dawning realization that unjust conditions could be transformed by struggle.

Toby shared what he'd been reading with Kathryn, and they could talk for hours about Freire's philosophy. "As long as the oppressed remain unaware of the causes of their condition, they fatalistically 'accept' their exploitation," Freire wrote. "Further, they are apt to react in a passive and alienated manner when confronted with the necessity to struggle for their freedom and self-affirmation. Little by little, however, they tend to try out forms of rebellious action. In working toward liberation, one must neither lose sight of this passivity nor overlook the moment of awakening."

Powerful statements like these resonated strongly with Toby, coinciding with his own personal evolution and his own intellectual awakening to the world. He and Kathryn inspired each other with their shared idealism about how things could change. Toby loved to discuss the books he was reading, including ones by John Locke, Jean-Jacques Rousseau, and Aristotle as well as more contemporary works on liberation theology, and found that Kathryn was an attentive listener, with strong opinions of her own. On the weekends, the two of them would go camping or fly-fishing. One evening they sat out under the stars by a campfire, drinking wine and talking about the future. It was at this point that Toby decided that the best way to effect social change was to become a lawyer.

Meanwhile, Kathryn was keeping her diary. In one entry on January 24, 1993, she broke down the entries into different categories—spiritual, mental, creative, physical, educational, professional, and social. Under the spiritual category, she wrote:

> *meditate once a day*
> *be continually cognizant of God and the energy and love we are all a part of*
> *be more clear—clarity acting out of heart center*
> *acknowledge and listen to words from my intuitive higher self*
> *make time to listen to nature. Sedona, Canyon, all the beautiful areas in AZ*
> *turn off the TV*

The next day, Kathryn mapped out a fairly complete plan for the future: "What is my vision and what actions do I take to achieve it? I feel the power in my heart. I feel pregnant with possibilities. When your whole life is at the tip of your tongue."

In due course, the years of thinking, planning, and dreaming by the canyon came to an end. In the mid-nineties, Toby and Kathryn moved to Saint Paul so that Toby could attend the William Mitchell College of Law. He graduated and became a member of the Minnesota bar in 1997, with the intention of putting his new legal skills to good use. Soon he found a job as a lobbyist for the Minnesota Catholic Conference, a nonpartisan Catholic lobby group focused on social-justice issues such as funding for low-income housing, health care, and the economic welfare of small farms. This was Toby's first experience working with lawmakers on a state and federal level, including the governor, state-level representatives and senators, as well as U.S. senators such as Paul Wellstone, and Mark Dayton (a wealthy Democrat with his eye on a Senate seat). These were formative years when Toby learned about working on legislative bills, how the system worked, and how to effect change.

Soon Toby started working for the National Catholic Rural Life Conference on social-justice issues facing rural Minnesota. One of the highlights was the Federal Farm Bill, which Toby learned was arguably the single most important piece of legislation affecting the nation's food environment. Every five to seven years, Congress passes this massively complex piece of legislation that authorizes billions of dollars of taxpayer spending and provides support for American farmers as well as funding the food safety net for the country's needy. Now Toby was looking ahead to the next bill scheduled for passage through Congress in September 2001.

Meanwhile, there was a lot of grassroots work to be done. Toby traveled around Minnesota, listening to farmers in rural communities talk about their anxieties and what they needed from the bill. A good listener, he'd duly note everything they said. On one memorable occasion, Toby found himself in a small plane with Senator Wellstone, flying over the vast fields of

Minnesota, discussing the issues at stake. Toby liked and admired this Democratic lawmaker with a conscience who genuinely cared about the community he lived in. A former college wrestler, Wellstone demonstrated intensity and a passion for the little guy, having devoted his political career to issues of economic justice for the community. Wellstone became known as the conscience of the Senate, and he was always happy to see Toby when he visited him and his staffers on Capitol Hill.

By now, Toby and Kathryn had found a measure of stability, and while they weren't changing the world in a radical sense, they felt happy. It was time to start a family. On September 27, 1998, Grace was born. It felt like a fitting name for their first daughter. After all, Toby admired Grace Kelly, but there was also the spiritual connotation of the name. As a new mother, Kathryn exhibited calmness and serenity from the beginning, a relaxed state of being that seemed to radiate to her newborn. Everyone loved that roly-poly Grace was a beautiful, good-natured, and joyous baby.

After Grace's first birthday, the Pearsons decided to try for a second child. In the first trimester of her pregnancy, Kathryn wrote in her diary: "I see my baby growing strong—healthy thriving—so secure and protected in my womb. And later I see this baby happy and content—grateful to be here. Easy kind and sensitive to others. Talented a writer, musician or artist who communicates with and touches the souls around him." Soon Kathryn learned that she was not going to have a him but a her—a second daughter. On July 28, 2000, Lily was born. Lily was baptized as Elizabeth, a name from the Pearson side of the family shared by Toby's sister and grandmother. But upon seeing her newborn infant, Kathryn insisted she was a Lily, which then became her name on everything but legal documents. Grace, now almost two years old, was brought to visit the new baby in the hospital. She wasn't sure what to make of this new bundle being cradled by her mom. She reached out her hand to touch Lily, but her fingernail accidently scratched her sister's cheek. Later on, Lily liked to remind her older sister, "You scratched me from the start."

Despite this, Grace and Lily quickly established a close sisterly bond. Toby and Kathryn observed how the girls would figure things out together, which fit with their easygoing parenting philosophy. They encouraged Grace and Lily to be unafraid of making little mistakes and stood back in amused amazement when the girls, on a summer's day, decided to drag their plastic slide into the wading pool to create their own miniature water park. On a summer's day, the girls learned to help each other out with their mom and dad standing there, watching and smiling with pride.

No one knew then that, on another summer's day in the not-too-distant future, the girls would again have to rely on each other under very different circumstances. As the trees burned, Mom and Dad would not be there. What lessons would Grace and Lily learn from Kathryn, their tender and fearless, wise and loving mother? When she was pregnant with Lily, Kathryn made this diary entry: "Many times today I have had the thought to 'go forward unafraid.' When someone dies at a young age I can't help but ask 'Why?' and 'Why Not?' There are no guarantees that my loved ones or I will be here tomorrow—yet I can't be afraid of life for fear of dying. The only thing I can do is live better, love stronger, deeper and laugh harder."

3

NOT ENTIRELY PLEASED WITH GOD

The summer before the plane crash, Carolyn was driving toward the family cabin on Pequaywan Lake, outside of Duluth. Grace and Lily were in the car with her, sitting quietly in the back. Traffic came to a stop. Up ahead, a load of hay being pulled by a tractor had caught on fire. It was such an unusual, almost surreal sight, that Carolyn and the two girls watched the flames for a while. Grace spoke up and said, "Why don't we go past the fire?" Carolyn explained gently that no, it wouldn't be a good idea to get so close, and instead opted to take a detour. At the time, the whole incident was a minor inconvenience.

Now, days after the plane crash and the girls' inexplicable survival, Carolyn thought back to this moment and the "ring of fire" from which Grace and Lily had been pulled. She wondered, through the haze of her grief, whether the burning hay was some kind of foreshadowing. There was no satisfactory answer as this weird mix of superstition, religion, love, and fear stirred in her mind. Perhaps Grace had learned some kind of lesson about the danger of fire from this seemingly inconsequential moment. Or maybe Grace and Lily were somehow protected. But if that were true—if it were some kind of miracle, as many people liked to assert—why did Charlie and Kathryn have to die? And now, within a matter of days, she would have to bury them both, husband and sister.

Two funerals had to be planned. Carolyn's best friend, Karen Allison, dropped everything to help, forgoing her own family camping trip with her husband and children to provide support for Carolyn. The day after the crash, Karen took charge of the vulnerable Carolyn to help her navigate the next few days. She took her cell phone away, telling her friend, "I'll decide who you're going to talk to." At the hospital, she made sure Carolyn and her mother, Marilyn, drank water and ate bananas to sustain them. She also took charge of the funeral details that had to be planned.

"I don't even know where Charlie's body is," Carolyn said.

Karen called Chief Deputy Sheriff Mark Falk in Grand Marais and discovered that Charlie's and Kathryn's bodies had been removed to the University of Minnesota, Duluth, for autopsy, a required procedure after an accident. Karen consulted with Toby's sister-in-law Anne, who was helping him plan the funeral arrangements for his wife as he kept vigil at the bedside of his injured daughters. The somber director of a local funeral home, Dan Dougherty, arrived at the hospital in his dark suit to discuss the details of Kathryn's visitation and funeral the following week. Meanwhile, Carolyn suggested to Karen that she call a firm in Minneapolis, Washburn-McReavy, to conduct the funeral for Charlie. Carolyn then wrote a short obituary for Charlie, including the details of the visitation and funeral, and posted the news in the Minneapolis *Star Tribune*. They would be held Wednesday and Thursday; Kathryn's would follow on Friday and Saturday in Duluth.

Inevitably, Carolyn had to go back to Minneapolis, to the house where she and Charlie lived. Karen and another friend, Carrie, traveled with her. Karen sensed that after the last few days of keeping her composure in the blur of friends and family, Carolyn was ready to collapse in her bedroom, "to lie down in the sheets and to smell Charlie." But when they went back to the house they discovered, unusually, that the cat had peed on the bed. When Carolyn realized what had happened, she buckled, exhausted, distressed, and weeping. Carrie held her grief-stricken friend while Karen quickly remade the bed. She looked in the laundry hamper and found one of Charlie's old shirts, still infused with his scent, and gave it to Carolyn as a comfort. Then the three friends climbed into bed together, held each other, and cried.

Everybody liked Charlie. He was charismatic, handsome, and intrepid. Carolyn met him in 1991 on her thirtieth birthday in Bayfield, a coastal sailing town in Wisconsin, a couple hours' drive from Duluth. Carolyn, along with two friends, first encountered Charlie walking along the dock of the marina, carrying a case of beer. Struck by his curly blond hair, his twinkling blue-gray eyes, and his athletic physique, Carolyn thought he resembled a young Steve McQueen. He invited everyone to join his group of sailing buddies at a local bar, where Carolyn and her friends quickly felt welcome. Later on that day, Carolyn and Charlie found each other, got talking, and hit it off immediately.

Charlie, who was about fifteen years older than Carolyn, had already been married and divorced. He had three daughters, all of whom were in elementary school at the time. His passions in life were sailing and skiing, activities that Carolyn loved, too. Although Karen cautioned Carolyn that Charlie would never settle down, she was not to be deterred, and their relationship soon became serious. They complemented each other. Where Carolyn was introspective, empathetic, and gentle, Charlie was bold, physically strong, and reassuring.

He was also entrepreneurial. In the early nineties, he invented a safe storage box for medical syringes, designed especially for use by diabetics at home. Up to that point, the practice of disposing of used syringes in private homes was far less organized than in hospitals and clinics. Charlie saw the business opportunity and applied for a U.S. patent in 1994 (which he was ultimately granted in 1996). Around this time, he teamed up with his brothers to found his own company, UltiMed, to manufacture and distribute the safe storage boxes. He established a production facility for the products in South Dakota, a good five-hour drive from Saint Paul, where the company had its headquarters. It made sense for Charlie, who'd first been granted his private pilot's license in 1981, to get a small plane to fly to and from the facility.

The plane also allowed Carolyn and Charlie to take trips. Together they would travel to ski resorts out West, including a memorable trip to Alta, Utah, one of the oldest ski resorts in the United States, famous for its spectacular views, challenging terrain, and powder snow. Charlie loved to hike up the mountains away from the resort trails to find the fresh snowfall, and ski down these unsullied runs. He would go down ahead of Carolyn to check out the run and, having progressed partway down, turn back to Carolyn and reassure her, "Yep, you're fine. Follow me!" If Carolyn showed any trepidation or fear, he would tell her, "You can do this!"

On the day of Charlie's funeral, Carolyn drew strength from this invocation, "You can do this!" She wondered if Charlie's death wasn't another version of his protective tendency to go on ahead while she hung back on the lip of an unknown run. *You're fine. You can do this.* Carolyn planned much of the service, which took place on September 4, 2003, at the Hennepin Avenue United Methodist Church. After the opening prayers, Charlie's friends reflected on his life as a sailor, a man of action, and a good guy. Then Charlie's three daughters read selections from the scriptures, which they'd chosen for their dad. Instead of somber hymns, Carolyn chose two songs that she loved, including an old Carly Simon song from the early days of their relationship, "Never Been Gone." For Carolyn, the song evoked their mutual love of sailing and captured the sensual rhythms of being out on the water.

> It's night on the ocean I'm going home
> And it feels like I've never
> I've never been gone

The service concluded with an organ postlude, Widor's Toccata from Symphony No. 5, a dazzling and uplifting piece of music that had a bittersweet significance for Carolyn. It was the same piece she and Charlie had chosen for their wedding back in 1994.

At the reception after the funeral, an old friend of Charlie's, a retired airline pilot, approached Carolyn to offer his condolences. Carolyn knew he carried his own share of grief—his wife had died, leaving him with two young sons, one of whom later died from an accidental gunshot wound. He hugged Carolyn and he offered a few considerate words that Carolyn found important. "You'll be afraid you won't remember them, or how they look," he said. "But you will."

In the days following the crash, Toby struggled to maintain his equilibrium, caught between grief and gratitude. The girls had almost immediately been transferred from Saint Mary's to the burn unit at the Miller Dwan Medical Center in Duluth. Surrounded by a flurry of doctors and nurses, he spent his waking hours at his daughters' bedsides, trying to grab some sleep when he could in the annexed sleep room. By now, the story of the crash and the girls' survival had made the local news, and the hospital updated the media about Grace's and Lily's conditions. On September 1, the Pearson family released some photographs of the girls and Kathryn in happier times, which were featured during a report on the ABC local affiliate's *Eyewitness News* by Sandy Drag. She called the news "a tragedy and a miracle all in one day."

For Toby, it was an emotional conundrum that was impossible to fathom. "Imagine the worst news of your life and the best news of your life all in one go," he told his close friend Greg. Publicly, Toby managed to compose himself for the media, for his family, and most of all for Grace. But privately, the loss of Kathryn left him reeling. He lay awake at night under the taut hospital sheets, wishing he could talk to her. That's when the acute loneliness of his state would hit him; as attentive as his family was, his primary support and the love of his life was gone.

Grace remained conscious and continued to offer up little clues about the crash to her dad, but how such a trauma would manifest itself in a four-year-old wasn't yet clear. Meanwhile, Lily remained in the intensive care unit, heavily sedated, with a breathing tube, and swaddled tightly in bandages that covered much of her body. Toby would sit next to his daughter and talk to her gently, or read to her from her favorite book, *On the Day You Were Born*, by Debra Frasier. The inscription in the book— now painfully poignant—read: "To our radiant Lily, July 28, 2000. We love you. Welcome! Welcome! Love, Mom and Dad."

A day or two after Lily had arrived, the medical staff wanted to see if she could breathe on her own. With Toby standing by nervously, they removed the tube. It didn't go well. Toby watched in horror as his daughter started wheezing and gasping for air on the hospital bed while the doctors tried urgently to reinsert the tube. To Toby, it seemed like minutes went by before they managed to stabilize his little girl again.

On another occasion, Lily accidently dislodged the breathing tube on her own and again stopped breathing. Toby's brother Tony was sitting with Lily when this happened. A doctor himself, Tony knew exactly what was happening. He reacted quickly and called a "Code Blue" to alert the medical staff a patient was in need of resuscitation. At the time Toby was in another part of the hospital talking to a burn surgeon about operating on Lily when he heard the emergency code broadcast hospital-wide over the loudspeakers. He knew instantly that this must be Lily—she was the only patient in the hospital in such distress. Down the corridors, there was a blur of action as nurses and doctors in white coats flapped toward the unit where Lily was now being monitored.

When they arrived at the bedside, Tony had already managed to reinsert the tube in enough time to prevent any brain damage from lack of oxygen. There was relief but also annoyance that a doctor who wasn't part of the hospital staff had run the code and saved the day. That wasn't supposed to happen. What mattered most to everyone, though, was that Lily was breathing again. That night, alone in his room, Toby went through private agonies bargaining and begging God to let Lily live.

Grace kept asking questions about her sister who, requiring a different level of care, was hooked up to machines in another room. *What's Lily doing? Is someone in the room with her? When can I see her?* Toby tried his best to give her concrete answers. Grace wanted to see Lily's room, and after checking on the wisdom of this with his parents and the hospital social worker, Toby decided to take his daughter to the unit for a visit. He had explained that Lily was having problems breathing and that was why she had a tube. Also, she couldn't eat and that was why she had another tube for food. Grace seemed to understand all of this. None of the equipment in Lily's room—the flashing lights,

the monitors, and the gentle shush of the respirator—fazed
Grace. But one thing concerned her the most. "She needs a
doll," said Grace firmly. With the deluge of gifts being sent to
the hospital from well-wishers, the family quickly found one.
Grace laid the doll next to her sleeping sister's hand with the
help of her dad. "Here you go, Lily," she said. "We love you!"

Decisions had to be made about Kathryn's funeral. Toby
hardly wanted to think about it. He didn't want to say good-bye,
but his sister-in-law Anne gently worked with him to decide on
the practical elements of the visitation and the religious service.
He decided that it would be done at Saint Michael's, the local
Catholic church, and Father Bill Graham would celebrate the
funeral mass. Kathryn had recently converted from Lutheranism
to Catholicism for the sake of the family, but not without questioning the dogmas of the faith with her usual feistiness. Once,
when a Eucharist minister in the church challenged her with a
question—"Are you even Catholic?"—before communion, Kathryn privately fumed. She wrote about the moment in her diary.
"The dogma, doctrine, the arrogance! Whatever feeling of community I had with the Catholic Church vanished in an instant.
My heart turns cold as I think of it. But I decided to go to
church with Toby at the last moment, relenting to the feeling
that it is important that Toby and I do this together."

Once the date was set for Kathryn's funeral, Toby had to
decide whether he should take Grace. He talked to his family
and to a grief counselor, Ben Wolfe, at the hospital and the consensus was that it probably wouldn't hurt her to be there but it
might have an impact later on if she missed it. In fact, doctors
suggested that once she got older, she would come to appreciate the fact that she had attended. Toby spoke gently to Grace
a few days before, feeling nervous, scared, and sad about explaining the impossible to his young daughter.

"Mommy's funeral is going to be happening. It's going to be a ceremony in the church and everybody will be there," he said. "Do you want to be there to say good-bye when all the people are saying good-bye?"

Grace nodded. She asked who else would be there, and Toby said that her grandparents would be there, as well as Auntie Carolyn. She asked where she would be sitting, and Toby explained she would be right next to him at the front of the church.

"Mommy won't be there because she's in heaven," he said.

Toby knew this concept would be difficult for Grace to understand. Of course, after such a catastrophic accident, there would be no body.

"So none of Mommy will be there?" said Grace.

"Yes. She's in heaven."

Grace started crying. Toby held her in his arms and cried, too.

Traditionally at a Christian visitation, the casket bearing the deceased is on view, but this wasn't the case at Dougherty Funeral Home in Duluth on Friday, September 5. However, there were many images of Kathryn on display as friends and family crowded into the room. Her father, Jack, had spent hours creating a video celebrating his daughter's life, channeling his own grief into this project. It showed photographs of Kathryn as a baby as well as more recent images—glamorous in a mauve shirt, smiling in front of the Grand Canyon, on skis atop a snowy mountain vista, or as a beaming mother with Grace and Lily. Especially poignant were sequences filmed at the Shady Rest cabin the previous summer, peaceful images of Kathryn resting in an armchair with baby Lily wrapped in a blanket asleep on her chest, or walking with Grace toward the water's edge as a young chocolate Labrador, Boo, tried to get their attention with a stick.

The last time Toby and Kathryn's friends had gathered like this was at their wedding. Everyone was in shock, but there was a comfort in being able to reconnect with old friends. Todd Richter, who had been with Toby the night he met Kathryn at Grandma's Saloon and Grill, felt as if this were a somber college reunion—almost, he thought, like the movie *The Big Chill*, where a group of seven former college friends gather for a weekend reunion at a house in South Carolina after the funeral of one of their friends. It was then that Todd realized that Kathryn was the glue that kept everyone together. When Toby entered, Todd gave his old friend a hug and offered a few words of comfort. But given the magnitude of Toby's loss, there was little he could say.

One by one, friends got up to say a few words. Cathy, Kathryn's friend from junior high, recalled what she nicknamed 'Kathy Wallisms.' She talked about Kathryn's love of learning and her habit at school of randomly choosing a "word of the day" from the dictionary. The game required her to use it as many times during the day as possible, but when poor Cathy tried to imitate her friend, she landed on the word *serendipitous*. Cathy concluded her humorous and touching tribute by saying, "I do not cry for Kathy but for myself and the hole left in my heart that only time can mend. I celebrate the life of a woman like no other. Although I have been made keenly aware over the last week that there are two other women still on this Earth that share not only Kathy's strength but also her zest for life. I hope one day I will be able to tell Grace and Lily what a truly beautiful person their mother is."

The funeral, a more somber affair, took place the next day, September 6, at Saint Michael's Church with Father Graham leading the service alongside Catholic and Lutheran bishops from Minnesota. Toby's mentor and friend from Saint John's University, Father Rene, also co-celebrated the mass. When Toby walked in, pushing Grace in a wheelchair, there was an audible gasp in the church before people spontaneously started to clap. This was the first time anyone outside the family had seen Grace since the crash, and it seemed to many to be a hopeful moment. Grace's hands were wrapped in bandages because of the burns, and there was a fluorescent pink cast on her left leg; her knee had been fractured in the crash. Toby and Grace went to the front of the church and took their seats near the rest of the family. Observing everyone in the church, Grace was a little impressed. "I didn't know my mommy had so many friends," she said to her Grandma Mar.

Father Graham began with traditional prayers before giving his eulogy, which sought to answer the question Why did Kathryn die?

> It is no doubt safe to presume that I am not the only one in the assembly this morning who is not entirely pleased with God . . . displeased, or even angry. We speak of the Lord and Master of all creation, the one who fashioned all things, creating from nothing all that is. The one who upholds and sustains all life in a mighty but gentle hand. Where, we want to know, was that God on Thursday, August 28? How hard would it have been to sweep away the clouds and rain, and grant a safe and gentle landing for that small aircraft?

Of course, the questions that Father Graham raised did require an answer, and not necessarily a spiritual or a philosophical one about human suffering, or why the plane had crashed. Following such an aviation accident, the National Transportation Safety Board would investigate the cause of the crash. Was it a mechanical failure or pilot error? At this stage, it wasn't clear to Toby what had happened. He knew neither why Kathryn had died, nor why Grace and Lily had survived.

Then Carolyn stood to say some words. Many in the congregation were astonished that she had the strength after her ordeal. But she started to read from the famous children's book *Guess How Much I Love You*, in which a young hare searches for the words to tell his father how much he loves him. Carolyn addressed the reading, and the book's sublime conclusion, "I love you right up to the moon," to Grace, who at this point had curled up in her dad's lap. It was an appropriate but heartbreaking moment for the congregants reeling from the sadness of the occasion.

After the funeral, Lynn Grano, a longtime friend of Charlie and Carolyn, approached Toby to offer his condolences. Grano offered legal counsel to the Erickson family in business and other matters; the joke was he was the family consigliere, but he'd also known Kathryn since she was a little girl. After the crash, recognizing that there would be insurance policies pertaining to the aircraft, Grano began examining the various policies against which money could be claimed. There was the "hull policy," which related to the loss of the actual property of the plane, the proceeds of which would ultimately go to the lender who had financed part of the aircraft. Then there was the liability policy, which related to negligence or mechanical failure and a host of other causes of loss. Grano knew this would be a delicate situation, not only because Charlie was a friend but also because Charlie and the Erickson estate could be the target of any lawsuit if the crash was caused by pilot error. In effect, one side of the family would be suing the other for damages. Grano was determined to head this off at the pass, and without any acrimony. The worst-case scenario would involve a direct claim against Charlie's estate, with Toby having to prove in a lawsuit that

Uncle Charlie had killed Kathy and badly hurt the kids. That seemed—in Grano's estimation—like an awful exercise for everyone.

At this point it wasn't clear why the plane had crashed, and Grano spent a good deal of time thinking about possible causes, apart from pilot negligence, that might have contributed to the crash, such as a faulty GPS navigation system, inaccurate weather broadcasting, or possible aircraft fuel defects. Grano also talked to everyone he knew who had visited the crash site to get a clearer picture of what had happened.

In the days leading up to the funeral, he'd also held several conversations with the insurance company about Charlie Erickson's policy and he'd been reassured by a representative that everything was in order, and that the company was on the verge of writing a check.

Since the accident there'd hardly been a chance to talk to Toby about such matters, but now Grano took the opportunity to offer Toby this little piece of good news in the midst of the darkness. Grano was acutely aware that Lily was still in critical condition in the ICU. He hoped this information would help assuage some of Toby's concerns about the inevitable medical bills.

"We have been in contact with the insurance company and they will definitely pay out," said Grano. "Right now, it's more a matter of deciding whom it should go to, and we can discuss that stuff later."

Toby looked at Grano and thanked him. At this point in time, questions about aviation insurance payments seemed far from important. Toby was putting on a brave face for the funeral as his family and friends rallied around him. He wanted to get back to the hospital to see Lily.

Another encounter after the funeral started Toby thinking about the next steps for treating the girls. They both had third-degree burns—Lily's were much more extensive—and it became clear that both would have to undergo skin-graft surgery. Eileen Reardan, the doctor who had delivered Grace and Lily, approached Toby, offered her condolences, and asked him where the girls would be having surgery. "Right here," said Toby. "No," she responded. "Go to Regions. They're the best." Toby was startled by this bold declaration, but he trusted the doctor and started investigating Regions Hospital in Saint Paul, which houses one of the biggest burn units in the United States.

Toby felt conflicted about this move. After all, the medical community in Duluth had taken Grace and Lily to their hearts, and it had a vested interest and pride in the continued well-being of these high-profile survivors. Toby's father-in-law, Jack, had been a prominent doctor in Duluth and was still connected to many of the institutions. He knew moving the girls would be seen as a rejection of Miller Dwan. Furthermore, going to Regions would mean being away from his home in Duluth, and also away from one set of grandparents.

"If these were your daughters, what would you do?" Toby asked Tony and Maureen, his mother.

They were emphatic. "Go to the best place possible."

Tony placed a call to a colleague at the hospital to inquire about space. They replied, "We've been waiting for your call." It was a relief. Knowing that Lily would have to undergo some grueling skin grafts, Toby found himself reassured by the chief surgeon at Regions, Dr. William Mohr, whose team of specialists typically performed twenty-five to thirty operations per month. There were no more questions. They would leave within a day or two.

The Gold Cross ambulance—carrying Toby, Grace, and the

still-sedated Lily—sped down I-35, emergency lights flashing, toward the Twin Cities. Grace asked a lot of questions, some of which Toby struggled to answer for himself, about the concept of death. Yet he knew he had to provide concrete answers for the little girl to understand. Metaphysics had to be superseded by practical explanations. But Toby asked his daughter questions, too, to gauge the level of her understanding.

"Where's Mommy?"

"What do you think?"

"Is she in heaven?"

"Yes, she is."

"Where's heaven? Why can't I see her?"

"Mommy's dead."

"Does that mean she's with Jesus?"

"Yes."

"Is Jesus going to let her come back?"

"Well, no. Once you go to heaven you don't come back."

"Will Mommy be at this new hospital?"

"No. The funeral was our way of saying good-bye to Mommy."

"Is Lily going to be okay?"

Toby paused at this question. He didn't know the answer.

"We're going to find the doctor to deal with her injuries and your injuries."

"Is Lily going to live or go to live with Mommy?"

Again, Toby paused. Grace looked out of the ambulance window as they sped past the cars, the trees, the sky. All a blur.

"Boy, we're going really fast," she said.

4

CRASH PHYSICS

When Grace described the crash to her dad, grandma, and aunt, it was in brief fragments. Nothing was absolutely clear, even as the adults craved the details. Was there panic in the cockpit? Did the girls suffer? Were they even aware of what was happening? With gentle coaxing, Grace revealed high-speed glimpses of the experience inside the cabin of Uncle Charlie's plane. Mommy gave them dolls to play with. At one point, she went to sit next to Uncle Charlie. A four-year-old child's perspective on a dramatic, traumatic experience is essentially unfiltered. Grace mentioned seeing the clouds through the windows of the plane. The girls felt excited because they'd never flown before, so they had no idea there was anything unusual happening. They were on their way to their grandpa's birthday party on the lake. But then, said Grace, it felt like they were traveling down a bumpy road in a car. All of a sudden Lily noticed the trees out of the window, so close she could almost touch them. The girls forgot about the toys Mommy had given them. Something was wrong. The trees came into the plane.

Surviving a plane crash is possible, but it's an event that still has the power to astonish. Each crash has its own unique set of factors, but every year there are crashes with fatalities where passengers survive the impact. It may be chance, and there's little science to support the theory, but some observers suggest that children, even teenagers, and crew members on commercial flights are more likely to survive an air crash than adults. It may be just the nature of kinetics (*kinetics* is derived from the ancient Greek word *kinesis*, meaning movement)—children are often seated in the rear seats away from the cockpit—but then again, their survival could be sheer dumb luck, as one aviation attorney put it. The word *miracle* is nearly always thrown around in such instances, but perhaps this is just an attempt to rationalize a fluke. Ever since Icarus, mankind has been trying to defy the certainties of gravity, and that prototype flight proved that things could quickly go wrong in the air. "Down to the sea he tumbled from on high, / And found his Fate." It is the fate of those who survive a fall from the sky to inherit a startling legacy for the rest of their lives.

Francesca Lewis was twelve years old when the small single-engine plane she was aboard crashed into dense jungle in a mountainous region of Panama. On the morning of the flight—December 23, 2007—Francesca had been in high spirits because she and her friend Talia were going on an adventure to a coffee plantation high up in the mountains, where they anticipated a day of horseback riding. Francesca, better known as Frankie, and Talia were on winter break from their school in Santa Barbara, California, and were spending time on the Panamanian resort island Isla Secas, which was owned by Talia's dad, Michael Klein, a wealthy California businessman. They traveled all together on a charter flight, with twenty-three-year-old local pilot Edwin Lasso, who took off in the Cessna 172 and headed due east toward the little town of Volcan. But soon the clear skies of the Pacific coast gave way to clouds and the little plane hit turbulence. Sitting in the back of the plane with Talia, Frankie had been happily taking photos until she became aware of frantic activity in the cockpit between Michael and the pilot. From her vantage point in the backseat, she could clearly see a red needle moving erratically on the GPS device attached to the cockpit, and though she couldn't hear anything over the noise of the plane's engine, she sensed something wasn't right up front. Michael pulled out a map and showed it to the pilot, began gesturing and making hand signals to the right. Outside the left side of the aircraft, Frankie could now see clouds, though on the right she could still see bits of green terrain, glimpses of a river, and a runway far below.

Judging from the activity in the cockpit, she surmised they were lost and started to feel scared. She stopped talking to her friend, keeping her eyes fixed mostly on the two men in the cockpit who were talking. She wondered why they weren't heading toward the runway she'd seen, and she wasn't sure what was happening. Then they entered a thick cloud bank and, in the seconds before the plane crashed, Frankie remembers Michael punching the pilot in the arm.

When she woke up it was night and she was freezing cold. Trapped upside down and pressed against her seat with suitcases on top of her, she called out to see if anybody could hear her, but there was no answer. She had no sense of how much time had passed since the accident and the present moment. Aware of the pain in her body, she drifted in and out of consciousness. Disoriented and imagining herself back in California, she wondered why there was a piece of aluminum wing sticking through her bedroom. When Frankie awoke again, she could hear the sound of rain and something else, some kind of animal "stomping around." She felt scared but could do nothing to free herself and drifted back to sleep again.

Unbeknownst to her, a massive rescue effort was being planned, with a possible search area of more than two hundred square miles. It was cold, overcast, and raining, so efforts to find the missing plane were severely hampered. Beginning at dawn on December 24, volunteers armed with machetes trekked up the mountain, slashing their way through the dense jungle to areas where it was believed the plane might have gone down. The weather conditions worsened, and the search was suspended until Christmas Day, when rescue teams persisted, climbing higher up the mountain until many were exhausted. Then one of the volunteers, Miguel Vurac, heard a faint cry: "Help me." It was Frankie, the only survivor of the crash, calling from inside the smashed-up body of the plane, facedown and desperately cold. The rescuers extricated her from the wreckage, wrapped her in a blanket and a garbage bag to protect her from the rain, and gave her a local sugar cane drink to keep her strength up. They stayed with her through the night until first light, when they struggled down the mountain to a clearing where a helicopter could land to take her to the hospital.

Although Frankie suffered hypothermia and bruising, amazingly she didn't have any broken bones from the crash. But the legacy of the trauma would include psychological scars, which manifested themselves over time. During a deposition later on (part of the inevitable postcrash litigation), Frankie revealed that she felt sad and even guilty about losing her friend, Talia. Her school in Santa Barbara set up a safe room, where she and her classmates could go to talk about their feelings, especially around the time of the memorial for Talia. But Frankie and her friends rarely discussed the accident and what had happened. "It's so hard for me to think that it's even true, even though people are telling me," Frankie told reporters at ABC News just after the crash. "It's like, 'No, that's not true. It's just a dream. Or a nightmare.'" It was complicated, perhaps too much for a twelve-year-old girl to process. Later, Frankie told her parents that she was having suicidal thoughts, and they took her to counselors to help.

Just like Grace and Lily, she was a miracle child, marked for life as not just lucky but blessed. Surely, her rescuers thought, some higher power must have intervened to save Francesca. The effect of this thinking is pressure on the survivor to feel grateful for this gift, even as she suffers the psychological, emotional, and physical traumas of survival. "She is like an angel, an angel from God," said Miguel, Frankie's rescuer.

In the standoff between chance and purpose, life and death, survivors often find themselves struggling with the meaning of their own lives. Some fare better than others. When Bill Hansult looks back on the crash that almost killed him, he considers it luck that he survived the impact, although everyone said it was a miracle. Hansult, a fifty-one-year-old lawyer, was a passenger in a four-seat Piper Cherokee being piloted by a friend, Joseph Terrell "Terre" Owens, along with another friend, Carol Maki. On January 8, 2006, the three friends were returning to the San Luis Obispo County Regional Airport after a ski trip to Mammoth Lakes, a resort town on the east edge of the Sierra Nevada. Hansult had flown several times with his friend to and from Mammoth, and on this occasion, sitting in the right rear seat, he noticed nothing unusual as the plane lifted off into clear skies and climbed to an altitude of six hundred feet. Then, about two minutes into the flight, something went wrong. Without warning, the plane turned hard right and plunged toward the bright white snow of a mountain slope. Owens attempted to regain control with the yoke, but nothing could stop the inexorable descent. Hansult saw the ground coming up very fast through the windshield and shouted, "Oh my God, Terre!" Beyond that moment, he had no recollection of the actual crash.

When Hansult regained consciousness, he realized he was

in very bad shape. He could feel the bones of his left arm grinding together and could taste the saltiness of the blood in his mouth. He'd obviously bounced around the plane on impact, and felt his head touching Terre's shoulder. He called out his name but saw immediately that Terre was dead, as was Carol, the other passenger. But now Hansult realized he was trapped "like a sardine in a broken sardine can," as he later told a local journalist. Hansult, dressed only in a T-shirt and jeans, tried to kick open the door of the plane, but it was jammed tight. Snow from the mountain had plowed its way into the plane through the shattered windows, and although it was a bright, sunny day, up on the mountain it was extremely cold.

Exposed to the elements, Hansult soon developed hypothermia. Until that moment, he had never been in a life-threatening situation, so he was hyperconscious of his reactions to this predicament. He had a strong will to live, but as the hours passed, he found out that his will would go only so far. "I'm dying here," he said to himself. "I just need to come to terms with that." He closed his eyes, ready to drift into oblivion.

As soon as he accepted that notion, he heard voices outside the plane calling out: "Hello! Hello!" He was amazed that his will to live returned immediately, with renewed vigor, even after he had accepted that he would die on this mountainside, even after thinking that he might never be found. With its white underbelly, the plane would have been difficult to find embedded in a snowbank. "Over here, over here!" said Hansult in response.

The voices belonged to two women who were cross-country skiing, shocked to come across the silent violence of a plane crash. One of them had a cell phone and called the emergency services. While they waited, the two talked to Hansult, though they were afraid to come too close to the mangled wreck, which had a powerful odor of aviation fuel. But their conversation and encouragement were comforting to the badly injured Hansult. Eventually a snowmobile arrived, and rescuers pried open the fuselage like a tin can using the hydraulic Jaws of Life, freeing Hansult.

Though he survived the crash, Hansult's ordeal was far from over. His right arm was broken, and his left arm was literally shattered; in the initial surgery, it required twenty-three pins and screws to hold it together. He'd broken his back in three places, which meant wearing a body cast for six months, followed by painful years of physical therapy. He also suffered head injuries, including a severe concussion, that caused frightening brain seizures. Such seizures would occur at night or in the day, exacerbated by stressful situations. Later he developed severe vertigo and could collapse to the floor without warning. He had to give up his career as a lawyer, a high-stress job, and devote himself to his physical therapy, which Hansult discovered was a full-time job anyway. His determination to recover kept him going, and despite bouts of deep, engulfing depression, Hansult found a way to work through the darkness of this survivor's legacy. He refused to take antidepressants and discovered a radio station that broadcast mostly stand-up comedy, which made him laugh. This he found to be the best medicine for his mind and soul.

Eventually, the National Transportation Safety Board issued a report about the cause of the Mammoth Lakes crash. They determined it was pilot error, a conclusion that shocked Hansult since, on that fateful day, he'd watched Terre fly the plane perfectly. On takeoff, he had not risen at an excessive angle or pitched up, then down, and up again, as some witnesses had reported. Baffled by this finding, Hansult started to investigate other small plane crashes using data from the National Transportation Safety Board, the federal agency charged with determining the probable cause of all civil transportation accidents, including aviation. What he discovered alarmed him.

Hansult noticed the large disparity in accident rates between commercial and noncommercial flights. Each year, the NTSB investigates every aviation accident, large or small, and maintains a national database of its findings, broken down into different categories for the type of flight. Commercial airlines are regulated under the general operating rules of Part 121 of the Federal Aviation Regulations (FAR); on-demand charter flights (with no set schedule) are conducted under FAR Part 135. Noncommercial flights—flights that generally do not provide direct revenue to the aircraft's owner—are ruled by FAR Part 91, known as general aviation. Often characterized by private and recreational flying in small planes, this category also includes professionally piloted corporate flights in high-powered aircraft. Part 91 rules set restrictions—everything from aircraft speed to safe altitudes to fuel management—under which these noncommercial aircraft must operate. But because the rules are looser than those for commercial planes, the risk factor is much higher in the world of general aviation. Under Part 91, one reporter pointed out, "Caffeine-swilling pilots can fly your aircraft around for days without ever taking a break."

In 2011, the National Transportation Safety Board found that 92 percent of that year's fatal aviation accidents occurred in general aviation. Of the 1,466 accidents involving private planes reported that same year, 263 had fatalities. Most of the accidents were attributed to pilot error. As a comparison, there were 31 commercial accidents with no fatalities. Meanwhile—according to figures compiled by the Federal Aviation Administration—the diverse fleet of private planes operating in the United States is composed of more than 224,000 aircraft, which includes the most popular civilian makes—Cessna, Cirrus, Mooney, Piper, and Beechcraft.

The NTSB found that more than three-quarters of the aircraft involved in accidents were single-engine piston planes flown during personal flights. The accident rate is significantly less for multiengine aircraft like the Beechcraft Baron, which Erickson was flying. According to pilot and aviation attorney Ladd Sanger, the accident rate of single-engine piston aircraft is about 53 times higher than that of commercial aircraft; statistics show single-engine piston aircraft average 8 accidents per 100,000 flight hours compared with commercial airlines, which average 0.15 accidents per 100,000 hours flown. "That safety record is abysmal compared to commercial airlines," said Sanger. "It's very risky to be in that airplane."

Nevertheless, the safety of general aviation is a relative matter. In comparison to commercial plane crashes, the statistics look very worrying. Compared to car crashes, the numbers are far less startling. After every high-profile plane accident, there is often a flurry of reports analyzing the potential risks of general aviation. The fatal 1999 accident involving John F. Kennedy Jr., who crashed into the Atlantic en route to Martha's Vineyard, prompted many comparisons, using a variety of statistics, to automobile travel. In its annual report on accidents and trends in general aviation, the Aircraft Owners and Pilots Association (AOPA), which tends to be highly protective of the culture of small planes, published the following assessment:

Motor vehicles have about 10 times as many accidents per mile as do general aviation aircraft, but the aircraft have about seven times as many fatal accidents per mile as the motor vehicles. Flying in light aircraft is not safer than driving your car, but, as with all statistics, the comparison should be put into context. Airplanes travel two to four times faster than cars. That is one of the primary reasons we fly. However, should an impact occur, crash physics, unfortunately, work against us. Double the speed, quadruple the impact; triple the speed and the impact force goes up nine times. Add the vertical component introduced by altitude and one has to marvel that aircraft protect their occupants as well as they do. On average, only one aircraft accident in five results in fatalities. To state it another way, the fleet flies almost 10 million miles before there is a fatal loss.

Crash physics means that when accidents happen, they are more likely to be newsworthy. Another factor that contributes to the high-profile nature of general aviation accidents is the demographic of who flies—musicians, sportsmen, and politicians are often numbered among the fatalities in small-plane crashes. Over the last two decades, general aviation accidents have claimed the lives of singer-songwriter John Denver, John F. Kennedy Jr. and his wife and sister-in-law, noted aviator Steve Fossett, New York Yankees pitcher Cory Lidle, U.S. Senators Paul Wellstone and Ted Stevens, to name just a few. It's a roll call of well-known names that stretches back into the twentieth century and continues to this day.

One of the most infamous small-plane crashes took place on February 3, 1959, shortly after takeoff from Mason City, Iowa. Perhaps America's first rock star death involving a private plane (though certainly not its last), Buddy Holly died along with fellow rock and roll musicians Ritchie Valens and J. P. "The Big Bopper" Richardson. After a cold and grueling bus tour through the snowy Midwest, Holly had decided to charter a plane to take them to the next gig in Minnesota, instead of driving the

365 miles. At the time it seemed like a good idea for the exhausted group, already ten days into their midwinter tour. In fact, even the Civil Aeronautics Board (which eventually evolved into the NTSB) mentioned the tour conditions in its report on the crash: "Because of bus trouble, which had plagued the group, these three decided to go to Moorhead ahead of the others."

It's now a well-known story that two other musicians were scheduled to travel on the plane with Holly. The singer's bass player, Waylon Jennings, was supposed to fly but surrendered his seat to The Big Bopper, who was suffering from the flu. Meanwhile, Holly's guitarist, Tommy Allsup, flipped a coin with Ritchie Valens for the remaining spot in the four-seater Beechcraft Bonanza. He lost and Valens claimed the fateful seat. The plane took off, piloted by Roger Peterson, and flew directly into a blizzard, lost visual reference, and crashed into a cornfield at 170 miles per hour. There were no survivors.

A few years later, a similar situation occurred on December 10, 1967, when the singing star Otis Redding and his band flew from Cleveland, Ohio, en route to Madison, Wisconsin. An entry on the NTSB database records the accident. The aircraft listed is a Beechcraft, the type of accident is "Undetermined," and the explanation concludes that the "Aircraft crashed in lake 3 miles from the runway." The accident claimed seven lives, including that of the twenty-six-year-old Redding and nearly every member of his band. The NTSB report is a rather formal summary that doesn't do justice to the horror of the crash, and it's easy to miss the fact that there was a sole survivor: Ben Cauley.

At the time of the crash, Cauley played the trumpet in the Otis Redding band, the Bar-Kays. He and his fellow musicians, most of them high school buddies in their late teens and twenties, were having the time of their lives touring the United States with the superstar Redding. The day before the crash, Redding and his group had filmed a TV show and then played a concert in Cleveland. They got up early the next morning to go to the airport, bound for Madison, Wisconsin. Aboard Redding's twin-engine Beechcraft, they eventually took off. Still tired from the previous night's gig, the passengers soon drifted off to sleep. But Cauley woke up with a start because he couldn't breathe. Then he heard his bandmate, who was sitting across the aisle from him, say, "Oh no!"

"And I turned to say something to him, but I couldn't because I couldn't breathe. I reached down and unbuckled my seat belt. I don't know why. I just reached down and unbuckled it. This may have saved my life. I don't know. God must have been with me," Cauley recalled in a 1967 interview with *Jet* magazine. "Otis was sitting directly in front of me in the co-pilot's seat. I didn't hear him say a word. Didn't see him do a thing. The next thing I remember is bobbing up in the water holding this cushion."

The plane had plummeted into the icy waters of Lake Monona, a few miles short of the runway in Madison. Cauley found himself floating in the frigid water, clutching a cushion as a float; he couldn't swim. He heard one of his bandmates about twenty-five feet away yelling out for help. He tried to paddle over but watched his friend disappear beneath the swirling surface. He saw another friend, the drummer Carl Cunningham, emerge for a moment and then, wordlessly, sink away in a matter of seconds. Struggling to stay conscious in spite of hypothermia, Cauley felt he, too, "was fixing to go." The next thing he remembered was being pulled from the water by rescuers on a police boat. A witness on the shore had seen the plane go down and immediately alerted the authorities. Cauley was taken to a local hospital with relatively minor injuries but in a state of shock. He kept inquiring about his friends: "Are they all right?" The answer: "Son, you're the only one alive."

More than four decades have passed since the crash, but for Cauley the horror of that December day—the cries of his friends, his utter helplessness, the silence that followed—hasn't faded easily into the past. Even now, he seeks counseling for the trauma he suffered, and which he still cannot recount without tears in his eyes. His survival conferred upon him a dubious status, something talismanic perhaps, as the living link to the triumph and the tragedy of the musical legacy of Otis Redding. Forever connected to this moment in time, Cauley is a man with a haunting story that everyone wants to hear. Now in his late sixties, Cauley continues to play and perform soul music with his new band despite having suffered a massive stroke that doctors believed he would not survive. Amazingly, he recovered, but these days his family takes care he doesn't talk too long about the crash, for it's a deeply traumatic experience that, says one of his close associates, causes his blood pressure to rise, time to collapse, and events to replay themselves all over again.

On the fortieth anniversary of the crash, Cauley returned to Madison to the site of the crash for the first time. During a small ceremony honoring Otis Redding and the lost members of the Bar-Kays band, Cauley performed elegiac renditions of "Try a Little Tenderness" and "(Sittin' on) The Dock of the Bay," which Redding finished recording just days before the crash. It was an important moment of return for the musician, who dressed in black to pay his respects to his long-lost buddies. "Lord knows, it just really touched me to be there," he said in a 2007 interview with Memphis's newspaper *The Commercial Appeal.* "You know, for a long time I used to tell my kids, 'One day I'm going back.' I just had to see the lake. I had to see it."

———

For Toby, the question of why Grace and Lily survived was fraught with hidden dangers. Why, Grace would ask, did Mommy die? Toby also sensed that the question had a silent second part: Why did we survive? He tried his best to give an honest, rational answer that might satisfy a four-year-old, something about Mommy being in the front of the plane and Grace and Lily being in the back. Something must have happened to let you get out, he would say, and we don't know how that happened.

A number of people would comment, "It's a miracle that Grace and Lily survived," or they might say of Kathryn's death, "Jesus needed another angel." Toby recognized that the miraculous nature of their survival was tempered by a harsh truth: There was no miracle for Kathryn. "People tell me there's a reason the girls survived and that they're meant to do X, Y or Z—that we don't know what it is but that there's a reason they survived," Toby told the *St. Paul Pioneer Press*. "Well, they are special. But I still think Kathryn had a reason to be around. That's the hard part for me, the difficult part."

Toby concluded that miracle comments, while well intended, were probably more about making the speaker feel good. In the end, maybe life and death was just a matter of crash physics. For a child, this whole notion—as one of the Pearson girls later summed it up—was "just a weird deal."

5

ONE STEP AT A TIME

In the first few days at Regions Hospital in Saint Paul, Toby found himself shuttling between his daughters, who were installed in separate rooms due to their different medical conditions. Still in an induced coma, Lily was hooked up to life-giving machinery on the intensive care wing of the burn unit, where nurses could observe her from behind big glass windows. When Toby first looked in to locate his sleeping girl, surrounded by the tangle of equipment that monitored her vital signs, he felt horrified by the image. He was numb, haunted, staggered by these unnatural circumstances. He would walk back from Lily's intensive wing to Grace's room, where he might find her sitting up or looking at one of her books, her hands tightly bandaged. At least she was alert.

Toby tried to fortify himself against the reality of his daughters in the burn unit, against the sterile environment of the room, against the white noise by putting up smiling pictures of the girls from happier times, carefree summer snapshots from the far side of the crash.

Still, Toby felt he had done something right by moving the girls to Regions, whose highly reputable burn center became one of the country's first in 1963, back when specialized care for burns was a brand-new idea. Since then, the unit had developed a highly skilled team of doctors, nurses, and therapists who treated all kinds of burns and wounds—including thermal burns, electrical and chemical burns, and frostbite. One of the busiest burn units in the country, it admits approximately 250 to 300 burn patients per year to its inpatient facility and provides outpatient treatment to an additional 400 people. Toby thought he and the girls were in good hands, although he felt completely disoriented in this new world where acute pain was a daily fact of life.

On day two of his daughters' hospital stay, Toby met with a team of doctors led by David Ahrenholz and William J. Mohr. They explained the nature of Grace's and Lily's burns and mapped out a detailed plan for surgery. Lily was obviously in the worse condition, with "massive" third-degree burns on her arms, legs, and the right side of her face—about 30 percent of her body. She was also breathing with a tube due to atelectasis, or loss of lung volume due to swelling in her body. Grace had suffered third-degree burns on her hands and a broken leg (now in a cast) from the crash. With the girls already more than a week out from their initial injuries, the doctors proposed surgery as soon as possible to remove all areas of burned skin that were not going to heal. This would involve an intensive series of operations and would require skin grafts. Dr. Mohr explained that the biggest risk for burn patients is always infection. With severely burned skin, it's only a matter of time before it gets infected, so this was a matter of urgency. But then the removal of the skin itself also carries its own risks. As Mohr explained it, "to heal a burn you have to make more open wounds."

Very quickly Toby had to become knowledgeable about operating on burns and skin grafts. He knew enough, even at this stage, to know that when the doctors said they would perform a "full-thickness" skin graft, this would be the better option for the girls because it offers a better cosmetic and functional outcome than the alternative—and the more commonly used—"split-thickness" graft. The full-thickness graft requires removing a deeper layer of the skin from a donor site on the body, often close to the burned skin so that it offers a similar color and texture to the surrounding skin. Ultimately, this skin heals with less scarring, which was particularly important in Lily's case since she'd be receiving a facial skin graft. The doctors laid out the risks of this procedure, explaining that sometimes patients do reject their own skin, but that this would be unlikely because the children were both so young.

Toby asked about the cosmetic outcome for Lily and the rehabilitation required. The doctors walked him through their procedure. For the facial grafts, the doctors intended to remove skin from the back of Lily's head, the closest match in terms of color and texture to the face. However, they warned that when a patient is young, the wound healing happens faster but the likelihood of scarring is greater than in an adult. To counteract scar tissue, Lily would have to wear a transparent face mask to apply pressure to the tissue. Mohr explained that scar tissue is essentially abnormally arranged healing tissue, comparing it to lumber scattered in a big pile. Applying pressure to this higgledy-piggledy collection of skin tissue encourages it to "stack nicely" and thus minimizes scarring. For the hands and body, pressure garments are created, but when it comes to the face, the task is more complicated.

Mohr explained it was the burn unit at Regions that first developed the transparent flexible mask, sometimes called a TFO or transparent facial orthosis, that Lily would ultimately have to wear following her surgeries. Doctors would take an impression of her face to build the plastic mask so it fit tightly over her features, and this process would have to be repeated regularly as she grew. The maturation process for scar tissue is around a year, but it continues for a longer period in children; Mohr estimated that Lily would have to wear the mask for eighteen months to two years.

Toby swallowed hard listening to this sobering information, knowing they were in this for the long haul. He was glad to have a time frame around everything, but even so he couldn't think that far ahead. These scientific, medical explanations were plausible, even reassuring, but when it came down to it, his daughters had to get through some seriously grueling surgery.

The night before Grace's first surgery, Toby sat on the hospital bed next to his daughter to explain how the doctors were going to make her better. "Gracie, the skin on the back of your hands doesn't work anymore, so the doctors have to put new skin on them," he said as his daughter looked up at him with her big hazel eyes. "What they're going to do is cut your hair, shave it, and then take the skin from your head and put it on your hands. Your hands are going to be very sore."

Toby touched Grace's hands and legs where she was going to get new skin. "They're going to come wake you up very early in the morning to take you down to fix your hands," Toby said.

Grace asked her dad if he would be there. He nodded, seeing how frightened his daughter felt by the prospect of this scary journey. She wanted to know if it would hurt. She wanted to know if she would wake up.

"I'll be there all the time," he said.

That night Toby slept again in Grace's room, as he had insisted he do since they had arrived at the hospital. She wanted him to be there. As usual, Grace woke him up with the nightmares she'd starting having after the crash. Often, she'd cry in her sleep, shake her head, crying out "Mommy!" She'd wake up screaming, startled, confused, and unable to remember the details of the dream. Toby would watch her drift off again, to land where unknown creatures waited to torment his daughter. He felt helpless.

The next morning, the medical team arrived to take Grace down for the surgery. What surprised Toby was not his daughter's fear of the unknown, but her fortitude. Perhaps Grace sensed her dad's anxiety, but around this time she started to deliver a line adapted from the Winnie the Pooh movie she'd recently watched. "Dad, I'm stronger than you think I am," she said. He was astonished that Grace was able to adapt A. A. Milnes's original line—"You are braver than you believe, stronger than you seem, and smarter than you think"—and deploy it at exactly the right moment. It's amazing, Toby thought. Here's my four-year-old reassuring me.

Burn injuries have always been especially difficult to treat. An ancient Egyptian scroll, the Ebers Papyrus from circa 1550 B.C.E., prescribed a mixture of cow dung and black mud as a kind of putrid ointment for such injuries. Over the centuries, physicians have argued about the most effective ways of treating burns, including the application of bizarre salves made of bear fat soaked in red wine, roasted earthworms mixed with moss from a dead man's skull, to the painful use of boiling-hot oil to cauterize wounds. In the sixteenth century, Ambroise Paré, a French surgeon who honed his profession on the battlefield, devised new treatments for soldiers burned by gunpowder. He developed gentler types of treatments using emollient salves for wounds, with such mixtures as egg yolk, rose oil, and turpentine, which were less painful and more effective than the traditional methods.

In the early seventeenth century, the celebrated German physician Wilhelm Fabry published his comprehensive work on burns called *De Combustionibus*, which included a new classification system of burns into three degrees according to their severity, a system still used today. A first-degree burn is considered a mild burn, which results in pain and reddening of the epidermis. A second-degree burn affects the epidermis and the dermis (the lower level of skin) and causes pain, redness, swelling, and blistering. A third-degree burn penetrates deep into the dermis and can affect connective tissue, muscle, and even bone. Much progress was made in the twentieth century with the development of antibiotics to fight infection, the main killer, and especially after World War II, when burn units started to approach burns in a multidisciplinary way with teams of experts—not just surgeons but also nurses, psychiatrists, and physical and occupational therapists. Remarkably, but perhaps not surprisingly, advancement in therapy for burn victims is typically accelerated during a war. In the early 1950s, prompted by burn injuries during the Korean War, the U.S. government established a burn center at the Institute of Surgical Research, Brooke Army Medical Center, in San Antonio, Texas, where skin grafting became the preferred treatment for those who'd survived. The Burn Center at Regions was also instrumental in developing treatments and technologies that are used all over the world, such as the clear plastic masks for facial burns and a treatment for frostbite that saves fingers and toes.

Toby was entering this new territory, learning about burns and burn survivors; the acute pain and surgery were just the beginning of a much longer process. In the early days at Regions, Toby would occasionally glimpse other patients, some of whom had suffered terrible, disfiguring injuries—a shock to his senses at first. But he began to understand that even people with 80 percent of their body burned could survive. Still, there was a great deal of risk, especially for Lily. With the 30 percent burns on her body, Lily's chances of survival were much stronger than they would have been decades earlier. As Mohr explained, forty years earlier it would have been fifty-fifty whether she survived. Fifty years ago, she wouldn't have made it.

After Grace had her first surgery on her hands, it was Lily's turn. On the night before her first operation, Lily was brought out of the induced coma and was able to sit up in bed. Toby, relieved that she was out of her drugged-up state, was able to hold her and even watch one of her favorite movies with her— Disney's *The Lion King*. While she sleepily watched the television, Toby watched Lily as she wiggled her foot this way and that on the bed. It was an image that touched his heart, a brief respite from the relentless medical imperatives.

Lily underwent the first of five scheduled surgeries for her burns and, despite all the reassurances from the physicians, Toby felt weak with worry about what lay in store. Mohr had explained the procedure in detail. Over the course of the surgeries they would remove all the areas of the burned skin that weren't going to heal. In the first operation they would replace that skin with cadaver skin to allow blood vessels to grow back, as well as providing coverage to exposed nerves. This was to be a temporary procedure to enable a "graft bed" to develop over five days, in preparation for the skin graft. To remove the burned skin was a three-hour procedure, which inevitably involved a very high blood loss and therefore required several transfusions. For anyone, not just a three-year-old, this kind of surgery placed tremendous physical strain on the body. There was also a degree of time pressure for the surgeons, as a child cannot stay "under" for too long. Later, in another operation, skin would be harvested from the back of her head for the facial skin graft, and from her back to replace the ruined skin on her legs and arms.

The first surgery went well, but afterward Lily had to go

back on the ventilator. Because the body needs to build all sorts of new proteins to develop a new blood supply, heal tissue, and fight off infection with new white blood cells, the body's metabolic rate increases dramatically. A burn is the most metabolically taxing injury there is, explained Dr. Mohr, and the body requires twice the amount of protein ordinarily necessary to function. For this reason, Lily also had a feeding tube, augmented with protein-rich nutrition to promote recovery.

Grace would often ask her dad about Lily, and Toby's response would be something like "She's still on her medicine." Grace liked to look through the glass windows at her sister, though she couldn't go to her bedside and touch her and see how she was doing. She was mostly sleeping. In her own way, Grace was ever vigilant and protective toward her little sister. After all, she was the one who'd saved her life.

With the daily focus on Grace and Lily, Toby barely had time for his own grief. He was exhausted. The hospital recommended that he sleep in his own room, not in the same room as Grace. Although solitude was difficult, moving allowed better rest and self-reflection. Every night before he went to sleep, he would say the same prayer as a mantra:

God, grant me the serenity to accept the things I cannot change,
the courage to change the things I can,
and the wisdom to know the difference.

Several times a week, when he could find the energy, Toby would go running. It was some relief from the anguish and the medical claustrophobia of the hospital regimen. He ran from Regions along Summit Avenue, past the State Capitol in downtown Saint Paul, with its triumphant dome rising over the city skyline. He knew the building well from his work as a lobbyist with NCRLC. He was grateful that his bosses were more than understanding about his new situation—he could work a couple of hours a day and, they said, not worry about it. They had him covered. This was some relief. He ran up the hill toward the massive Cathedral of Saint Paul with its bright exterior walls of Saint Cloud granite, past the grand Victorian mansions on the street—houses where the railroad and lumber barons and even F. Scott Fitzgerald once lived. He ran beneath the old trees, whose leaves were turning yellow in the cool autumn air, a route that, under any other circumstances, offered lovely vistas at every turn. But Toby was not focused on the exterior world. Instead, running provided a kind of simple therapy, a way of dealing with the invisible but astounding forces of grief and hope, finding the energy he needed to press on against the past, against the constant loop in his head. Kissing his wife good-bye, the blue Ford Explorer driving away to the airport. A smiling face framed by the window. The last time he ever saw her. As he ran, he would not listen to music, but instead listened to his breath, his only form of control in a world that was suddenly chaotic. One step at a time, he told himself. Keep moving forward.

"There's a hole in the middle of my life and I don't know where to go next," Toby told a reporter from the *St. Paul Pioneer Press.* "The days all blend together and it's hard to keep them separate. So when I run, I wish life was as simple as just putting one foot in front of the other. I don't know if there's a support group for men whose wives die in plane crashes and leave them with two little girls."

Of course, local and national reporters were all clamoring for news of Grace and Lily. Despite his need for privacy, Toby recognized people were interested in the fates of his daughters, maybe too interested. He'd been unsettled by certain rumors that were circulating—that the girls were all on their own, that people wanted to adopt them. Even strangers felt they had a claim on the "miracle girls." Toby thought the time was right for a press conference, which he and Dr. Ahrenholz held on Tuesday, September 16, 2003. TV cameras from the four major networks showed up, as well as reporters from the main Minnesota newspapers, including the *Star Tribune* and the *St. Paul Pioneer Press*. He hoped it would satisfy the curious and put a stop to any unpleasant hearsay.

Toby brought Grace down in her wheelchair to the press conference, and she sat in his lap and snuggled close to her dad as the cameras flashed away. Her hands and right foot were bandaged, and her left leg was still in its fluorescent pink cast. Before the conference, Toby spoke to his daughter and explained carefully that a lot of people wanted to know how she was feeling. He told her that she didn't have to say anything, and that he would be with her all the time. She understood. There were also ground rules for the media: Toby would talk, Ahrenholz would talk, but no one would be allowed to ask Grace anything directly.

Toby started by answering the question on everyone's mind.

"They have no explanation as to how the girls survived," he said.

Ahrenholz concurred. "This doesn't happen very often. . . . Even people who are 'seatbelted' don't often survive," he said. "It's amazing. But it doesn't minimize the loss."

At one point, Grace leaned over to her dad and whispered in his ear. She wanted to say something. "What do you want to say?" said Toby quietly. She explained to him, and then to the gathered reporters in a quiet but audible voice.

"We were a little bit scared of the accident, and I took good care of my sister," she said.

"Yes, you did," said Toby. "What did you do?"

Grace explained that when Lily wanted to go home, she told her, "We can't."

"I protected her," said Grace.

Toby was impressed that his four-year-old, seemingly timid and clutching a good-witch rag doll she called Glenda, spoke on topic in front of an intimidating crowd of reporters and photographers. Grace was right: She was stronger than even he knew.

While Grace pressed her head into his shoulder, Toby went on to express his deep gratitude to the rescue pilot, Dan Anderson, who went up in bad weather to search for the wreckage. "It was nothing short of heroism. Rescue workers on the ground wouldn't have been able to find the site if he hadn't spotted it. Who knows what would have happened overnight?"

That night, Grace kept telling the same story a few more times, about how she unbuckled her sister from the seat and moved away until the fire went down, about how they felt scared, about how they realized that Mommy wasn't there, and how they didn't know where she went. He listened carefully each time for the possibility of a new detail.

Toby understood Grace's repetitive storytelling was her way of dealing with the trauma she'd experienced. Early on, Regions assigned what they called a child-life specialist to Grace and Lily, a psychologist trained to deal with children who'd experienced the trauma of a burn injury, not to mention surviving a plane crash. The child-life specialist would spend time with Grace, talking and playing, trying to get a read on her emotional state. Sometimes Toby would ask the specialist about the best way of explaining concepts to his daughter, concepts like life and death. He was advised to speak in concrete terms. It was very important not to lie to her, or sugarcoat reality. Would the surgery hurt, for example? If Toby said no and she felt pain, Grace would never trust his word again.

Yes, there would be pain. But there was also hope and recovery. Toby learned this from Christine Gilyard, another counselor assigned by the hospital to Grace and Lily. She worked at the hospital two days a week to offer support and advice to families of burn victims. Her official title was Burn Survivor Peer Support representative, which she admitted didn't exactly roll off the tongue. She introduced herself to Toby as he stood next to Lily, who lay sleeping.

"She looks so sad," said Chris.

"She's got a lot of things to be sad about," said Toby.

Gilyard knew from her own experience what it meant to be injured by fire. In 1979, when she was seventeen, she was badly burned in a car accident. Her small car, an AMC Gremlin, was rear-ended at night during a snowstorm. The gas tank exploded. A man came along and dragged her out of the passenger-side door. She discovered later he was a welder who happened to be wearing protective clothing that insulated him from the heat. Chris ended up at the Burn Center at Regions Hospital, where she spent two months being treated for severe burns to her face and body. Back then, in the late seventies, burn treatment wasn't as evolved, and the benefits of early excision had yet to be realized. The thinking was to wait for a few weeks before a skin graft, and that meant the excruciating hell of the tub room—painful debridement baths with little to no anesthetic—where burned skin would be sloughed off. A nurse thought it would be a good idea to hold a mirror up to Chris so she could see her face without any skin. It was unbelievably shocking. Likewise, when Chris saw her face immediately after grafting, she thought, I don't look like a girl anymore. Her cartilage had melted; her eyebrows were gone. Another crushing thought: *Who is ever going to love me?*

Chris was seventeen when it happened. Lily was three. But Chris could offer Toby advice, comfort, and reassurance. She'd been one of the first patients to wear the transparent face mask that Regions Burn Center developed to prevent scarring. In fact, Regions even had a display showing Chris's journey from survivor to advocate. She was living proof that a patient could not only survive but could have a life, despite the scars and the trauma. "I really have a good outcome," said Chris, who learned that her physical presence was good news for families of burn survivors but observed that patients were not always so pleased when they saw her scars.

In those first two years outside the hospital wearing the mask, Chris had suffered. Strangers stared, teased her, and someone even looped back along his route to sneak another look at her face. When she did venture out wearing the mask she both needed and hated, she felt vulnerable and exposed and lonely. Once she dared to go out to a mall with her sister. A young guy across the space, walking around with his buddies, shouted, "Hey, what's with the mask? Halloween's over." Chris's sister flipped and started yelling at him. "What the fuck are you looking at?" she said, shaming him in front of everyone with the shocking explanation; he came over to apologize. That was just one incident. But people were rude—they gasped, they pointed, they whispered. Sometimes parents pulled their children away. In the face of this cruel barrage, it was a struggle for Chris to remember who she was.

Chris certainly knew about the pain of social reentry for burn patients, and right now, looking down at Lily lying there, she could empathize not only with her current pain, but also anticipate her future anguish as a burn survivor. Chris had recently described her own experience in a book, *Walking Through the Ashes*, which revisited her severe burn trauma in a series of short, vivid poems. She traced her story from the car crash to the hell of treatment to rediscovering her identity after being scarred. Her words, which she shared with Toby, offered an insight into survival.

> The day began as the day before
> Something new, nothing more.
> Sun so hot, snow so white
> Day was day, night was night.
>
> But everything changed
> In the wink of an eye
> And though I understood how . . .
> I often asked why?
>
> For I was burned by fire you see
> And after tasting fire
> It's hard to be free
>
> Free from the innocence of knowing pain,
> Free from the fear it might happen again.

During the weeks at Regions, Toby would engage in longer conversations with Chris, learning from her experience, arming himself with knowledge and vocabulary—the language of "cosmetic differences" and "pressure garments" and "post-traumatic stress syndrome"—for this long journey back to normal life. Right now, it seemed things would never be normal again, but Chris offered hope. Now in her early forties, more than two decades after the horror of the crash, here was a woman who had regained beauty, confidence, and grace after being so badly injured.

Days after the press conference, the Minnesota newspapers ran stories about the Pearsons, one of which in the *Star Tribune* caught everyone's attention, "Amazing Grace." Of course, Grace had captured everyone's heart. More offers of help for the Pearsons came in. When word got out that Toby's sister, Beth, had a roster of friends and family who would bring in home-cooked meals for Toby, more volunteers stepped up. A local running shop called Run N Fun donated designer running apparel for Toby, including short and long pants for when the weather turned cold.

Toward the end of that week, something unexpected happened. Toby received a phone call from the Cook County Sheriff's Office. Chief Deputy Sheriff Mark Falk wanted to drive down from Grand Marais to see how the girls were doing, and also to deliver something important to Toby. They set a time to meet on Thursday, September 18, when neither Grace nor Lily had any surgery scheduled. Toby was eager to meet the man who had found his daughters alive in the forest exactly three weeks earlier.

Toby waited alone in the family room at the Burn Center, feeling nervous. The deputy sheriff walked in, dressed in his uniform. The physically imposing thirty-seven-year-old Falk approached Toby and gave him a bear hug, or so it seemed to the smaller man, but it was genuine and heartfelt and overwhelming. Toby thanked him profusely for saving the girls, and for all the work that the sheriff's department had done to keep the girls alive. His blue eyes shone with tears. Falk, too, felt his stoic reserve crumble faced with the gratitude of this man who'd "lost his lovely wife," and whose daughters were now without their mother.

Falk, who was married with an older son and two teenage daughters, felt deeply moved by Toby's sorrow.

Toby listened, for the first time, to the whole story of the rescue, about how the pilot Dan Anderson had taken his plane back up despite the clouds and the ongoing bad weather, to look for the missing plane. Falk explained how Anderson had spotted the wreckage and radioed down to the rescuers, telling them, "There'll be no survivors. Just bring body bags." But of course there were survivors, at first mistaken for dolls, two little girls lying there on the seat, waiting, strangely calm. Nearby the ruined cockpit and its occupants, the burning trees, the intense heat even five hours after the crash. Falk had picked up Lily, and his partner picked up Grace, and they carried the girls to the awaiting ATVs, which rushed them through the trees to the service road.

Falk explained he had something valuable to give Toby and it only seemed right to present it in person. He put his hand in his pocket and drew out a heart-shaped white enamel case. It was about the size of a bar of soap, decorated with a fine gold lattice and a gold clasp. Falk opened it to reveal a ring with a double band of white gold and a diamond. Toby immediately recognized it as the ten-year anniversary ring that he'd given Kathryn, a ring she'd been wearing when the plane crashed. Overcome with emotion, Toby took the case in his hand.

Falk explained what had happened. Two weeks after the crash, he'd received a call from a friend of Toby's, Jim Metry, who wanted to know if the sheriff's department had recovered any of the rings. Falk reported that they hadn't found anything, but the inquiry started him thinking. He decided to return to the scene of the crash to have another look around. He went up there alone and walked back into the forest, eventually finding his way back to the clearing. It looked different. The big pieces of the wreckage were gone, removed by the NTSB for post-crash investigation, but there was still debris scattered on the forest floor. Falk recalled the location of the cockpit and tried to remember the position of the bodies. He wasn't really sure, but he knelt down and started scraping the soil with a piece of Plexiglas he had found nearby. It seemed like a hopeless task, an attempt to find a needle in a haystack, and anyway surely the intense heat of the fire would have melted any piece of metal.

After a minute, Falk said something out loud. There was no one else there to hear him, but he said it anyway. "Kathryn, help me find your wedding ring."

He kept digging, uncovering the soil in the same place. Then he saw it. Just a few minutes after he'd started digging, he saw the ring. It was covered in dirt but essentially undamaged. He couldn't believe it.

Falk said he took the ring to a friend who owned a jewelry store in Grand Marais to get it cleaned up. Falk shared the story of his incredible find with his wife, and with his close friends, all of whom were equally amazed by the story—was it luck or a miraculous turn of events? Falk knew immediately that he had to deliver the ring in person.

Toby cried as he listened to the story, stirred by tender feelings of gratitude and by the sharp reminder that Kathryn wasn't there. Toby took the ring back to his room and placed it safely in his suitcase. Then he went to collect Grace and wheeled her to the family room to meet a man who had saved her life. Toby wondered if Grace would remember this big man with a moustache who'd found Lily and her in the forest. She didn't seem to at first, but when Toby explained who he was, Grace said a quiet "thank you."

Falk spoke very quietly and tenderly to Grace, asking her how she was doing.

"Pretty good, but my hands hurt," said Grace in hushed tones.

"I hear you're getting out of here and going to your grand-parents'," said Falk, who'd learned from Toby that Grace would be staying with his mom and dad, Mimi and Tom, in Mankato.

"Yes, I'm leaving Lily here," she said. "But I'll come back and visit."

"Recovering from a burn is like a marathon," said Dr. Mohr. This much was clear to Toby as he measured his days at the Burn Center one run after another. In the first two weeks at Regions, Lily had undergone five major operations to remove the burned skin and to receive the skin grafts. She was out of immediate danger, and Toby could feel more confident that she would re-cover. When Grace turned five years old on September 27, Toby arranged for a little party in the family room. Mimi and Tom drove Grace back from Mankato for the event. Grace had been discharged from Regions on September 18 and was now being cared for by her grandparents while Toby continued to live at the hospital. Lily watched Grace blow out the candles on her birth-day cake. It was truly a birthday to celebrate.

But yet another threat to Lily's health suddenly loomed. Be-cause of the constant need to draw blood to monitor her progress, Lily had a catheter going into one of the large central veins of her leg. This allowed the nurses to draw blood from her painlessly, without having to constantly tap veins with a needle that chil-dren's bodies can't tolerate for long. The downside to this meant an increased chance of bacterial infection, which is what hap-pened next.

A specialist was brought in. Toby could tell by her expression, and the urgency with which she worked, that this was serious. It was, the doctors said, a bloodstream infection called MRSA, a "very resistant organism." It was—it went without saying—life threatening. Now, with a raging temperature, Lily was put on the antibiotic of last resort, vancomycin, used to treat aggressive penicillin-resistant infections. Given intravenously, the drug required yet another tube, yet another breach of the skin. Toby called his older brother, Tony, to get his doctor's insight into MRSA and what would happen if the drug didn't work. Tony confirmed that it was potentially fatal, especially for a three-year-old already in a weakened state.

Toby felt numbed by this intelligence. There was no way out of this. It seemed unfair for Lily to survive a plane crash, third-degree burns, and skin grafts only to succumb to something invisible.

Sitting in a chair by her bedside, Toby stayed awake all night, willing and praying for Lily to pull through and wake up. The doctors said, "We'll know within a day."

Overnight she burned with fever. Then morning arrived.

Lily woke up.

Her temperature apparently was dropping.

The specialist confirmed it.

The drug had worked.

She had survived again.

That week, Toby went running again, parsing out his pain in steps. He almost ran into a car exiting a driveway near the cathedral. A man—a familiar face—jumped out. It was the archbishop, who called after him by name, "Toby!" The archbishop wanted to know about the girls and how they were doing, offering Toby his prayers, his blessings. The encounter seemed fortuitous. The community was rooting for him and his girls. Tragedy had conferred upon him a dubious kind of fame.

There were still more trials ahead, and another medical digression.

One evening as Toby held Lily while she sat on his lap, he

looked down her body and noticed that her legs were bent at a funny angle. He mentioned this to her doctors and, sure enough, they determined that both legs had been broken. Because of the catastrophic nature of Lily's burns, and reports that both girls had been walking in the forest after the crash, the break had remained undiscovered. No wonder, Toby thought, that Lily didn't want to walk around even though she was feeling better.

An orthopedic specialist—Dr. Steven Koop of Gillette Children's Specialty Healthcare, which was located on the fourth floor of Regions—was added to the list of doctors attending to Lily's injuries. A decision was made not to rebreak the legs but to observe Lily's progress as the bones continued to heal. It would be something to keep an eye on—there was some nerve damage that meant Lily couldn't properly flex her foot. The doctor suggested fitting an orthopedic boot to see if the nerves would heal along with the bones.

Six weeks after her arrival at the Burn Center, the day arrived when Lily was to be discharged from the hospital. Grace had been coming back with her grandparents most days for treatments and because she wanted to see her sister. Their departure was a poignant moment, since everyone in the unit had fallen for the sweet-natured Pearson girls and their attentive father in running shoes. Days before they had to leave, Toby learned how to use the snug-fitting compression garments both Grace and Lily were required to wear until their scars healed, as well as the transparent plastic face mask that Lily needed to wear twenty to twenty-two hours a day for two years. She was to take it off only for eating, care, and face exercises.

Toby had watched in amazement as craftsmen created this mask. A mold of Lily's face was turned to plaster of paris, a startling white monument to this moment in time, cast into a solid bust for the mask makers. Now it stared out from a cabinet of hundreds of similar sculptures, the silent faces of those who came before, all afflicted by fire. Near Lily's face was an earlier incarnation, the head of the seventeen-year-old Chris Gilyard.

On the day he left Regions, Toby buckled Grace and Lily into the backseat of the Ford Explorer, just as he had done on that late summer morning when they'd left for the airport. His brother Tony was there to help. Looking in the rearview mirror, Toby could see his daughters—wounded and motherless—but still the same Grace and Lily, safe in their car seats. As he drove, he talked to Tony about the days ahead. Halloween was just around the corner, and then Thanksgiving, and then Christmas. As they got closer to Duluth, Toby started to feel severely anxious about the future. He hadn't been back to the house—*their* house—since the day of the crash. It was now late autumn. The leaves had gone. He wasn't ready.

6

A PERIOD OF WILD SUSPENSE AND UTTER BEWILDERMENT

Weeks after the crash, the wreckage of Charlie Erickson's plane ended up in an aircraft salvage yard in an area of South Minneapolis known as Phillips. This was a facility called Wentworth Aircraft, billed as "the world's largest aircraft salvage operation for single engine and light twin general aviation aircraft." Hidden away behind a tall wooden fence topped with barbed wire, the lot provoked curiosity in the midst of this otherwise leafy residential neighborhood. Had people actually died in those planes? One local nicknamed Wentworth "the Midtown Phillips Light Aircraft Graveyard." Inside, the white cabins of defunct planes—Cessna, Piper, Beech, and Mooney—lay side by side, crushed and deformed like huge bugs without their wings.

In November, John Dornik paid the place a visit. He was interested in the remnants of the Beechcraft Baron, which he knew had been brought here by investigators from the National Transportation Safety Board. As was routine after any aviation accident, the NTSB had already examined the wreckage—a teardown and investigation—for evidence of why the aircraft had crashed. It had yet to issue its report, which typically took the overworked federal agency a year. Dornik was also looking for evidence, but his motivation was different from the NTSB, whose primary goal is to develop factual records and issue safety recommendations. The forty-two-year-old Dornik was now acting in his capacity as Toby Pearson's lawyer, doing his due diligence as an experienced attorney who knew that where there was a plane crash, there were possible legal claims to be lodged against a manufacturer, a pilot, even air traffic control. It all depended who, if anyone, had made a mistake.

Shortly after the crash, it had become clear that Toby would need help with legal issues arising from the accident. Since Charlie Erickson was the pilot and the named insured on the policy, the Erickson estate would be the conduit through which the insurance settlement would be paid to Toby—compensation both for his wife's death and the injuries to Grace and Lily. Dornik quickly filed a claim in probate court handling the estate.

From his first involvement in the case, Dornik felt a personal connection to Toby and his daughters. He'd been referred to the Pearsons by one of Toby's college friends who'd vouched for Dornik as a "good and honest attorney." Dornik and Toby also shared a common background, having both been raised Catholic in the sixties and seventies, which, Dornik said, meant they were anything but strict adherents to the faith. Still, they shared that cultural bond as well as a common interest in social justice.

Dornik didn't set out to become a lawyer. In fact, he was a chemistry major at Saint Mary's College in Winona, though he quickly decided he didn't much like science. But with his natural eloquence and easy charm, Dornik discovered he had a gift for something else. When some of his classmates got hauled before the college disciplinary committee for drinking, Dornik stepped in to argue on their behalf. Whatever he said convinced the committee to go easy on the penitent students. Word quickly spread about Dornik's skills, and soon other students in trouble sought him out. "Get Dornik," they would say. These were early steps on his path to the plaintiff's bar. In Dornik's estimation, it was the only thing he was good at.

Dornik attended the University of Minnesota Law School and was admitted to the bar in 1989. He clerked for a while with the prosecutor at the Hennepin County Attorney's Office in Minneapolis, but soon realized criminal law wasn't for him because, as he saw it, most criminal defendants are guilty and he didn't want to spend his life defending "guilty folks." Instead, he accepted a low-paying job as a plaintiff's lawyer with Hvass, Weisman and King, a Minneapolis-based firm whose founder, Charlie Hvass, had flown bombing missions over Germany during World War II and now was a personal injury lawyer who specialized in aviation accidents. (He met his second wife handling a case involving her husband, who had died in a crash.) Hvass was renowned as one of the most thoughtful, logical, and prepared trial lawyers in Minnesota, something that made him a commanding presence in the courtroom. He set another important example for the young lawyers at his firm—be the nicest person you can be to both friends and adversaries alike. But, Hvass maintained, always be yourself. "Juries can smell a phony," he cautioned. Dornik took all these lessons to heart.

Success came quickly for Dornik. He took on a case of sexual abuse that he stumbled upon during his time at the prosecutor's office. A young woman who worked in the copy room had revealed to Dornik some painful past history—her high school teacher had repeatedly had sex with her when she was a student. At the time, Dornik was shocked but unable to help. It was a case of statutory rape, but a few years had passed and the statute of limitations prevented any criminal complaint from being filed. Dornik made a promise to help the woman if he was ever in the civil arena. Once he began working at Hvass, Dornik made good on the promise, following up with an investigation, and then issuing a complaint against the teacher and the school district, which tried to get the lawsuit dismissed. Dornik prepared well, finding other witnesses who supported the woman's testimony; the judge agreed that sexual misconduct had occurred. Before the case went to trial, the school district settled the case, awarding more than $1 million in compensation to the woman. Dornik was thrilled with the result, and saw his first major case written up in the Minnesota newspapers.

After seven years of honing his trade as a personal injury lawyer at Hvass, handling everything from medical malpractice to automobile accidents, Dornik teamed up with a partner to create his own law firm, Mackenzie and Dornik, headquartered on the twenty-fifth floor of a luxury tower in Minneapolis. Anyone who met Dornik could tell that he'd done well; he wore expensive Armani suits, exuded a boyish charm, and had a wicked sense of humor bolstered by a boisterous laugh. He also had a touch of the maverick about him and had been known to roll up to work on his vintage Honda 750cc motorcycle, although not usually in a $2,000 suit.

By the time Dornik started working with Toby Pearson, he'd handled many aviation cases and knew from experience there could be litigation arising from this kind of crash. He was hoping it would be a "product case," which would allow him to go after the manufacturer, but he also knew mechanical failures accounted for fewer than 15 percent of accidents in small planes like these.

One recent case loomed large in his mind. It was an aviation accident involving a thirty-eight-year-old dentist who had crashed his own plane, flying it right into the ground. He had died instantly. The pilot's tearful wife came to see Dornik and told him, "I don't know what happened. He was a good pilot." After an investigation, Dornik discovered that some of the teeth on the crankshaft gears were missing, which meant the propeller wouldn't turn. It doomed this single-engine plane. Dornik brought a wrongful death suit against the aircraft manufacturer and won $4.5 million in damages—a figure that, in 2003, was the biggest wrongful death settlement in Minnesota history. It was some consolation for the grieving wife, and a vindication, too. "You were right," Dornik told her. "Your husband didn't crash his plane."

Dornik moved down the rows of smashed-up fuselages at Wentworth Aircraft, each a twisted tale of woe, looking for the Beechcraft Baron. That one flew into a thunderstorm, while another apparently ran out of fuel. He found Erickson's plane inside the warehouse, concealed under a tarpaulin. Although he wasn't an expert, experience had taught him to return to the scene of the accident and to examine the wreckage. Sometimes serendipity provided an answer in the form of a broken piece of equipment. But when he lifted the tarp to look at the charred hull, he saw it was burned, destroyed beyond the point that it could reveal anything to him. He later called the lead investigator of the NTSB, Mitchell Gallo, to get his read on what had caused the crash. Although the official report would not be published for many more months, Gallo told him everything pointed to a case of pilot error.

Beginning in August 2003 and continuing through to April 2004, the NTSB conducted a study—"Risk Factors Associated with Weather-Related General Aviation Accidents"—that it eventually published on September 7, 2005. Investigators collected data from seventy-two general aviation accidents that occurred in weather conditions characterized by IMC, or instrument meteorological conditions, a flight category that describes weather conditions bad enough that the pilot must fly by reference to instruments only. Typically, this means a pilot is flying in clouds or bad weather, with no external visual references. "Historically, about two-thirds of all general aviation (GA) accidents that occur in instrument meteorological conditions (IMC) are fatal—a rate much higher than the overall fatality rate for GA accidents," the study noted. The investigators wanted to make a statistical comparison of these so-called "accident flights" with "nonaccident flights," which had experienced similar weather conditions around the same time, the significant difference being they had not crashed. Tucked away in Appendix G of the study, one of the accident planes listed is a Beechcraft 58P that crashed on August 28, 2003 in Grand Marais, Minnesota—the "accident severity" reported as "fatal." Kathryn and Charlie had already become statistics.

In order to pilot an aircraft on an instrument flight rules (IFR) flight plan in bad weather conditions, pilots must add an instrument rating to their pilot certificates by completing additional training and passing both knowledge and practical tests. Pilots who aren't instrument rated are said to fly by visual flight rules (VFR)—that is, by using the horizon and features of the earth as a constant reference point. Much of the IFR training is focused on how to use aviation weather reports and forecasts before a flight, as well as the safe and efficient operation of an aircraft under instrument flight conditions. Federal regulations stipulate that receiving an instrument rating requires forty hours of actual or simulated instrument flight, including at least fifteen hours of flight training. It also requires periodic practice to maintain proficiency. If a person is "pilot-in-command" of a plane under IFR, that pilot is required to conduct "at least six instrument approaches . . . in actual and simulated instrument conditions" every six months to be current.

Charlie Erickson's fatal example proved that even though he was an instrument-rated pilot, things could still go wrong under pressure. In fact, the main conclusion of the NTSB report was that reduced-visibility weather exposed weaknesses in a pilot's knowledge, training, and skill, which were the underlying causes of the accident. The NTSB would not speculate on individual pilot errors in its case studies, instead taking a step back to draw general conclusions. There were a number of factors of higher risk that applied to Erickson. It found that 42 percent of the fatal accident sample occurred during the "descent/maneuver" and "approach/landing/go-around" phase of the flight, and that 19 percent of the accident pilots had been involved in a prior accident (which, importantly, Charlie had). The report also notes that the median number of flight hours for the accident pilots was thirteen hundred hours—a significant amount of flight time. Many of the pilots who crashed were hardly rookies.

The study selected accidents that "appeared to have involved spatial disorientation, loss of control, or collision with terrain or object due to a lack of visual references or encounter with weather." Obviously Erickson did encounter reduced visibility due to bad weather on their flight, but was it likely the pilot suffered from spatial disorientation? It was more typical for pilots who didn't hold an instrument rating and suddenly, scarily, found they could no longer see the horizon. Charlie, as one pilot observed, had "nailed the needles pretty well." How could an instrument-rated pilot with more than a thousand hours of flight experience crash his plane?

In the history of flight, spatial disorientation (SD) is considered to be the number one pilot killer. It can cause someone to fly a plane nose first into the ground, even as the pilot thinks he or she is in level flight. It's a powerful sensory illusion that, according to William J. Bramble Jr., a senior investigator at the NTSB, "refers to a pilot's failure to sense accurately the attitude, altitude or direction of motion of his or her aircraft."

"Spatial disorientation is a pretty huge problem, if not the number one problem for pilots," said Dr. Fred Patterson, an SD expert with the Naval Medical Research Unit (NAMRU) in Dayton, Ohio. Over the decades, both military and civilian institutions have studied the phenomenon of "spatial-d," as air force pilots call it, in case study after case study. It manifests itself in different ways but can scare even the most experienced pilots. Inevitably, spatial disorientation has emerged as a factor in a number of major accidents, as well as near accidents, in large commercial airplanes. If it can fool professionals who fly frequently, it's surely potent enough to trick a weekend pilot.

Even nature's supreme aviators, birds, can suffer from spatial disorientation if they lose visual reference with the ground, especially in situations where artificial light hinders a bird's ability to orient itself. Several studies have shown that nocturnally migrating birds are especially susceptible, and that certain wavelengths of light on overcast nights, when celestial cues like the moon are not visible, can interfere with the "magnetic compass of migrating birds." In one famous case study, fifty Blackburnian warblers, flying on a night of low clouds, crashed into a hangar and were killed. Scientists said intense floodlights around the building confused the birds, and this invoked spatial disorientation.

While birds are designed for flight, humans are not. Man is a terrestrial being with a balance system that works well on land, where the force of gravity keeps the body stable. Good spatial orientation on the ground relies on three equilibrium components—the visual, the vestibular (balance mechanism located in the inner ear), and proprioceptive (receptors in the muscles and joints that sense pressure on the body). In the air, however, our reference points can be thrown off easily enough because gravity no longer seems constant. During flight, the body can misinterpret centrifugal force, which is caused by changes in a plane's acceleration or motion. The body reads this change as gravity, as Scott McCredie explains in his book,

Balance: In Search of the Lost Sense. It's a phenomenon most have experienced when traveling in a commercial jet. A passenger may look up from a book and notice the plane in a sharp turn, banked, with one wing dipped toward the earth. Visually, the brain can acknowledge it's at an angle, but the proprioceptive sensors suggest that the body is being pushed back into its seat by gravity. We're not falling toward the earth or into the passenger next to us. In fact, the force that keeps the body in place is centrifugal force caused by the plane's turning motion.

Further complicating this in-flight perception, the vestibular senses read only *changes* in motion or velocity. So if the turn continues at a gradual rate, the brain fails to sense this because the vestibular system has returned to the neutral position, believing that the turn has ended. Worse still, once the turn has stopped, the brain registers this as a turn in the opposite direction. Of course, these sensory discrepancies can play havoc with a pilot—and especially one who is flying blind, without the visual component of the horizon as an anchor.

Ever since those pioneer aviators, the Wright brothers, took to the air in the early twentieth century, pilots have been subject to the mind games and illusions played by the vestibular system. Wilbur Wright referred to the "disturbances of equilibrium" that occurred in the air. For this reason, during the formative years of flight, no civilian pilot would risk flying blind, at night or in the clouds. Military aviators, on the other hand, suffered tremendous casualties due to what some termed "ear deaths." After World War I, spatial disorientation started gaining wider recognition among pilots, and authors tried to capture the essence of the as-yet-unnamed sensation. A British professor of Aeronautical Engineering, Sir Bennett Melvill Jones, summed it up in an academic paper he wrote in 1920:

[The pilot's] first indication that something is wrong is, as a rule, either an increase or decrease of speed that is not counteracted by the accustomed movements of the controls. A period of wild suspense and utter bewilderment now follows, during which the pilot makes violent efforts to recover control, but without success. The next thing he realizes if he realizes anything at all, is that he is either on his back or spinning, and the next thing he knows is that he is out of the clouds with the earth standing up at a ridiculous angle and spinning round like a drunken dinner plate. Happy is he that has plenty of air room under those circumstances.

Gradually, the notion of flying with instruments started to emerge, although pilots still fervently believed in a macho creed—skill and instinct trumped the newfangled technology. But in the late twenties, things began to change. Building on the principles of the gyroscopic compass, developed by Elmer Sperry, scientists created a dial with an artificial horizon, which gave the pilot a graphic representation of the plane's attitude in relation to the horizon. In 1929, Army Air Corps Lieutenant James Doolittle—who also assisted with the development of this equipment—made the world's first flight solely by reference to the aircraft's cockpit instruments. It was a major breakthrough, although pilots still found it difficult to ignore the false sensations of "instinct" and preferred to fly "by the seat of their pants." Even as aviation technology has continued to advance, the vestibular and proprioceptive senses remain strictly and stubbornly terrestrial, of course. Since they will not evolve, only experience and training can overcome the hazards of disorientation.

Part of the problem with spatial disorientation is that pilots don't recognize when it's first happening, before it's too late to take corrective action. That's one of the key findings of a 2008 study, "Spatial Disorientation in Large Commercial Airplanes," by William J. Bramble Jr. of the NTSB, which documents fatal and nonfatal instances of spatial disorientation among professional pilots. Bramble calls the phenomenon "an especially insidious form of subtle incapacitation."

The accidents cited by Bramble shared common characteristics. They all occurred in reduced visibility conditions, at night or in bad weather, requiring instruments; there were often distractions that preceded an unexpected deviation from the flight plan; most of the accidents happened when the airplane was "turning and climbing, during departure, go-around or missed approach"— when flying is at its most involved. These factors can combine, or cascade, and set the context for a spatial disorientation accident.

This context also applies to general aviation flights. The fateful flight of Buddy Holly, Ritchie Valens, and the Big Bopper on February 3, 1959, is a case in point. According to the report by the Civil Aeronautics Board, the four-seater Beechcraft Bonanza took off into "an overcast sky, snow falling, no definite horizon, and a proposed flight over a sparsely settled area with an absence of ground lights." It pointed out that any pilot flying into these conditions would need to fly solely by reference to flight instruments. Unfortunately, the pilot, twenty-one-year-old Roger Peterson, had limited experience flying blind, and was yet to be instrument qualified. Because of that deficiency, it concluded, "he could have become confused and thought that he was making a climbing turn when in reality he was making a descending turn." The fact that the aircraft struck the earth in a "steep turn" suggested something else, too—that the pilot had found himself in the nightmare scenario of the so-called graveyard spiral.

The graveyard spiral or spin is a worst-case scenario for any pilot. The description of this phenomenon in the FAA *Pilot's*

Handbook sounds bloodless and academic—"The illusion of the cessation of a turn while still in a prolonged, coordinated, constant rate turn, which can lead a disoriented pilot to a loss of control of the aircraft"—for an experience that's surely characterized by panic and terror. Unaware that his plane is banked but sensing the nose falling through the horizon, a pilot may pull back on the yoke in an attempt to stop this loss of altitude. Because of the physics of a banking turn, this action does not help and serves only to tighten the circle and speed up the descent. It quickly becomes a runaway bank—an ever-tightening gyre heading toward the earth. By now, all those tiny gyroscopes in the ear are totally confused. An inexperienced pilot has virtually no chance of returning to stable flight, and after a certain point, any attempt to correct this rapid plunge will break up the aircraft. In other words, it's all over.

In 1954, the University of Illinois Institute of Aviation conducted a study, led by Leslie A. Bryan and Jesse W. Stonecipher, in an attempt to simplify instrument flight technique. The researchers chose twenty subjects—pilots who were not yet instrument rated—and watched their reactions as they flew into simulated instrument weather. Nineteen pilots went into graveyard spirals, and one went into a "whip-stall," whereby the plane pitches nose down after a steep vertical climb. The outcome in each case would have been fatal. The study also calculated the life expectancy of a noninstrument-rated pilot, flying into clouds or bad weather or darkness. It was 178 seconds.

It's been observed that accident sites of graveyard spiral crashes are breathtaking in their devastation. The aircraft is literally broken into hundreds of pieces. Such was the case when investigators recovered John F. Kennedy's Piper Saratoga, which crashed in the Atlantic Ocean a few miles short of Martha's Vineyard on July 16, 1999. Radar data released a few days later showed that the flight ended in a plunge that was ten times the normal rate for a descent. It also explained why authorities had a difficult time recovering significant pieces of wreckage—a recovery not helped by the fact that he went down at sea. After a long investigation into the crash, the NTSB concluded that the reason for the crash was "pilot error," which hardly explained the nuances of the catastrophe. Since then, a number of pilots have reconstructed the last flight of JFK Jr., surmising inexperience along with spatial disorientation along with a thick haze over the Atlantic, which all added up to the cascade effect that killed not only the pilot but his two passengers, his wife, Carolyn Bessette Kennedy, and his sister-in-law Lauren G. Bessette.

"While spatial disorientation makes only a modest contribution to the overall accident rate in general aviation, it is responsible for a high percentage of its fatalities," says a 2004 study by AOPA's Air Safety Institute. It also found that VFR-rated pilots were responsible for most of these accidents, while instrument-rated pilots were much less likely to be involved in an accident caused by spatial disorientation. With Charlie Erickson's experience, it seemed improbable that he'd lost his orientation in the clouds like Kennedy or other pilots with marginal IFR training.

An experienced pilot who'd known Erickson well visited the crash site a few days after the accident. He'd often flown with Erickson and considered him a "technically proficient pilot," so he was naturally curious about what had caused the man to crash. He tramped around the forest floor, examined the still-smoldering wreckage, and came up with another scenario—that Erickson broke out of the clouds too late to land and began the missed-approach procedure, which involved a climb to 3,000 feet, and then a climbing left turn to 3,500 feet before holding. The pilot thought that Erickson must have been turning to set up for another approach, but in doing so did not watch his speed control, which led to him stalling the aircraft. An aerodynamic stall occurs when there isn't sufficient air speed to produce enough lift for an aircraft. When that aircraft, like the Beechcraft Baron, is heavy and flying at a low altitude, it spells disaster. The plane—as one pilot put it—becomes a "brick in the sky."

Stall/spin accidents—that's how the Air Safety Institute classifies them—tend to be more deadly than other types of general aviation accidents. Even experienced pilots can stall the aircraft. In fact, less than a year before Erickson's fatal crash, Senator Paul Wellstone and seven other people had died in a plane crash on the approach into Eveleth-Virginia Municipal Airport in Minnesota. The NTSB report asserted a probable cause: "The flight crew's failure to maintain adequate airspeed, which led to an aerodynamic stall from which they did not recover." Although the pilots were professional, the board criticized them for failing to monitor the airspeed as they approached the airport. The plane stalled and crashed about 1.8 miles from the end of their destination runway.

The Erickson crash shared some similarities with the Wellstone crash. Both had happened during the maneuvering phase of an approach or missed approach. Also, both had occurred close to the ground, which meant in the event of a stall recovery was highly unlikely because of a simple fact—a lack of sky beneath the aircraft. The Air Safety Foundation examined 465 fatal stall/spin accidents (between 1991 and 2000) and found at least 80 percent of the accidents started from an altitude of less than 1000 feet.

There were few clues in Grace and Lily's fragmented recollections of the crash to confirm whether or not the plane stalled. One pilot likened the sensation of experiencing a stall to that of being on a roller coaster at the very top of a run, "a momentary freedom from feeling the effects of gravity and just dropping." Had the girls felt these strange G-forces? Grace's report of the plane "seeming like it was on a bumpy road" probably referred to what happened after that drop: hitting the trees and then the violent impact with the ground.

In the to and fro of postcrash investigation, lawyers like to look for tangible clues as to why a crash happened, which could be used as ammunition in a blame game—or in a courtroom. Dornik had searched the wreckage for something, anything that could explain this sudden way to die. He also traveled back up to the crash site, too, and met the Cook County sheriff, who was still emotional about the experience of finding the girls alive.

However, there was something else beyond the mechanical specifics of the crash. The culture of the general aviation world, a little bit maverick, seemed to attract a certain type of personality. Dornik—a motorcycle aficionado himself—recognized some of these pilots as Harley riders in the sky, cowboys up in the blue frontier. JFK Jr. surely belonged to this world, an adventurous thrill seeker, someone well acquainted with accidents who pushed on perhaps against better judgment. There was somewhere he absolutely had to be that evening, and that consideration was as disastrous for him as it was for Charlie Erickson.

"There is a vast amount of literature of pilots like Charlie who kill themselves because they push the envelope just a little bit too often," said Lynn Grano, the Ericksons' family friend and a pilot. "Regarding general aviation instrument-rated pilots there seems to be two classes of people who kill themselves. The first group has instrument ratings but low hours and haven't had the shit scared out of them," said Grano. "The second group, which probably includes Charlie, are the classic Type-A personalities— ambitious, hard-charging, impatient, competitive—and it's this group's tendency to fly in marginal weather conditions instead of more cautiously waiting on the tarmac, that has given rise to some high-performance small planes being called doctor or lawyer killers."

On paper, it looked like the crash that had killed Charlie and Kathryn and had injured her girls was a classic case of loss of control, spatial disorientation, aerodynamic stall, or otherwise. However, before Charlie found himself staring through the milky-white mist, before that period of wild suspense and bewilderment, perhaps he made a decision that he absolutely had to arrive on schedule, come what may. Said Grano, "I suspect, based on that type of person who flies, eventually the odds can catch up to you."

7

THE SECOND LUCKIEST PERSON OF THE YEAR

Back at his house on London Road, Toby awoke early. The environment was familiar, but also strange and disorienting, the marital bedroom transformed by Kathryn's absence and the new reality of being a single father. It was still dark outside as Toby lay on his bed, his senses hyperalert for the sounds of Grace and Lily in distress. Since they'd returned home, the girls' nightmares had become more frequent, and Toby was perturbed by what Grace called "the monsters." Toby would do his best to soothe whichever daughter was struggling with this invisible darkness. A few tender words and the orange glow of the night-light would help solve the immediate problem, but monsters kept returning night after night. Sometimes the girls wanted to climb in bed with their dad, and though Toby had been advised this wasn't the best solution, he sometimes relented out of sheer exhaustion.

He also considered his new economic reality, chasing his thoughts into dark corners. So far, he was surviving on the salary that his organization, the National Catholic Rural Life Conference, continued to pay, although he could work only sporadically because Grace and Lily needed almost constant attention. But Toby knew that this wouldn't carry on indefinitely no matter how generous his employer was. Further, the household income had dwindled because Kathryn had been the second wage earner, and of course that was now gone.

Since arriving home, Toby had started to calculate the rapidly mounting medical costs associated with the girls' burn injuries. He had reasonable health insurance for the family, but of course for such extensive treatments the family had quickly depleted the $10,000 maximum out-of-pocket expenses—deductibles, co-pays, and other uncovered expenses. Weeks after the accident, a potential avalanche of bills threatened to spill off the dining room table—the now familiar paperwork from doctors, hospitals, laboratories, and therapists who treated Grace and Lily. One thought did strike Toby as he worked his way through this complex maze of numbers and benefit calculations: He'd never had a bill from the Cook County sheriff's department for the search and rescue operation. He discovered that for a public rescue such billing wasn't permitted and he made a mental note that somehow, later, he would repay these first responders.

As the end of the year approached, Toby worried about the new out-of-pocket expenses that would reset in January. Treatments, especially for Lily, were ongoing and expensive—a specialist dentist was required, as well as physical therapy and psychological counseling several times a week in Minneapolis. Sometimes the insurance company would query a treatment like reconstructive surgery, refusing to cover the costs because it was, they insisted, elective. Toby spent many long hours on the phone with insurance representatives patiently explaining why all of this surgery was necessary.

He also worried about the longer-term costs for Grace and Lily, and the preexisting condition clauses and especially the lifetime cap issues, $2 million per child, which both girls could face in the future. Already, Lily's healthcare costs had cut deeply into her lifetime cap and she needed years more work. The notion that the coverage would run out before the girls even reached adulthood was distressing.

He'd received settlement money from Kathryn's life insurance policy, and it was a small mercy that the money came through quickly, which assuaged some immediate anxiety. The money was a gift bequeathed by a tragedy, and Toby hoped that some of it could go toward college for the girls, so it had legacy and meaning. He figured, with the mounting expenses, that he had about a year to establish a new professional and personal life plan before it would dwindle. Toby had used up his own sick days and now took a leave of absence from work at the forbearance of his employers, who were sympathetic and flexible. His job had required him to travel to Saint Paul to work at the Capitol, as well as outside the state, and obviously now that wouldn't be possible. The care that Grace and Lily needed took special knowledge, the intimate touch and treatment of a parent who could tend not only to physical injuries, but also to psychological ones. The girls absolutely needed their dad to stay close. Before going to bed every night, Grace would ask for constant reassurance: "Will you be there when I wake up?"

Then there was that plane insurance that Lynn Grano had said would soon be paid. Toby, as the trustee for "the heirs and next of kin of Kathryn" and as the father of two injured girls, was eligible under the terms of the policy for the maximum settlement of $1 million for the "incident." The knowledge that he might receive this money soon mitigated Toby's ongoing sense of dread about his financial future. It sounded like a lot, a godsend maybe, but into the black hole of grief and spiraling medical costs, who knew how far it would stretch?

These uneasy calculations swirled through the small hours. Inevitably the light would seep in through the curtains, and Toby would wait to hear the newspaper slide through the mail slot and fall on the doormat. That was usually his cue to get up, take a shower, and make himself a pot of coffee. He would read the *Duluth News Tribune*, letting news local and foreign drift abstractly in his mind: Six American soldiers died in Iraq when their Black Hawk helicopter crashed and burned along the Tigris River; Minnesota farmers suffered financial setbacks after a Midwest drought had shriveled the soybean crop; the liberal comedian Al Franken had floated the idea of running against Norm Coleman for senator. On November 19, Toby spotted a news item about the late Senator Paul Wellstone. He paid more attention than usual not only because Wellstone had been a friend but also because it was about the plane crash that had killed the senator a year before, in October 2002. The crash foreshadowed Toby's own experience. Was it an uncanny coincidence or something more?

As everyone knew, Wellstone and his entourage had perished when his campaign plane crashed as it approached a small airport near Eveleth, situated in a wooded region in Northern Minnesota. The fifty-eight-year-old senator was a Democrat and considered to be one of the Senate's most liberal members. He'd been locked in a fierce battle against his Republican challenger, Norm Coleman, with whom he was scheduled to debate later that day. Seven other people died in the crash, including Wellstone's wife, Sheila; his daughter, Marcia; three of his campaign staff, including Mary McEvoy and Tom Lapic (both of whom Toby knew well); and the two pilots. The death of Wellstone just eleven days before the election stirred up a powerful conspiracy theory that Wellstone was murdered. The reasoning went as follows: Although Wellstone had voted against the Iraq War Resolution in 2002, he continued to surge in the polls. This incurred the ire of the Bush administration and others who viewed his stance as factious and anti-American. Wellstone even received death threats from anonymous callers. Then suddenly, and conveniently, his plane crashed without explanation. The fact that the FBI immediately deployed agents to the crash site to investigate possible criminal activity only fueled this speculation.

However, a year later, the National Transportation Safety Board issued its report, laying the blame squarely on the pilots. Toby read the story with a sense of curiosity and alarm. At this point, he knew nothing about Dornik's investigations into the Charlie Erickson crash, but the Wellstone crash seemed to have similarities. It happened in bad weather as the plane approached the airport. The NTSB issued its report to Congress: "The tragic accident that took the lives of a respected U.S. senator, members of his family, staff, and the flight crew, shocked us all. It sadly and starkly points out the need for more aggressive action to improve safety in the on-demand charter industry."

The board also came to some grave conclusions about the pilots, finding that both had "previously demonstrated serious performance deficiencies consistent with below-average flight proficiency." This ultimately struck Toby as strange. It seemed unimaginable that a U.S. senator's life could be in the hands of lax pilots who essentially stalled the engine by flying too slowly. If that was the case, how then could anyone flying in a small plane, never mind a more regulated charter plane, know if a pilot was competent enough to fly a wife, a mother, a child?

In that moment, his sense of righteous rage, the quiet crusading impulse that he'd had throughout his career, was tempered by more immediate concerns. He had to get Grace and Lily up, make their breakfast, apply ointments and pressure garments. For the first few weeks, there was a routine. Several times a week the girls had medical appointments back at Regions in Saint Paul, a two-and-a-half-hour drive away, with various different doctors and specialists. It was a long trek each way, but this was a critical time in the recovery process, and besides, driving long distances felt vaguely therapeutic for Toby. He would think about Kathryn while the girls temporarily escaped by watching videos they liked—*Mulan*, *The Little Mermaid*, and *The Wild Thornberrys* were favorites—on the little TV in the back of the car. Toby often heard the Paul Simon song "Father and Daughter" featured in the *Thornberrys* movie and the chorus stuck, becoming a kind of mantra as he drove up and down I-35:

> As long as one and one is two
> There could never be a father
> Who loved his daughter more than I love you.

On other days, Grace would have preschool for a half day, and Toby would take Lily to her rehab treatment in Duluth. Then around lunchtime, Grace and Lily would be back at the house, playing together in the TV room while Toby made lunches or dinners. Toby could hear the games they played, and the scenarios they invented were telling. Sometimes the dolls would get hurt and end up in the hospital. Another time the girls pretended that Mommy came back to visit. Toby knew these games were an important outlet for his daughters.

In the afternoons, he made sure the girls did some stretching exercises to prevent scar tissue on the skin grafts from building up. The stretching exercises often felt brutal, intended as they were to break up the scar tissue, and the pain provoked much crying and screaming from Lily at first. The skin on one side of her face had become so tight she couldn't open her mouth wide enough for a lollipop. For a three-year-old, this was both a torment and an incentive, sucking the lollipop being the desired goal. Lily had to wear the face mask at all times, twenty to twenty-two hours a day, except for these exercises and when she ate. Toby noticed that she got into the habit of eating very slowly during mealtimes, a brief respite from the uncomfortable thing clasping her face. He could hardly blame her. Even now, with her blond stubble barely growing back on her scalp, she was still feisty and determined.

Sometimes Toby would take the girls out to the store, something he tried to avoid because people stared at Lily in her mask. Toby was often taken aback by the brazen questions that strangers asked him. Many times people quizzed Toby: "What happened?" Once, in the cereal aisle of the local supermarket, a man looked at Lily and said loudly, "Oh, my God! What happened to her? Why does she look like that?" Sometimes they had to leave a store in a hurry when Lily started to cry. It upset Toby deeply, but he had to temper his responses, fully aware that Grace and Lily would likely learn from his behavior. So he rehearsed the answer: They were burned in a plane crash. This was his matter-of-fact response before he moved on. Children were curious, too, but seemed to accept the answer with less horror than the adults. Once, when Lily was playing in the park, another little girl came up and gently touched her mask and asked if it hurt. Lily said "No. Not anymore." The girl accepted the answer and the two played for a while. The stares of strangers would be something that Lily would ultimately have to live with.

Despite this kind of insensitivity, there were many more people in the community who rallied around the Pearsons, offering to help in any way they could. During the first few months, Toby's mom, sister, and Carolyn took turns staying at the house to help. It wasn't just friends and family, but also people who'd heard about the family's plight who reached out, asking, "What can I do?" Especially attentive were those in Duluth's nursing community who'd known and worked with Kathryn. Volunteers cooked and delivered meals to the family several nights a week, thanks to a sign-up sheet posted by the church. One group of women even formed a volunteer cleaning service to help out.

It made all the difference to the grateful but mostly exhausted Toby. In the evenings after dinner, Grace and Lily required more physical therapy exercises for an hour, until bath time. It was important to keep their skin clean as it healed and then to moisturize it with lotion. Between the two girls, it took Toby a couple of hours to do all the necessary preparations before reading them a bedtime story in his room. Kathryn and Toby had split reading duties, Mom in one room, and Dad in the other. Now, however, the girls snuggled up to their dad as he read fairy tales and stories about princesses, and they listened attentively. Grace was just starting to read and sometimes insisted on "reading" a story to her sister, though Toby suspected she was simply memorizing the parts of the story she could remember and then adding in her own details, which made him smile.

After the girls had gone to bed, Toby would tidy the house and get ready for the next day. That's when he would feel most alone. When he retired to his bedroom—*their* bedroom—all of Kathryn's things suggested she was still there; her jewelry and perfume were on the dressing table, and her clothes hung on the closet. Plus, Toby was haunted by another discovery, which he'd made soon after returning to the house from the hospital. When he'd walked into Kathryn's closet, he saw all of Grace and Lily's baby clothes laid out, as if in preparation for another baby. They'd long been packed away since the girls had grown up, but here they were, arranged in neat little piles. Toby now wondered if, on that Labor Day weekend at the cabin, Kathryn was planning to share some wonderful news, that she was pregnant. He didn't know. He would never know for sure. He put the baby clothes away.

———

If Toby's grief was private, the world beyond his door remained curious. One day he received a call from ABC's *Good Morning America*, which wanted to interview him, and the girls, live on national television. Toby had resisted the persistent media calls, but this one seemed like an opportunity to satisfy a wide audience in one go, to tell people, "We've survived, we're okay." Lights and cameras were brought in for an early-morning live link-up with the ABC studio in New York, with Charlie Gibson as the host. Toby had dressed and prepared the girls for their appearance on television, trying to hold them close as the producer indicated they'd be on the air shortly. Then breaking news bumped the Pearson segment—law enforcement officials in Santa Barbara wanted to search Michael Jackson's Neverland Ranch following new allegations against the pop star of child molestation. Sitting at home, listening to the live studio sound, Toby found the whole thing surreal. Eventually Gibson introduced Toby and "the miracle girls," who were sitting uncomfortably on their dad's knee, yawning, sneezing, and talking to each other, mostly oblivious to being on TV. For viewers unaccustomed to the distortion caused by Lily's face mask, she was a sorry, even shocking, sight.

This appearance on television did not have the effect Toby intended. Instead, it merely added to the snowball effect of media curiosity. Despite Toby's caution, and against his better judgment, somehow the nationally syndicated news show *Inside Edition* convinced him to let the CBS cameras through his front door. They lured Toby in by promising him an introduction to the pilot, Dan Anderson, who had located the crash site by flying over the forest in bad weather. Toby felt hesitant about the proposed TV segment and, until the film crew arrived in late November, wasn't sure if he'd even agreed to it. At this point, running on very few hours sleep, he felt exhausted.

Then, with the cameras rolling, Anderson walked in through the front door to meet Toby for the first time. "Hi, my name's Dan Anderson. I'm Grace and Lily's rescue pilot." He came over to Toby and the two embraced. "Thank you very much," said Toby. "You saved their lives." Although this was a staged media moment, there was genuine emotion in the terse exchange between the two men. Dan was clearly moved as he crouched down to meet Grace and Lily, who came over to him and hugged him. Anderson handed the girls the gift bag he'd brought along, which contained two Angel Bears of Hope that he'd chosen to show how much he felt for these two little survivors. The girls delved in, excited to see what they'd got, and then ran off to play.

The whole endeavor attempted to capture a private moment with lights and cameras on one side of the living room, but later, both Toby and Dan reflected on the experience as frustrating and inauthentic. Dan recalled being spurred on by an upbeat producer who said of Lily, "Doesn't she look great!" Privately, Dan was shocked by the severity of her burns, her mask, and her special mittens, thinking to himself, Oh, my God. She has so far to go.

Carolyn slept uneasily, too, sometimes keeping the television on all night as company. She had taken a few necessary weeks off from work at Abbott Northwestern Hospital, where she worked as a nurse in radiation oncology. In this role she dealt with cancer patients undergoing radiation treatment and often encountered people who were scared, vulnerable, and in need of reassurance. Now she was struggling with those same feelings. She traveled back and forth to Duluth to stay with her mom, a proximity that allowed her to see Grace and Lily once they were out of the hospital. She deeply missed the girls, her precious nieces, who provided a vital connection to her forever-lost little sister.

Anguished as she was, it pained Carolyn to see Grace and Lily suffering. She recalled one visit to Regions when Lily was sitting in a little wagon and refusing to interact, turning her head away angrily. She wondered what was going on in her mind. Carolyn told her gently, "You can be angry, you can be mad, but I will always be here for you."

Back in Duluth, Carolyn would often drop around to the house. The girls were always excited to see Auntie Carolyn when she came in. Toby seemed grateful to have Carolyn, or his sister, Beth, help out with the daily challenges of looking after Grace and Lily, with all the complicated garment changes, as well as trying to re-create the fun mom stuff—arts and crafts and music—that Kathryn used to adore. Although, Carolyn observed, nobody really felt like dancing. Around this time, Carolyn reflected on the fact that she had no children. In the past, people had asked her whether she regretted not having any herself. Charlie had older children from a first marriage, but when he married Carolyn, they'd chosen not to have any kids of their own. She considered this question but couldn't bring herself to feel regret. Still, there was no doubt she had maternal instincts for Grace and Lily, and she felt some comfort that Kathy had known how much love she felt for the girls.

One night after Grace and Lily went to bed, Carolyn and Toby talked about the difficulties of being suddenly alone, especially when it came to making big life decisions. Both instinctively wanted to run these things by their partners, but that could never be. Talking about the crash was more difficult. For Toby, there were times when he wrestled with rage toward Charlie. What failures of judgment or care or control were responsible for this destruction? He had no idea what had happened in the cockpit—he imagined a dreadful scenario that played differently each time—but extreme emotions played fast and loose with facts. Even if Charlie wasn't entirely culpable, there was the question of God, the all-powerful, the all-knowing deity who seemed utterly indifferent to who lived and who died. For Toby, the good Catholic, it was a bitter pill to swallow. At times, he allowed a rogue thought to creep in: With friends like that, who needs enemies?

There was another dark ally to the anger—guilt. Why had he ever allowed Kathryn and his daughters to travel on that plane? When he'd been at Regions, he shared these tumultuous feelings with the grief counselor, Ben Wolfe, and also spoken to Father Graham. Both had acknowledged his quiet struggle with these potentially destructive thoughts, and both had encouraged him to channel those feelings into something productive. Obviously his energy was focused on the girls, but Toby also found redemption in running. When he sensed the creep of depression, he put on his sneakers, recovering the virtues of rationality out on a road, or a running path, or by the lake that filled the horizon. He had to learn to accept these feelings, determined not to let anger and frustration spill over into his relationships with Grace and Lily, or with Carolyn.

For her part, Carolyn expressed anxiety about Charlie being responsible for the crash, figuring his error (whatever it was) must have come down to split-second timing. Toby explained to her that he couldn't hold her accountable for Charlie's actions. Besides, he said, we still don't know what happened in the plane. Although the topic was charged with emotion, acrimony was always banished from their encounters. They cried and hugged each other, keeping the faith for both sides of the family.

Eventually Carolyn returned to her silent, empty house on Mount Curve in an upscale neighborhood in Minneapolis. She reeled in her grief, a widow at forty-two, not sure how to proceed. She would call friends to meet, but had what she called "a flake-out clause" that allowed her to stay home if she needed to. She cherished her spaniel Kalli—a birthday gift from Charlie—who her friends observed had become her rock and her comfort. So many good memories of Charlie and Kathy were linked to Kalli, who had been a puppy when Grace was a toddler. Later, Kalli was the one Carolyn hugged on the boat ride from the cabin, when she feared the plane was lost. She was the one that Carolyn cried to, this goofy and lovable spaniel who managed to make her laugh even during these dark days.

But in those first months, Carolyn's grief was deep and disorienting. She often called her friend Karen Allison, whose empathy and good sense helped Carolyn move forward.

"I don't know where to eat," she said. "Charlie and I always ate in the tree house, but the tree house is too sad." The tree house was what Carolyn nicknamed the three-season porch at the back of the house, surrounded as it was by big trees. It had a fireplace and, in the evening, the dark shadows of the trees fell outside the warmth of the firelight. Once, Carolyn saw the silhouette of a mother raccoon and her three babies flit beyond the screens, but now the glow of those evenings seemed lost in the past, and the looming shadows felt more ominous.

Karen listened.

"The dining room table is too big, and the kitchen counter feels like McDonald's," said Carolyn.

"Here's what to do," said Karen firmly. "Tonight eat in the tree house, tomorrow on the dining table, and the next day at your McDonald's counter."

On another occasion she called Karen about the winter broomball party she and Charlie used to throw when the snow was still on the ground. Broomball, a recreational ice game with similar rules to ice hockey, was especially popular in Minnesota. It had become an annual tradition at their house, but now Carolyn was unsure whether she could face a party.

"Do you want to have the party?" asked Karen.

"Well, yes, I think I would," said Carolyn.

"Then let's have the party!"

Carolyn agreed to it on the condition that Karen and her friend Carrie both came.

The party turned out to be a success, cathartic even, and a celebration of Charlie's life. Many of his friends came around, and Carolyn gave away some of Charlie's sailing trophies to fellow crew members, each one with a particular story that delighted the gathering. During the party, Karen discovered a bottle of wine that Carolyn had been storing—a fine red wine, a Brunello from an estate in Tuscany called Poggio Antico.

"Oh, my God," said Karen. "You and Charlie never opened this!"

This bottle of wine, which Carolyn had brought back from Italy in the summer of 2001, promised to yield wonderful, and now-painful, memories. For her fortieth birthday, she and Charlie had rented a villa near Siena for a couple of weeks. Karen and her husband, Garth, had joined them for this long and luxurious summer break. During the trip, they drove up winding roads to historic towns with romantic names like Montepulciano, Montalcino, and San Giacomo and sampled the local wines, buying up favorite bottles of red as they proceeded from vineyard to vineyard. They took a side trip to Elba and rented scooters to explore the island, laughing like teenagers, and later traveled north toward the Alps. One night they had dinner at their house near Siena on a patio fragrant with rosemary bushes. As the light fell, they sipped limoncello in small ceramic glasses and watched in wonder as green fireflies lit up the meadows. When the group returned to Minneapolis, they laughed again when they counted more than twenty bottles of red wine packed into their carry-on luggage.

That was then. Carolyn now thought about the wine, wondering, What the hell were we waiting for? Now she would have to wait some more to find the right moment to drink this bottle. Plus, there was yet another bottle of wine likewise charged with meaning. After the crash, one of the sheriff's deputies brought back several items recovered from the crash site—some children's water shoes (for paddling in the lake), and two of Kathy's books, one on wildflowers, another on the constellations. Carolyn thought it was just like her sister to want to identify the stars with Grace and Lily, especially up at Saganaga Lake, where stargazing was sublime. And then there was a resilient bottle of wine, probably packed by her sister. Caked with mud and with a scuffed-up label, it was a 2000 Louis Bernard Côtes de Rhône, consecrated by the crash.

During that first month back in Duluth, Toby found himself losing track of time. The accident had completely disoriented his calendar, and his days became a blur. Caring for Grace and Lily at home redefined his reality into one long day. He didn't recognize it while it was happening. Every now and then, the outside world would thrust its way into the domestic routine. Around Thanksgiving, he received two phone calls within a matter of days, one of them macabre, the other menacing.

Since his TV experience, Toby had become wary of the unexpected phone call, especially from the press, but this time he picked up. The caller introduced herself, a reporter from the *St. Paul Pioneer Press* writing an end-of-year piece about newsworthy people in Minnesota. She explained that the newspaper wanted to name Toby Pearson "The second luckiest person of the year." Toby was taken aback by the request, and slightly baffled as to what this designation could possibly mean.

"Who's number one?" he asked.

"A group of local cooks who won the lottery," she replied.

"Well, why do you want to put me as number two?" he said, struggling with the concept of being a lucky person. He hadn't won the lottery—he had lost his wife, watched his kids suffer terribly, and had his life torn to shreds.

"Is it lucky to lose your mom? No," he said to the reporter before he softened his tone a little. He realized what the reporter was looking for. His children survived a plane crash. "But we have a lot to be grateful for."

He offered a few details of the family situation before hanging up.

A few days after the phone call, Toby and the girls headed to his parents' house in Mankato, where they planned to spend Thanksgiving, a big family gathering with cousins coming from as far away as Colorado. It was a houseful of fifteen people, including six small children between the ages of three and five. After dinner, Toby joined his brother Tony and their father, Tom, in the kitchen to wash the dishes. As the kids ran around, the conversation turned to Toby's medical costs.

"What's your status with all the financial stuff?" asked Tony.

Toby explained the situation, how he'd been reassured by Lynn Grano that the money from the liability coverage for Kathryn's death, and for the girls' injuries, would be coming soon. Dornik was handling the legal side of things, having filed a claim in probate court against the Erickson estate for the insurance settlement. Thankfully, since it was the other side of the family, it was an amicable claim. While the insurance payment would be a reasonably substantial figure, almost nobody believed it would be enough to cover all of the cumulative losses associated with the crash. As yet, no one was sure of the ultimate value of the Erickson estate, because the largest part was Charlie's interest in his company, UltiMed, whose monetary worth some supposed was close to nothing. It seemed that Charlie's estate might be "judgment proof" in that even if negligence and ultimate liability were found, there would be nothing to claim. For the time being, the insurance money was all there was to pay the family's claim against the estate. Right now, Toby explained, he just had to be patient.

After Thanksgiving, he was back to his routine in Duluth when the phone rang again. It was Carolyn, her voice tight with emotion. Toby knew immediately something was wrong.

"It's bad news." That's all she managed to say before she broke down.

Lynn Grano, who was with her, took the phone and explained there was news about the insurance company payment. He dropped a bombshell.

"The insurance company is denying coverage," he said. "And they're going to sue the estate."

Toby was stunned.

"What does this mean? Isn't this some kind of legal wrangling?"

"No. This is much more serious than that."

Grano explained that the insurance company, Old Republic, had filed a complaint against the Erickson estate, as well as Toby and his daughters, because they were named in the claim. It was a declaratory action seeking a summary judgment, filed in federal court, which essentially asked the court to declare that Old Republic owed nothing to any of the defendants for the claims of wrongful death, personal injury, and hull damage made under the policy.

Why?

The company had found, Grano said, a "material misrepresentation" on Charlie's policy that rendered it void. Whether Charlie had actually lied wasn't clear, but the insurance company considered this as equivalent and damning as fraud. Knowing this was devastating news, which had all sorts of family repercussions, there was little that Grano could say to be reassuring.

"This could be a long fight," he offered.

Toby listened, unable to grasp this new reality. Whatever sense of security he'd established now felt threatened by forces beyond his control.

He hung up the phone.

In due course, the newspaper article appeared in the *St. Paul Pioneer Press*, headlined "The Lucky Ones." The article continued: "Each of these newsworthy people had a year to remember. Some years are better than others. At year's end, some people wind up richer—in a variety of ways—and happier to be alive. Yet the reality is, even a stroke of luck can come at a high price."

With the new knowledge of the pending lawsuit, the newspaper article seemed to Toby more absurd than ever, an ironic bookend to a tragic year. Everybody in Duluth read it, including Toby's sister, Beth, who wrote a scolding letter to the newspaper objecting to the semantics of the word *lucky* being attached to children who'd lost their mother. Fortunate, maybe, but lucky didn't feel right. She felt the urge to stand up on behalf of her brother and speak her mind. Days later, the paper published the letter. Now when Beth called Toby, she would ask him, "How does it feel to be the second luckiest person of the year today?" He had to laugh. Yet being dragged into court by a major insurance company didn't feel lucky at all.

8

THE RISK OF LOSS

Shortly after the crash, when Toby had first talked with Dornik about representing him in the claim, Dornik had thought it was a cut-and-dried kind of case. In fact, Dornik said he'd take the case pro bono, anticipating a fairly quick settlement, joking, "I'll get you the first million, and then let's go from there." However, the lawsuit changed everything, and Toby now needed to hire Dornik as his defense attorney.

"You're most likely fucked," said Grano, summing up the situation to Dornik. Grano had specialized in insurance cases, so when he heard the denial was based on "material misrepresentation," he felt strongly it was "game over." The easiest way for an insurance company to deny or rescind a policy was to discover a deliberate lie on the application form. The courts would typically back an insurance company in such a complaint against this violation, a basic breach of contract.

Dornik didn't despair completely, despite Grano's bleak assessment. As a plaintiff's lawyer, Dornik had come to understand the strategies often used by insurance companies to avoid paying out a claim. In particular, the notion of postclaim rescission was, in Dornik's experience, a common maneuver. He'd seen it before, and it didn't always end badly for his clients. Still,

Grano's warning had been sobering. Dornik warned Toby that fighting the lawsuit would be lengthy and would necessarily involve charging some legal fees.

In civil actions, it had been Dornik's practice to locate sources of money for plaintiffs, and very often an insurance policy would be the most obvious target. Dornik had proved himself skilled at nailing insurance companies that tried to wiggle out of settling claims. Earlier in his career, he'd handled a pedophile case involving a married man who was abusing the child next door; the man's wife said she knew nothing of the abuse going on under their roof. After the abuser was prosecuted for this crime, Dornik filed a negligence claim against the wife, claiming against her homeowners insurance. After all, Dornik figured, she surely knew what her "creepo" husband was doing sneaking upstairs with the neighbor's child. The insurance company argued that standard liability insurance would not cover intentional acts, such as sexual abuse. Dornik prevailed, however, insisting on coverage under the legal doctrine of negligent supervision, and won his settlement for the plaintiff.

This strategy proved successful, though insurance companies in Minnesota subsequently started writing specific exclusions for sex abuse into their policies. Another case with a similar dynamic involved a lawsuit against the parents of a young teenager who'd accidentally shot his friend with his dad's gun. Of course the teenager didn't mean to shoot, but the friend was severely injured for life. Dornik sued the parents for negligence for having left a loaded gun lying around. Under the homeowners policy there was limited coverage—about $500,000—but even Dornik was surprised by the strenuous efforts of the insurance company to get out of the case. What instilled a sense of righteous determination in Dornik was that the company in question didn't want to argue the case on the merits but opted to use exclusions after the fact to avoid payment. Given that an insurance company is in the risk business, thought Dornik, surely it must know it insures "a certain percentage of assholes." Moreover, the insured defendants wanted their insurance coverage to kick in, since it protected their home and other assets. From Dornik's perspective, the insurance company didn't care about the so-called insureds. Even though it had collected premiums for years, it never felt compelled to pay. Dornik took delight in winning this and other similar cases where he could hold an insurer's feet to the flame.

So his initial thought on the Old Republic declaratory action was considered within this context. What was the nature of Charlie Erickson's misrepresentation? Perhaps it was unintentional, ambiguous, or subject to more than one interpretation. He read Old Republic's complaint. In essence, it argued that Charlie Erickson had lied on an aviation insurance application about a previous accident in another plane. Was that the whole story?

According to the complaint, on September 18, 2002, Erickson and Quintessence Air Service, L.L.C. had requested a quote through a broker from Old Republic Insurance Company. (Quintessence Air Service, L.L.C. was created as a holding company for the aircraft, listing two other pilots on the form who would lease the plane for private use from the company). Erickson wanted to insure his 1977 Beechcraft Baron 58P aircraft, which was a more powerful—pressurized, multi-engine—aircraft than he'd previously flown. In the application Erickson revealed his total pilot hours as 1,300, but only 200 in multi-engine aircraft.

On October 17, 2002, Erickson signed an aviation insurance application for coverage through Old Republic, acting through its aviation insurance provider, Phoenix Aviation Managers, with coverage retrospectively effective October 4, 2002. The complaint, however, alleged that Erickson falsely answered two questions on the application form:

Has the applicant had any aircraft/aviation losses/claims during the last three years? Erickson had checked the "No" box.

Has any pilot named above ever been involved in any accident or incident?

Again, Erickson checked "No."

These statements were signed and certified as true, but Old Republic said they were false and cited a clause in the aviation policy as the basis for its denial:

Fraud or Misrepresentation. This policy shall be void if the Named Insured has concealed or misrepresented any material fact or circumstance concerning this insurance or the subject thereof or in the case of any fraud, attempted fraud or false swearing by the Named Insured touching any matter relating to this insurance or the subject thereof, whether before or after the loss.

In fact, said the complaint, Erickson had been involved in a "major accident" just a few months before the quote request and application had been submitted to Old Republic. "On June 6, 2002, Mr. Erickson was the pilot in command of a Mooney M20J that was totally destroyed when Mr. Erickson lost control of the aircraft while landing at Crystal Airport in Crystal, Minnesota," read the complaint. "The misrepresentation concerning Mr. Erickson's prior accident history materially increased the risk of loss to the plaintiff and voids the policy."

Old Republic argued that it would not have insured Charlie Erickson had it known about the previous accident. Ten months later, on August 28, 2003, Charlie crashed the Beechcraft Baron into the forest near Grand Marais. The complaint recapped the situation. Claims for the wrongful death of Kathryn and for the personal injuries of Grace and Lily were made against the Erickson estate and Quintessence Air Service, L.L.C., "and those claims have been tendered to the plaintiff with a request that the plaintiff defend and indemnify the estate of Mr. Erickson and Quintessence Air Service, LLC pursuant to the liability coverages under the policy."

Now, because of the apparent lie, Old Republic saw no reason why it should pay a penny. A lot of lives were suddenly affected by that misplaced *X*.

Even with Dornik's experience, *Old Republic Insurance Company v. Erickson et al.* promised to be a tough case. Dornik's strength and experience were honed at the plaintiff's bar, but this lawsuit suddenly thrust him into a defense role against a formidable challenger. In 2004, Old Republic Insurance Company was one of the nation's fifty largest publicly held insurance companies. The year 2004 was yet another profitable year, with net income of $650.9 million on total revenues of $3.492 billion. The stock ended the year just above $25, putting a valuation of more than $4.5 billion on the company, including its underwriting subsidiary, Phoenix Aviation Managers.

Maybe it was—as Grano warned—game over.

In early January, Dornik pulled up his Chevy pickup truck in front of Toby's house on London Road. He'd driven from Minneapolis, though conditions on the roads were far from ideal. It was a freezing day—twenty degrees below—a typically cold Minnesota winter, with icy blasts whipping across nearby Lake Superior. Dornik hurried into the house to see his client. Knowing he was the bearer of mostly "crummy news," as he put it, Dornik brought with him a bottle of Maker's Mark bourbon in addition to the legal documents, just in case the discussion called for a drink "to drown their sorrows."

The last time they'd met was mid-September, when Toby was living at Regions Hospital and Lily's burns were still life threatening. Then, he'd peered into Lily's room and was shaken by the sight of the suffering three-year-old, a bandaged bundle that made him think of his own little girl, Adeline, who was almost two years old at the time. Like Toby, Dornik was a family man. He'd met his future wife, Sarah, a couple of years after college and eventually they married and raised a family—two boys, Sean and Delaney, as well as Adeline.

Now, when Dornik entered the living room he met the girls in a different condition. They were obviously doing much better, but Lily's compression garments, her gloves, and the startling face mask still had the power to disconcert Dornik, an injury lawyer who had seen it all. When Lily saw Dornik, she said matter-of-factly, "I was in a plane crash and my mommy died." Lily had taken to saying this as an introduction, prompted in part by how self-conscious she felt in the mask. It was also a rehearsed response Lily had learned with her dad, something to say when people stared. Toby had told Lily she could say, "I was burned in a plane crash, but I'm okay now." If you want, he added, you can also tell them your mommy died. Lily efficiently compressed these responses into one swift sentence, often reducing strangers to stunned silence. Grace—older, wiser, and more cautious than her sister—often found herself following up on Lily's headline with a more detailed explanation, which she did on this occasion.

Dornik sat down and talked with Toby about the case. He'd laid out some of the preliminary information about that previous accident cited in the complaint. On June 6, 2002, Erickson had apparently damaged a single-engine aircraft while attempting to land at Crystal Airport in Minneapolis. No one had been hurt, but it hardly sounded like a "major accident," as the insurance company insisted. Dornik thought he would find out more about it. Maybe it was a mishap but not an accident, something that Charlie didn't even consider as serious. For a material misrepresentation to stick, it had to be shown to be a purposeful deception.

Still, thought Toby, the fact that he'd never heard about the accident, incident, or whatever it was, probably meant it wasn't such a big deal. As far as Charlie's competence in the cockpit, Toby figured, in order to fly a plane surely you had to be a good pilot. It went without saying. When he and Kathryn had first decided to send the girls up to Grand Marais in his private plane, there was no reason to doubt him. Uncle Charlie was an intrepid man—skier, sailor, and pilot.

Dornik broached the issue of the Erickson estate and its lack of money. He'd done further research and talked amicably with the estate lawyer, Rick Snyder, only to confirm what they already suspected: There were no substantial assets to satisfy the full extent of the Pearson claim. Dornik asked Toby if he knew of other insurance policies; for example, was there additional liability coverage in the form of umbrella insurance? Toby didn't know of such a policy, though he could follow up with Carolyn.

Then there was the tricky issue of subrogation. Dornik explained that even in the event of recovering some settlement from the estate, Toby's health insurance company had a legal right to be reimbursed for the medical expenses they'd already paid for Grace and Lily. Dornik explained that many personal injury plaintiffs are often surprised, if not outraged, that an insurance company has a right to claw back benefits already paid out.

None of this was good news for Toby, and a new financial picture started to crystallize: no money in the estate; a drawn-out legal battle in a federal court with the airplane insurance company; and even in the unlikely event of a victory, a high chance that the health insurance would make a subrogation claim against any settlement. Meanwhile, it was January. New deductibles had kicked in for Grace and Lily's treatments, and he didn't have a permanent job. It was a sobering moment of realization. The accident could ruin him.

Yet there was something about Dornik that Toby liked, that buoyed his spirits even at this grim moment. He wasn't a typical corporate lawyer and seemed determined to find a way. Indeed, Toby had spoken to a couple of his own attorney friends who'd all told him the same thing: You will lose this case. He was impressed by Dornik's realistic appraisal of the situation and surprised by a hint of optimism. Dornik suggested that during the process of discovery, maybe something would turn up.

"We've got nothing to lose," Dornik said. "If we don't try, we won't get anything, so I think we've got to fight."

Dornik shook Toby's hand, said his good-byes to Grace and Lily, and left. The bottle of bourbon hadn't seemed appropriate after all. Toby clearly wasn't one to drown his sorrows. There was serenity to his sadness. Most likely, Dornik figured, he had stoical Scandinavian genes. He noticed something else, too, about his client: his deep sense of responsibility, his absolute dedication to Grace and Lily. Come what may, Dornik wanted to help this man. It made him mad that an insurance company was trying to "stiff Toby Pearson and these poor little girls."

It was still snowing when Dornik got back into his SUV, so he decided to check in to a local hotel to avoid the hazardous trek back to Minneapolis. When he got to his room, he took off his coat, sat down, cracked opened the bourbon, and poured himself a strong drink.

Toby had spent much of his career lobbying politicians, both on the state and federal level, on behalf of the less powerful members of the community, to make sure they had a voice, so they, too, could get a cut of the pie. Now, in his current predicament, he was surprised by how little control, how little power, he had over the turn of events. A plane crash, the death of his wife, and his daughters' terrible injuries had opened up trapdoors into dark rooms in which he struggled for definition. If he was suffering in this place, he often wondered how other families, perhaps without the same political connections, would ever survive such catastrophe.

Then, out of the blue, he got a call from James Oberstar's office. The powerful and long-standing congressman from Minnesota was the ranking Democrat on the House Transportation and Infrastructure Committee. This overture from the congressman, whose home district included Duluth, seemed fortuitous. Oberstar wanted to meet with Toby, and they set a date for brunch at a local restaurant called Black Woods Grill and Bar. Toby could hardly believe the congressman had reached out to him. "Imagine that," he told his family.

Oberstar represented Minnesota's Eighth Congressional District, which covers the northeastern part of the state, and was the longest-serving member of Congress in Minnesota's history; by 2004 he had been reelected to the seat fourteen times. Having spent his entire congressional career on the Transportation Committee, Oberstar's primary focus was infrastructure—roads, rail, shipping, and, of course, air travel. In fact, so many considered him to be the most knowledgeable lawmaker in Congress on aviation issues that he was sometimes known as Mr. Aviation. Although he'd risen up the ranks on Capitol Hill, Oberstar managed to keep his profile as a practical populist. The son of a miner from the Iron Range city of Chisholm, Oberstar proved a strong ally for the labor movement and was regarded as an advocate and friend of the many blue-collar workers who populated his district.

One weekend in early spring, Toby met the congressman for brunch at the diner, where they took a table with views over Lake Superior. Oberstar was a genial, affable presence with a deep, booming voice. He asked about the well-being of Grace and Lily, offering his prayers and his sympathy for Toby and his family. The congressman had followed the story of the crash with interest and expressed amazement at the courage shown by the girls in the face of such tragedy. He listened as Toby talked about his new life as a single father, his anxieties, and also about being sued by the insurance company, which had voided the policy after the fact, leaving him with little to cover health-care costs.

When Toby met with Oberstar he was entering a wider world of aviation issues—mechanical failures, pilot errors, NTSB investigations, blame and recrimination, and stories of anger and heartbreak from the families of plane crash victims. For the congressman, the story of the Pearson tragedy unfolded in a genre he knew well. As a member of the House Transportation Committee, Oberstar oversaw the Federal Aviation Administration (FAA), which is charged by Congress with promoting and regulating civil aviation by issuing and enforcing safety rules; certifying pilots, aircraft, and airports; and managing the air traffic control system. He'd seen it all in his three decades on Capitol Hill and knew that much that concerned itself with safety was born in disaster.

Ten years prior, a 1993 accident had killed all eighteen people aboard when a commuter plane crashed in freezing fog as it tried to land in Hibbing, Minnesota. It thrust Oberstar into the middle of a local tragedy, which soon played out nationally. The NTSB report determined that the captain made errors of judgment, had failed to communicate with his crew, and had lost awareness of the plane's altitude. The plane, flying at night from

Minneapolis–Saint Paul International Airport, came in to land at too steep an angle, brushed the trees, and crashed into a ridge, scattering wreckage over an old iron ore mine and the surrounding woods. Around this time, Oberstar faced a major test as an advocate for victims' families who insisted on greater federal oversight of commuter planes, which had lower safety standards than those of their bigger airline partners. In fact, one woman from Minnesota, Lorilei Valeri, who'd lost her father in the Hibbing crash, sought out Oberstar on Capitol Hill and challenged him to bring about safety changes more quickly. She lobbied the lawmaker in person, with a mixture of anger and tears, because, as she told a reporter at the time, "He knew my father. I mean, if anyone is in a unique position to bring about change, Oberstar is."

However, as Oberstar knew only too well, change in Washington was infuriatingly slow; even heartbreak and tears failed to move lawmakers to action. Under pressure, the congressman defended his position as an advocate for change, as someone who could push the FAA into action. "I'm the only person in the whole Congress who held hearings on commuter airline safety," he told the *Star Tribune* in 1994. "If I were running the FAA, you're damn right there would have been a lot of stuff done a hell of a lot sooner." After the investigation into Hibbing, Oberstar led efforts to write legislation to tighten regulations for commuter pilots. Then, in 1994, the Democrats lost control of the House and his efforts fizzled. "The Republican majority was reluctant to enact new regulations," Oberstar lamented—his comments recorded by the Federal News Service, which transcribes political events on Capitol Hill. The chance was gone. It would take another sixteen years—and another major plane crash in New York State—before the House passed Oberstar's airline safety bill in 2010.

With his wealth of aviation knowledge, Oberstar asked Toby

if there was anything he could do to help. Toby wasn't sure what action the congressman could take, if any, on a federal level, but he outlined some of his general concerns. He worried that an insurance company was denying his claim based on the fact that a previous accident had been unreported on the insurance application. Surely, he wanted to know, a company should have to do due diligence in checking the background and record of a pilot? In Toby's mind, this lack of requirement meant that anyone could tell whatever lies they needed to get pilot's insurance, and the insurer could, in the event of an accident claim, void the policy. Toby pointed out that this wasn't just about collecting damages for Grace and Lily; both the state and federal governments seemed fairly lax about who was flying private planes. With the terrorist attacks of September 11, 2001, as a backdrop, wasn't this a potential national security issue? To what extent could an insurance policy inhibit civil or criminal violations?

Oberstar knew from firsthand experience that an insurance company could police a risky pilot or commercial operator. In the 1980s, Oberstar had led an eighteen-month-long congressional investigation into Galaxy Airlines after a fatal crash on January 20, 1985. Galaxy Flight 203 was a charter flight flying back to Minneapolis after a gambling trip to Reno, Nevada. Shortly after takeoff, the plane failed to gain altitude and crashed about two miles from the airport. The fiery crash left hunks of metal and bits and pieces of wreckage strewn across the main highway out of Reno. Of the seventy-one passengers on board, only one ultimately survived—seventeen-year-old George Lamson Jr. Somehow he was thrown from the fuselage into the middle of the highway, still strapped into his seat. (After two decades, Lamson spoke about his survival in a documentary called *Sole Survivor*, which examined the phenomenon of lone plane crash survivors. Said Lamson, "I think if it was blind luck, I would feel better about it.")

The NTSB investigation into the cause of the crash criticized Galaxy as a slipshod and potentially dangerous operation, run by its owner, Phillip Sheridan, whom Oberstar considered to be a "shifty character." The airline became the target of several government investigations in addition to the NTSB inquiry into the crash, receiving heavy fines from the FAA for violations of aircraft maintenance requirements and crew flight-time limits. During the investigation, Oberstar came to realize Galaxy was a "phony operation . . . with a fleet of aircraft that included one operating aircraft and two Hangar Queens"—a grounded plane with a bad maintenance record—"from which he scavenged parts to keep the one aircraft flying." He tried to get the airline shut down but, noted Oberstar, the pro-business Reagan administration wasn't about to shut down anybody at that time.

Oberstar was even more dismayed when Galaxy won a contract from the U.S. Air Force as a cargo operation. Despite his personal warning to the Air Force to keep an eye on Sheridan, Galaxy continued to operate with impunity. Only when the insurance company revoked its coverage for Galaxy did the FAA finally act. Being responsible for certifying the airworthiness of an airline operator, the federal agency had no choice but to shut down Galaxy. Sheridan forever blamed Oberstar for putting him out of business. At the same time, Oberstar lamented the fact that it took a private insurance company to stop Galaxy and not the federal regulatory structure, despite his efforts. The whole episode had proved to the congressman that insurance could be a powerful factor in determining who could fly and who could not.

Oberstar sat and listened carefully to everything Toby laid out, alert to the complexity of this topic. It was a personal tragedy with traits that could ultimately impinge upon federal aviation liability laws, the U.S. Constitution Commerce Clause, and the Tenth Amendment's limits on federal power—a heady mix for any legal brain. In time, Oberstar believed if the FAA could require pilots or aircraft owners to obtain insurance in their home state, then it would be a major step forward "to righting the wrong that hung over the Pearson case."

At that time, however, sipping coffee over brunch at Black Woods, the possibility of a federal remedy for Toby's situation did not coalesce, and the topic was not broached. Oberstar was realistic about the politics of the time. With the Republicans once again in charge of the House, effecting any change in the insurance industry implied, as Oberstar well knew, a huge battle. Moreover, the pilots' lobby found the status quo—low premiums and little regulation—acceptable.

Oberstar had to be honest. He explained that it was not the best time for Congress to investigate the bigger questions raised by the Old Republic lawsuit. For Toby, too, with Grace and Lily still recovering, it was impossible for him to be an advocate for anything other than his children's well-being. Yet the conversation with Oberstar was reassuring and planted some seeds. While Toby held out little hope that much could be done for his current predicament—at least on a national level—the conversation caused him to reflect on the lax liability laws that had dumped a federal lawsuit in his lap. As the two men parted, Toby had a strong sense that he'd be dealing with James Oberstar again.

9

FALLING THROUGH CLOUDS

Grace and Lily wanted to send a message to their mom. It was
a desire they often expressed in their therapy sessions with
Dr. Constance McLeod Hvass, a pediatric therapist whom they'd
started seeing at Regions after the survival phase of their burn
treatment. The two girls shared sessions at first, and eventually
went to individual sessions every week, then every month. By the
spring of 2004, the girls felt comfortable with the psychologist—
they called her Dr. Connie—who was anything but a formal
presence. In fact, Lily told Connie she liked coming to see her
because she was "so goofy." It was true she cultivated playful
activities in the sessions to reveal what the girls were thinking
and feeling.

Lily suggested she could send a message to her mother by
bird, because "the bird flies in the blue sky toward heaven." Or,
said Grace, "We could just look up into the sky and talk." Both
girls agreed that their mother was now their "guardian angel."

Dr. Connie found it gratifying to work with Grace and Lily,
not only because of the level of engagement she received from
Toby, but also because they were both such verbal children.
Given the small but significant difference in their ages, Connie
also understood the girls had experienced the trauma of the crash

quite differently. They would grow and respond at separate developmental levels, so the individual sessions made a lot of sense.

At first, Lily was obsessed with blankets and needing to be warm and comforted. She created rituals with baby dolls, and nurtured them. As she became more assertive in 2004, she would play the role of a mother who brings her six children to see the doctor. The children, Lily explained, had been in a plane crash and got burned. The person who had died in the plane crash, she said at first, was their mother. In the scenario, Lily realized she was the mother, and she quickly corrected this to say it was the dolls' grandmother who had died. From Dr. Connie's point of view, this was good progress. Although Lily mostly ignored the topic of the plane crash, this was her way of exploring traumatic events, refracting her own experiences through her imagination.

Grace, on the other hand, better understood the events of the plane crash as a narrative. She had first introduced the topic of her mother's death to Dr. Connie by asking her if she watched the TV news, explaining that she'd been in the plane crash, but "my mother didn't survive." She told Dr. Connie there'd been a special ceremony for her mom—struggling to pronounce "funeral"—and talked directly about the crash, though in elliptical ways.

"No one saw it," said Grace.

"What was it they didn't see?" asked Dr. Connie.

"No one saw the tree and then it hit us."

Grace began a ritual that continued for several months. She would make something and in some way it would be adorned with a symbol for her mother. It might be a drawing of an angel, featuring the letter K for Kathryn. The technique also helped Grace confront the troubling issue of monsters and how fearsome they were at night; she saw them moving around in the dark. Grace worked hard on making a sign for each side of her bedroom door, warning the monsters to stay away. Grace drew many elaborate symbols that looked like knights, swords, and special animals. On the signs she wrote, NO MONSTERS ALLOWED. She also made some smaller signs to give to Lily in case "she had monster dreams." At the next session with Dr. Connie, Grace said that the signs had helped keep the monsters away, all except for one certain monster who was light blue and navy colored. Dr. Connie wasn't sure what those colors represented.

Grace was attentive to Lily's medical problems, still conscious of her protective older sister status. As Dr. Connie understood it, Grace had kept Lily from running back to the burning plane to get her teddy bear, and that was the act that had saved Lily's life. But her vigilance, and the ongoing awareness of Lily's medical problems, were now sources of anxiety for Grace, who told Dr. Connie, "I feel bad for Lily because people don't know the story and they always ask her about the scars." As the big sister, she'd inadvertently been thrust into an adult role, a responsibility that naturally provoked some ambivalence in the five-year-old Grace.

At times, Grace desperately wanted to remove the pressure garments she was obliged to wear on her hands, but then she remembered Lily, who was so compliant about wearing hers, as well as the face mask. Once Lily told Dr. Connie she didn't like to wear the garments, before adding, "But I will never give up!" The psychologist was amazed to see her "characterize her power struggle not with her father or doctors who laid down these restrictions but a power struggle with the survival of her body and not giving up."

It was encouraging language.

———

Regarding his own emotional well-being, Toby had spoken to very few people. Since he'd returned home from Regions, he'd continued talking to the counselor, Ben Wolfe, about his feelings. While he felt the pain of loss, he wasn't about to surrender to his emotions. Not that he had the option. He told his mother about his discovery of the baby clothes, and they cried together quietly about this. Then it was never mentioned again. When his old mentor, Father Graham, returned home to Duluth for a short break, Toby took the opportunity to talk with him about his worries. The two men traveled up Highway 61 for dinner at the Lakeview Castle. It was hardly therapy in the conventional sense, but the priest was sensitive to Toby's needs. On the way home, Father Graham gave his friend some advice. He warned him to be wary of women who would "target" him as a grieving widower, an attorney with two little girls. "You're an attractive person to get to know," said Father Graham.

"I did receive some strange letters from women," said Toby, impressed by the priest's insight. He explained that after he'd returned home to Duluth, he received letters from women offering to help with the girls. One woman had even included her picture as an inducement, and proposed that she move to Duluth to help the family, which Toby found to be both a "remarkable offer," and also "kind of weird."

Father Graham expressed astonishment at Toby's ability to maintain his poise in the face of what he saw as "an insurmountable loss." He observed that while his friend was grieving, his profound sense of duty to his girls had kept him stable. From the beginning—in the devastating days just after the crash when Father Graham talked more frequently with him—Toby had seemed calm, reasonable, and filled with grace. Father Graham couldn't figure it out, wryly observing that Toby's strength was clearly drawn from more than just a "good Catholic upbringing."

Over time, Toby revealed more troubled thoughts that he'd so far kept private. He continued to struggle with guilt, still wanting to blame himself for allowing his girls to fly with Charlie. Shouldn't he have known about the previous accident? Shouldn't he have been a bit more diligent about Charlie's safety record? Father Graham waved this away.

"If Kathryn wanted to go on that plane, you were not going to stop her. She would never have gone if she thought this would happen. There was no way to predict this crash could or would happen," he said. "What you can do now is to be the best dad you can be."

Coming from Father Graham, it was an absolution of sorts.

It wasn't just Toby who suffered. The crash had rocked his entire family. Toby's mom, Maureen, and his sister, Beth, suggested everyone needed to talk about it together. Beth's husband, Mike Peterson, Toby's college friend who was a student counselor at the College of St. Catherine (known locally as St. Kate's), recommended a place in Saint Paul he knew—the Center for Grief, Loss and Transition—which provides specialized therapy in areas of "complicated grief." They made an appointment for one family counseling session at the center. Toby dropped Grace and Lily off with Carolyn so that he could attend. He joined his mom, dad, brother Andy, and Beth, in a big room with a counselor present. Everyone took turns talking, sharing feelings about the crash, the loss of Kathryn, the insurance company's conduct, and the unknown aspects of Grace and Lily's physical and psychological health, as well as Toby's future. For the usually reserved Pearson family, the session was emotional and cathartic, a way—as Toby saw it—to throw it all on the table. It brought them closer.

That spring, Toby was conscious of all the rapid changes that Grace and Lily were going through, the process of physical and mental healing that would show up in ways large and small.

They were more verbal than ever before, and in the critical first year of their emotional recovery. Toby wanted somehow to capture the girls at this stage, without being too intrusive. At Father Graham's suggestion he turned to a local freelance writer, Molly Stein, who had collaborated with the priest on a lighthearted guide—*The Catholic Wedding Book*—all about getting married in the Catholic Church. Toby felt an immediate bond with the fifty-one-year-old Molly; she was warm, gentle, and the mother of three adult children.

When Molly arrived at the house, Grace and Lily were curious about this new lady at the door. Toby explained.

"Do you know what Molly does? She's a writer."

"So you're like a narrator?" asked Grace.

Like most people in Duluth, Molly had heard the story of Grace and Lily, though she had never actually met the girls. Now, when she walked into the house, she felt no sadness, or shock, or drawing back. She thought the girls were lovely. "Not as in 'you could tell they had been beautiful,' or 'they were beautiful in spite of . . .'" She could see at once that people who loved Grace and Lily had worked hard to preserve their inner loveliness. They are beautiful. They are Snow-white and Rose-red, she thought.

Just like the sisters in the fairy tale by the Brothers Grimm, Grace and Lily had survived an ordeal in the forest.

And when they looked round they found that they had been sleeping quite close to a precipice, and would certainly have fallen into it in the darkness if they had gone only a few paces further.

Molly felt immediately welcome and comfortable, and observed that the accident had placed more of a burden on Toby, the poor dad in a house full of girls! She started her tape recorder and took notes, attempting to capture Grace and Lily's freewheeling energy at home—a portrait of innocence with vivid glimpses of the fiery catastrophe they had experienced.

Toby had started to tell Molly about the insurance issue and his recent meeting with Oberstar. It had prompted a question: If his brother-in-law had been truthful on the application form, might he have been denied his pilot's insurance? If that had been the case, thought Toby, Charlie would never have been in the air that day with his sister-in-law and his nieces. Then Grace climbed up onto her dad's lap and insisted that together they look at a children's book on anatomy, with big colorful pages.

"When the doctor puts a stethoscope on your back, he or she is listening to your lungs," explained Toby gently. "It's where the air goes in and out."

Molly listened, watching Grace as she stared at the picture book. Toby explained that Lily was having a hard time getting enough air into her lungs. (She had extensive scarring inside her windpipe from the constant intubations—75 percent closure in her throat, which was like "breathing through a straw." They had scheduled another procedure at Regions, which would use laser technology to clear out the scarring.) This was said carefully, sotto voce, as Lily's radar was always on.

He switched his attention back to Grace.

"You know a lot about the body because of your experiences, don't you?" Toby said gently to his daughter.

"No more doctors! Only nurses and Connie!" said Grace.

"It will be another year before you're done with doctors. And you'll be done with your garments."

And then out of the blue, Grace offered a flashback, an explanation, almost a haiku, for the benefit of Molly.

"I protected my sister. It was foggy. We were falling through clouds. People can't fly the plane when it's foggy."

On Molly's second visit to the house, a few days later, the girls wanted to watch the wedding video of their mom and dad.

In fact, they'd taken to watching it quite frequently. Thanks to a birthday present for Kathryn on November 13, 2000, a video camera, the Pearsons had been diligently recording scenes of family life, which now seemed carefree, prelapsarian, and untainted by tragedy. (The video camera had been destroyed in the crash.) Grace and Lily giggled as they observed their younger selves. There was Grace sledding at Northlands, or singing "Do-Re-Mi," or splashing around with her little sister at Big Elbow Lake. Grace on her first day of preschool, innocent and wide-eyed—on September 10, 2001—curtseying like a ballerina. There was Lily lying flat on her back on the vast acreage of Mommy and Daddy's bed as her older sister clambered up to give her a tender kiss on the cheek.

And there was Mommy, curled up with a book at Shady Rest, or waterskiing with the sunlight dappling the lake, or walking into the church, beaming, dressed in white to join Toby at the altar.

"Knock knock? Who's there? Kathryn."

"Kathryn who?"

"Kathryn had a wedding dress!"

This was Lily's joke. Molly observed that she was eager to be a part of the story, but it was clear her memory of certain events with her mom were fuzzy and frustratingly out of reach. But now Grace wanted to tell the story.

"My first word was 'mommy.' My second word was 'daddy.' And my third word was 'Lily,'" said Grace.

"What did you love most about Mommy?"

"She loved us. And she loved gardening. Mommy's favorite flower was lilacs and lilies. I held stuff for her and planted flowers," said Grace.

"Did I? Did I plant flowers with Mommy?" said Lily.

"What did you cook with Mommy?"

"Fish. Cooking the crappies we caught from the lake."

"Do you want to tell more family stories?" Toby said.

"I want to tell about when Mommy died," said Grace. "When we looked out of the window, we only saw clouds."

"Mommy gave us a toy on the plane."

Another thought.

"The person on the ambulance told me to grit my teeth to keep from hurting so much."

"Dad, let me talk!" interjected Lily.

"Grace unbuckled both the seat belts," said Toby.

"So we could walk around a lot, and we didn't even notice the looks of our hair. There were lots of twigs in our hair. And it was foggy, and there was fire and lots of trees. And I saw a couple of trees falling down. It was hot. It was in the summer."

"How did they find you?"

"I heard some twigs breaking and I popped my head up. And they were glad that they found some survivors. We're like survivors."

Grace continued, deeper into her memory, deeper into the forest.

"We were looking for Mommy because we thought that we accidentally dropped off the plane and the plane went without us to the airport. And that Mommy survived. We were calling her. It didn't hurt."

Darkness if they had gone only a few paces further.

When Grace said, "We didn't even notice the looks of our hair," Molly immediately sensed that this was a female household. She understood that Kathryn must have spent time on Grace and Lily's hair and clothes, as well as her own, making sure everyone looked nice. As Molly saw it, poor Toby was struggling to navigate this baffling world of "purses and scrunchies and tights and jellies and clothes that were supposed to somehow match."

Women's magazines still arrived in the mail—Kathryn's subscriptions had yet to run out—and Toby noticed the girls loved to look through them. Lily especially adored pulling out the perfume samples and smelling them over and over.

Although he had many weightier things on his mind, Toby felt aware of his dual role. In fact, Grace understood this, too, telling him, "Daddy, you're a pretty good mommy and daddy."

In a series of one-on-one conversations with Molly, Toby talked about what he missed most about Kathryn. "The hardest thing I've noticed so far is the lack of adult conversation that can be intimate; something beyond the hockey scores—that's what I miss most about her being gone," he said. He explained that he and Kathryn had a regular routine of putting the children to bed, having Grandma Mar come over to babysit, and going out for dessert and a drink and just talking for a couple of hours. Toby now felt the weight of making every decision on his own, from the routine to the life-changing choices about health, insurance, and work.

Still, Toby was careful not to complain. He felt grateful for his advantages—his legal training, his family, and his professional connections. In his capacity as a lobbyist for the family farms and health care associations, Toby had seen poorer communities and now he thought of them. "How would somebody who can't read English figure this all out?" he said to Molly.

"There's a lot we take for granted, but when I step back and take a look at it, boy, if I wasn't raised the way I was raised with the benefits that I have, I don't know how I would have handled the whole situation. Of course, we probably wouldn't have known someone with a private plane. But stuff happens to everyone."

As the summer approached, Toby's anxieties about work and money required more drastic action. His current situation, doing part-time work from Duluth, was becoming unsustainable. He considered the options and even weighed the possibility of going to live with his parents in Mankato as an interim measure. He started to look for a job there and interviewed at a couple of law firms, but he could only work part-time, on account of the girls' regular medical appointments, and the law firms preferred someone who could rack up substantial billable hours. Toby knew he needed a job that would provide ongoing health insurance; this was the main source of his anxiety. If he lost it, he'd have to pay to continue the family's health plan via the federal plan known as COBRA, which would likely be more expensive than his mortgage. Of course, given the ongoing health concerns for his daughters, maintaining insurance coverage was critical. In May, Lily had the laser surgery to remove scar tissue in her throat, and the important sessions with Dr. Connie continued indefinitely.

Toby feared the worst-case scenario would be bankruptcy, and that would mean losing the house. Something had to give. For Toby to maintain his position with the National Catholic Rural Life Conference, he would have to be closer to friends and family who could help care for Grace and Lily while he went off to work; in addition, a new part-time contract as a lobbyist for the Catholic Health Association opened up another opportunity. Both would require his presence in Saint Paul. Not only that, because of the girls' medical needs (at Regions, Gillette Children's, and with Dr. Connie), he was traveling back and forth to the city frequently. It made sense to leave Duluth. It would be a big risk and a major upheaval—giving up the family home—but at this stage it seemed to be the best option. It was closing a door on a life that he and Kathryn had dreamed about, and planned, from the beginning: to live near the forest, near the lake, to have time—as Kathryn once put it—to listen to nature.

Before then, however, the August anniversary of the crash loomed. Over the summer, one of Kathryn's closest friends, Teri Metry, had suggested to Toby a trip together to the crash site. He had demurred at first, but now that he would likely be leaving Duluth, he called Teri and said, "I'm ready. Will you go with me?"

Ever since Toby had proposed to Kathryn at Teri and Jim's wedding, the couples had remained especially close. Teri always delighted in coming over to Toby's house and spending time with Grace and Lily. She'd known Kathryn since they were little girls, and shared all sorts of funny and entertaining experiences with her. When she showed up, inevitably Lily would say, "Tell me about my mommy!" Teri would oblige them with stories from their teenage years, talking about the dance lessons they took together, or sneaking out at night for a secret swim. She would even imitate Kathryn's jaunty way of standing, with one hip thrust forward. The girls would watch, enamored, Grace with a solemn expression and Lily with a broad smile, giggling, as Teri brought their mom back into the room.

The girls wanted to keep their mother's image crystal clear in their head. So did Teri. Just after Kathryn's funeral, Marilyn gave Teri something that Kathryn had written as an assignment for her nursing class in 2000. It was headlined, "A Hypothetical Eulogy" and essentially imagined what people—her husband, her coworkers, her friends—would say of her after she'd died. Written at the time with no shadow of the darkness to come, no sense of fear, the eulogy now read like a portent of loss. Kathryn wrote:

My husband would say:

Kathryn was a wonderful wife, mother and friend. She lived her life with the intention to each day live a little better, to love a little deeper and laugh a little easier. And she did just that. She was not afraid to die, as she knew each day was a day well lived. She had no regrets. She had a passion for life and living. We were all beneficiaries of her love, of her laughter and her undeniable life spirit. She inspired us to be more, to love more and to be thankful for all we have. Although I can't bear the thought of living without her, I know her spirit lives on forever. I am grateful for the time we spent together. I am grateful for the ways in which she impacted my life. I am a more compassionate, patient and loving person because of her.

Steeped in such thoughts of Kathryn, Toby and Teri drove up to Grand Marais. They reminisced about Kathryn and about the trip to Berlin together. Teri had been on that trip, too. They shared a warm memory of a party at Pequaywan Lake when twenty people gathered at the cabin, all standing in the glow of a bonfire after a day of waterskiing on the lake. Teri recalled Kathy playing a record by the Indigo Girls, which had been the catalyst for her reunion with her boyfriend Jim, who eventually became her husband—lives and memories all intertwined.

In Grand Marais, they stopped at the sheriff's department for the exact location of the crash. Everybody knew Toby, the story, and asked about the girls. Officers drew them a map. Toby felt anxious as he drove the car up Gunflint Trail, but he knew he had to see the spot where it had happened. They parked and hiked the rest of the way into the forest, disturbing the occasional grouse as they pushed down the deserted trails. The area was overgrown with new-growth trees, which made it difficult to access the crash site, but they knew it when they arrived. They saw a big tree split like a Y, with a charred black trunk. "That's the tree," said Toby and Teri, almost in unison.

They looked around, slightly overawed by the experience, a peaceful space with the memory of sudden violence. Toby could still see bits of debris that hadn't been cleared away—seat belt parts, fiberglass, and hoses. The two visitors went to a spot twenty yards from the trunk, standing silent under the cloudy sky. A light drizzle began to fall.

"I bet this is where the girls were," said Teri.

"I think you're right," responded Toby.

They walked around, brimming with emotion, contemplating this damaged patch of wilderness, imagining the event, amazed also by the fact it was ever found by rescuers. It still seemed unfathomable that Grace and Lily had survived. Then they put up two small crosses, one for Charlie and one for Kathryn, and holding hands, said an Our Father.

As for Grace and Lily, the anniversary held unseen anxieties. Dr. Connie had warned Toby of the strength and tenacity of the anniversary of the trauma, and she took special care to note the girls' mood changes as the date approached. Lily became more scattered and unable to focus on play, while Grace appeared more anxious but obsessed with planning her September birthday—probably, thought Dr. Connie, as a way to avoid her feelings. The anniversary was one trigger, but Toby also told the therapist that even a foggy or overcast day reminiscent of the day of the crash seemed to make the girls more irritable and emotionally unpredictable. It was, explained Dr. Connie, a testament to the power of sensory memories, which are a lot stronger than conscious ones. She summed it up in one sentence, citing a seminal work on the neurobiology of trauma by Bessel van der Kolk: "The brain never forgets."

Toby scheduled the big move from Duluth to Saint Paul on Labor Day. The days leading up to the date caused distress, not just for Toby and the girls, but also for Marilyn and Jack, Kathryn's mother and father. Toby knew the girls loved their grandparents, and he knew it would be hard for Marilyn and Jack to lose proximity to these two precious grandchildren in whom so much love and hope and redemption resided. Grace in particular was sad about leaving Duluth. She would miss the playground in the back garden that her dad had built. She also worried about her Grandma Mar because, she told Dr. Connie, "She is small and lives alone." During one of her sessions she made a broken heart card for her and asked Dr. Connie to write a message: "I will miss you, Love, Grace." At the heart of their anxiety, the girls would be leaving the home that held dear memories of their mother.

Toby sensed all of this. Even he was dragging his feet. Before the movers arrived to pack up the house, Toby's mother suggested they hold a yard sale to shed some household things, furniture, clothing, and any other items that would only clutter up their smaller place in Saint Paul. Toby's father sat outside the house waiting for customers to drive up and make an offer. When someone did, and expressed interest in an item, Tom Pearson would go in to double-check with his son. Sure you want to sell it? he'd ask. Toby would mostly shake his head, reluctant to let anything go. The yard sale was a flop; Toby kept his stuff.

On Labor Day, Toby, Grace, and Lily left the family home on London Road for the last time. The family's move to the Highland Park neighborhood of Saint Paul was even reported in the local newspaper. "It's been amazing—the whole community of Duluth and Grand Marais and even Saint Paul has been incredibly supportive," Toby told the *Duluth News Tribune*. A few weeks later, he told a reporter, Steve Kuchera, that his daughters handled the move well. "One of the things that made the move easier is they got what they call their 'girls' suite' upstairs—'no

daddies allowed,'" he said. "That's what they sometimes decide."

The day after arriving in Saint Paul, the girls started at new
schools—preschool for Lily, kindergarten at Highland Catholic
School for Grace. For children who'd suffered burns, this was a
transition that needed careful management, especially for Lily,
who continued to wear her mask. Children would ask questions.
The Phoenix Society for Burn Survivors—a national nonprofit
organization—had developed a school reentry program admin-
istered by Regions Hospital, which sent a representative to talk
to Grace's and Lily's new, naturally curious classmates about
burns, scars, and why the girls had to wear the pressure garments.
Toby—who'd done this once before when Grace returned to
school in Duluth—sat and listened to the talk. In one classroom,
he was surprised when another boy, peeling up his sleeve, wanted
to show his own, albeit much smaller, scar. This prompted some
of the children to hunt for scars on their own bodies. Toby
thought it was a wonderful moment of solidarity for Lily, and
felt teary eyed because of the children's simple acceptance that
everyone has scars, no matter how big or small.

Back in Duluth, momentum had been building for a few weeks
to hold a fund-raiser for the Pearson family. After the move, word
had spread about the family's immediate financial difficulties.
The *Duluth News Tribune* even cited a figure: "Repairing the physical and psychological damage has thus far cost about $850,000,
not all of it covered by insurance," it stated. It was a startling
figure to many, although due to the staggering costs of health
care perhaps a low estimate, given the extent of the girls' medical and psychological treatment.

So long as the insurance money remained firmly out of reach,
Toby needed financial help. His sister, Beth, and his friend Greg
McGee forged ahead with the fund-raiser, bringing in other

close friends like Tricia Mattson to help. Toby felt very reluctant to accept such charity, but the tight-knit group insisted. He finally agreed to it, thinking to use the event to thank the community for the support he and the girls had been given. "We're trying to raise funds for Toby to make it a little easier for him to care for Grace and Lily," Tricia told the newspaper. "In the future, some of Lily's surgeries might be considered plastic surgery and not covered by insurance. So hopefully we can have something set aside for that if he needs it."

On September 26, the Spirit Flight Kite Festival in memory of Kathryn Wall Pearson took place at Grandma's Sports Garden, with its spectacular views of Lake Superior and proximity to the iconic Aerial Lift Bridge. Just a few weeks after leaving Duluth, Toby was back at the familiar spot where he'd spent many a night as a young man. After all, this was a stone's throw from the place where he'd first set eyes on Kathryn, when he'd vowed she was the one. Now here he was celebrating her in very different circumstances, with the entire community buoying him up. Toby felt humbled by the overwhelming pageant of support, which included the Duluth Fire Department, the K9 police unit, a roster of clowns, a children's booth with arts and crafts, face painting, and temporary tattoos (which Lily liked to deploy strategically on her own skin, a good sign). Several hundred people attended, including Dan Anderson and Chief Deputy Sheriff Mark Falk, who'd driven down from Grand Marais. As Grace and Lily flew kites outside with the many other children, Toby greeted the numerous well-wishers who'd come to support him.

Local businesses donated their services for a silent auction. On offer were more than two hundred items, including a vacation condo in Hawaii, tickets to major sporting events, sculptures and paintings from Minnesota artists, jewelry, and many other items.

The event raised more than $40,000 for the Pearson girls.

Toby's sister wanted to create the kite festival as a tribute to Kathryn, whom she remembered as a happy-go-lucky person who'd adored flying kites. Plus, thought Beth, she's up there in heaven, so it was entirely appropriate for everyone to be looking up. On this sunny September afternoon, Beth and Toby felt a sweet sadness as they watched the spectacle of dozens of kites fluttering high in the late summer skies, held aloft by the breezes off Lake Superior.

10

DISCOVERY

Rodney Roy remembered the day of the crash. As the manager of the little Grand Marais Airport, he didn't see a lot of drama. But on that late August day, after the thunderstorms had rolled through and left a legacy of cloud, he'd been outside when he heard a "routine" radio call come in on the Unicom asking about the ceiling. He went back to the radio, located in his office. With an eye on the sky, Roy asked the pilot of aircraft N285V if he needed a ceiling report. The pilot radioed back, saying, "Let me get my approach together and I'll get back with you." Shortly afterward, Roy observed the bottom of the plane, "just barely," as it flew over the runway, executing a missed approach. Roy never heard from N285V again. That in itself wasn't unusual, since if a pilot determined he couldn't land, he typically would fly on to an alternate airport.

Everything Roy saw and heard that day, he told to NTSB investigators. He said everything sounded normal with regard to engine sound and the pilot's voice. He told investigators that the cloud ceiling was "varying a lot," but at the time of the radio call he determined it to be three hundred feet. The investigators noted that the minimum descent altitude for this approach into Grand Marais Airport is 544 feet. The pilot, as Roy later put it, "darn near busted that minimum by three hundred feet." From a professional standpoint, Roy said, this was "a major mistake."

When he heard that a plane had crashed a mile or so from the airport, he figured that the pilot had "tried to do it again and he got disoriented." Shortly after that, Roy had become heavily invested in the search and rescue, driving around trying to locate the signal being emitted by the Emergency Locator Transmitter that had been activated when the plane crashed. Hours later, Roy was as amazed as everybody else when he learned that two little girls had survived the fiery crash. He heard about their burns from his wife, Dottie, who worked as an E.R. nurse at the North Shore Community Hospital, where the girls were first treated. For Rod and Dottie Roy, it was undoubtedly a traumatic and memorable day.

Weeks after the crash, Roy told the NTSB that he'd spoken to a friend of Charlie Erickson, whom he now knew to be the pilot of N285V. "The friend told Roy that Erickson had the reputation for flying below approach minimums on numerous occasions," according to the NTSB's initial brief of the accident.

Almost a year later, most of this information appeared in the NTSB's accident investigation report, published on September 1, 2004. It asserted the probable cause of the accident to be "The continued descent below the minimum descent altitude and the altitude/clearance not maintained by the pilot during the approach to the airport. The low ceiling was a contributing factor."

As was usual, the investigators had compiled some narrative detail about the elements of the crash. "Ground scars and impact signatures on the wreckage show that the aircraft was inverted when it hit." It continued, "After the initial ground impact, the wreckage broke some 12 to 15 inch diameter trees off at the base.

The wreckage broke up into two main sections and was severely damaged by fire. The first section included the right wing, right engine, turbocharger, empennage, left propeller and inverted cabin section. The two front seat occupants remained in the cabin section of wreckage and were fatally injured. The two little girls were in the aft facing seats (seats 3 & 4) and were thrown clear. They survived with serious injuries."

The *Duluth News Tribune* wrote up the findings and interviewed Toby and Dornik for the article. "It doesn't change the outcome at all," said Toby. "It's still sad that I lost my wife. But at the same time it's still nice and somewhat miraculous that Grace and Lily survived." It was a tepid response for a reason. Toby certainly didn't want to project any animosity in the newspapers even if they goaded him, trying to get him to point the finger of blame.

From Dornik's point of view, this finding opened up the possibility of a lawsuit against the estate, but he expressed caution when he spoke to the reporter. "There are three years to do that," said Dornik. "And the girls have until their 19th birthdays and they haven't even come close to recovering from their injuries so it's really premature to pursue their cases."

Dornik felt he was tap-dancing around the issue, still not wanting to commit to such specific legal action, which would limit him to one source of recovery: the Erickson estate. He was buying time. "The liability claim may or may not ever have to be filed against Mr. Erickson. It depends on whether it is something that can be resolved," he said.

Yet now that the accident was officially deemed to be pilot error, it seemed the only potential source of recovery for Toby and the girls would be the aviation insurance. Privately Dornik despaired. One of his lawyer friends told him bluntly, "You don't stand a chance in hell of surviving summary judgment."

But then, in January 2005, Dornik made an intriguing break-through on the insurance case. During the process of discovery, he'd personally gone through the voluminous files he'd requested from the insurance company and their affiliates. It seemed like a huge task, but Dornik put in hours of time, reviewing every piece of paper related to Charles Erickson's insurance policies. One day, he noticed that the name of the underwriter on Erickson's insurance policy with Phoenix Aviation Managers, a subsidiary of Old Republic, was the same as the one on the prior policy, which had covered, and settled, the damages on Erickson's accident in June 2002. Oh my God, this is the same guy, thought Dornik. If he could connect the dots, then Dornik could argue that the company had the necessary information in its files to assess the risk, despite its protests that it didn't know about the older accident involving Erickson.

Dornik's sliver of hope rested on a legal fiction known as constructive notice. The doctrine of constructive notice, used in both common law and civil law, says that a person or legal entity is presumed to have knowledge of a fact even if they don't have actual knowledge of it. Constructive notice is often used in "slip-and-fall" cases, where an injured plaintiff doesn't have to prove, say, that a supermarket had actual notice of a slippery substance on the floor, but can argue it should have had knowledge of its presence (if there's enough evidence to prove it was there for a while and no one cleaned it up). In this situation, the supermarket is said to have constructive notice and can therefore be held liable for negligence.

Dornik quickly made plans to depose the underwriter, Steve Knowle, who arrived at the law offices of Mackenzie and Dornik on the morning of April 1, accompanied by the lead attorney representing Old Republic in Minnesota, Michael Lindberg. Dornik knew Lindberg from the Twin Cities legal community and thought him "an excellent attorney and a truly nice fellow," but he also knew in the adversarial context of litigation Lindberg could be a tough opponent. His client, Steve Knowle, was an experienced underwriter with Phoenix whose job it was to assess the insurance risk on planes, leasing companies, and pilots applying for coverage.

Dornik first questioned Knowle about insuring Erickson, who had applied for aviation insurance to cover him and the two other pilots under his limited liability company called Quintessence Air Service L.L.C. Dornik established that Knowle had provided a handwritten quote for coverage on the Quintessence aircraft on September 23, 2002, and showed him documents bearing his signature. Knowle didn't argue with this; he'd obviously signed off on the policy.

At this point, Dornik asked Knowle about the insurance company's decision to raise the rates on the leasing company— Northland Aircraft Services—from which Erickson had leased the single-engine Mooney he'd crashed on June 2, 2002. Northland had filed a claim that was settled for $97,500, after which the insurance company had recommended a 30 percent rate increase for Northland when it renewed its policy. Now Dornik produced his ace, introducing the document that proved Knowle was the very underwriter who'd issued the renewal policy. At first Knowle denied reviewing the file, but Dornik persisted, much to the dismay of the underwriter and Lindberg, who seemed genuinely surprised by this information.

"Isn't that your handwriting?" asked Dornik, showing the document to Knowle.

"Yes."

"Okay. So do you want to rethink whether you were involved

in the—that underwriting file or does this not change your answer?"

"I just—I guess I was involved."

Dornik produced another two documents linking Knowle to the renewal, which meant that he would have reviewed the file containing information about Erickson's first crash.

"My guess is that I was aware of the Mooney accident, that it involved the Mooney, because I'm increasing the hull and liability rates 30 percent," said Knowle.

"Okay," said Dornik.

"But again, this is a long time ago. I normally would not bump an account, we would not bump an account 30 percent unless there was an accident. So I would guess that I was aware of the accident."

"So in your opinion, you most likely were aware of the accident?"

"I would think so," said Knowle.

"Most likely had access to the information regarding the accident?"

"I don't know."

"So you maybe didn't have access to that information?"

"I just don't recall. It's been a long time ago. I'm thinking that I probably did, was aware of the accident because of the rate increase that I gave them."

Surely, Dornik argued, when it came to insuring Quintessence weeks later, Knowle must have reviewed Erickson's file, which contained all his personal details, including his pilot's license, his Social Security number, his name and address, and information about the first crash. He must have seen that Erickson was involved in a prior crash and factored that into the Quintessence quote. Moreover, the underwriter had required Erickson to have further training in a flight simulator because of his low airtime in the more powerful twin-engine plane, the Beechcraft Baron, he sought to insure. This suggested to Dornik that the company was aware of the risks when it insured Erickson. However, Knowle countered that Phoenix relied entirely on the information on the application form. How was he to know? After all, Erickson had indicated that he'd never been involved in any other incident or accident.

"The increased risk because of the Mooney accident was not known to me when I underwrote the Quintessence file," said Knowle.

Dornik found this hard to believe. Were they really arguing that it was hard to keep all this information straight, information that could have been checked with a few, swift keystrokes. Erickson's name was on Northland's sworn statement, showing proof of loss. Dornik pointed out there were other ways to do background checks and showed a letter he'd recently received from the FAA following his request for "all accident records involving Charles W. Erickson." The letter provided information on both the 2002 and the fatal 2003 accident.

"Have you ever utilized the Federal Aviation Administration's service through the aviation systems data branch where you can access pilots' accident records?" asked Dornik.

"I have never," said Knowle.

"You're aware of it, though?"

"No, possibly our claims department or someone else were aware of it, but I'm not."

"All right. So as far as you know, you didn't even know that the service existed through the FAA, where you just write them a letter and ask for a pilot's history?"

"I didn't think it was available," said Knowle.

"Okay. And I wrote to them, and they told me about both of

Mr. Erickson's accidents, had all the information. So in your experience, that's nothing you've ever done?"

"No. I've never done it."

Knowle said even if he had known about this, it wouldn't have been foolproof. "It would be time-consuming, and I'm not sure how accurate the data would be, anyway, because pilots' names are given to us in all different fashions. There might be a Charles Erickson, there may be a C. E. Erickson, there might be a Chuck Erickson."

Dornik thought this absurd reasoning. "Okay. But I bet there's only one Charles Erickson, Chuck Erickson, Charlie Erickson with Mr. Erickson's flight certificate number. Wouldn't you agree with that?"

"Yes."

"Okay. The same with Social Security number. That would be unique. Correct?"

"That's correct."

"Address maybe? That's probably pretty unique. Correct?"

"Correct."

"Okay. So in the end, you extended coverage on this Quintessence airplane on a high-performance aircraft to a pilot who had no experience in this aircraft, who had relatively low time generally, in which you did absolutely no background checking, other than to read the application?"

Dornik was on a roll. Lindberg interrupted him, saying it was an argumentative question, but that didn't matter. He'd managed to rattle their cage. "Isn't that true?" he pressed.

"That's true," said Knowle.

Excited after the depositions, Dornik called Toby and told him, "I think we struck gold." The deposition meant Old Republic could no longer claim they did not know or could not have known of Erickson's prior accident. Even if he gave the underwriter the benefit of the doubt—that he'd simply forgotten the name Charles Erickson in a blur of paperwork—this provided the basis for a constructive notice argument. Old Republic maintained these records on file at its headquarters in Atlanta, Georgia. Toby received this news with caution, taking Dornik's enthusiasm with a grain of salt. He recalled warnings from some of his attorney friends who painted a starker picture, affirming Toby's worry. They explained it would still come down to basic contract law. He lied. It's void. However, another attorney friend of Toby's offered a scrap of hope, saying that with the imputed knowledge argument he could maybe get past summary judgment. "You've got a shot now anyway," said the lawyer.

Dornik, on the other hand, had smelled blood.

Now that he lived in Saint Paul, Toby had more frequent access to Dornik. In fact, they struck up an easy friendship. From time to time, the two men would meet for a beer at a local pub, the Loon Café, near Dornik's office in downtown Minneapolis. They would discuss the legal situation, and then conversation might veer from Toby expressing feelings of frustration to Dornik trying to cheer him up. He was good at that. If there was an attractive woman in the bar, Dornik liked to tease Toby with a "Go on, have at her! You're not married." Toby would shake his head, still laughing at Dornik's well-meaning antics. "No, I'm a widower. I would never!"

Meanwhile, Toby's female friends were scheming. They decided the time was right for him to consider dating again. Back in Duluth, when he was still in the house on London Road, it seemed an impossible concept. Kathryn was the love of his life. He was indeed a widower, a pretty good mommy and a daddy, not to mention struggling to stay solvent. When close friends pressed him to start dating, he wondered if this desire to see him with someone new was less about his own happiness, and more a way of reestablishing some kind of familial order. Maybe it was just too uncomfortable to see him on his own, raising his two girls. It was lopsided. Maybe he needed a female figure in his life, in Grace's and Lily's lives. Even Teri Metry had urged Toby to keep his heart open to the possibility. That meant something, because Teri was one of Kathryn's oldest friends. She told him Kathryn would've wanted him—a young dad with young kids—to remarry eventually. It was the closest thing to Kathryn herself giving him her blessing.

"If you're looking to date, we know somebody you should call," read the e-mail that appeared in early January 2005 in Toby's in-box. It appeared to be from his good friend Greg Mueller. Actually, it was from Greg's wife, Meg, who'd secretly used her husband's e-mail to send the message. One of Meg's friends, Katy McCormick, had recently moved to the Twin Cities. She was thirty-eight years old, attractive, athletic, and working on a graduate degree in counseling at the University of Minnesota. Katy had heard the whole story of the plane crash and knew Toby's situation.

Toby decided to call Katy. They set up a lunch date, arranging to meet the next day at a Chinese restaurant called the Rainbow. As she parked her car, Katy saw a man walking across the street toward the entrance. She didn't know if it was Toby, and thought to herself, No. He's too cute. He'd walked straight in without looking around for an anticipated guest, so presumably not. After waiting around ten minutes in the foyer for her date to appear, she went inside and saw no sign of him. Maybe he was a no-show. Meanwhile, Toby was waiting inside the restaurant at a table. He saw someone he thought could be Katy start to leave the restaurant, and he hurried over to catch up with her, introducing himself. Katy was pleased to see he was indeed the handsome man who'd crossed the street. As they walked back to the table, Toby said, "When you're meeting someone in a restaurant, you just come in and sit down." Katy smiled. "Oh, is that what you do!" she said. When the lunch arrived, they laughed at the huge pieces of broccoli that defied the grip of the chopsticks. For both Toby and Katy, the conversation flowed easily, naturally.

Katy was the youngest of six children, born into a big Irish Catholic family from Madison, Wisconsin. Her father, Bill McCormick, ran a lumber business with his brothers, Mike and Pat, a successful firm founded in 1934 by Katy's grandfather, Gregory McCormick. Katy loved growing up in Madison, which offered an incredible range of outdoor activities for the McCormick children and their many cousins. A highlight of the winter was to go iceboating on one of Madison's four lakes, a thrilling variation on sailing where an iceboat fitted with runners could achieve speeds of up to one hundred miles per hour as it sped over ice. In the summer, there was swimming, sailing, and trips to the family cottage in the countryside. Katy considered the great outdoors to be her "classroom in the wilderness."

After college, Katy began life as an educator and adventurer. She taught in the South Pacific, lived and taught in the wilderness with Outward Bound, was a special education teacher, and led a cross-country bicycling expedition called Girls on the Move—a coast-to-coast bike ride for women of all ages that raised awareness about Outward Bound's goals—in this case to celebrate the power of girls and to provide strong role models for them. When Katy met Toby, she was still as intrepid as ever, embracing travel and adventure with friends, studying resiliency, and enjoying her new life in the Twin Cities.

Toby loved the concept of Girls on the Move. He was impressed by Katy's energy, intelligence, and integrity. When she mentioned she was taking a class that semester called Resiliency and Spirituality, it was obvious they shared the same values. The subject was close to Toby's heart. As a student, he'd been drawn to the politics of nonviolent action and the resiliency of people who survived oppression. Resiliency had become the watchword of Toby's own life.

"Are you interviewing me?" said Toby with a smile.

"No!" said Katy. "But you are kind of the poster boy for this."

They laughed. Two and a half hours flew by.

"Should I call you again?" Toby said.

"Yes, I'd like that."

"Do you mean you really want me to call you or are you just saying that?" asked Toby.

"No, I'd really like for you to call me," said Katy.

Toby called the next day, and they arranged a second date. Again, the conversation was easy and spontaneous. Then he talked directly about the plane crash and what was going on with his girls, tearing up as he told the story. Katy was amazed not only by Toby's strength of character, but also by his ability to communicate so openly and honestly. Toby had a life, and a story, and that made him real. She told a friend, "I met this man. I've never been so present in my whole life as I have been in the last two weeks."

Although Katy thought about marriage, she had already made peace with what some in the Midwest considered her "nontraditional" lifestyle—that is, by remaining unmarried beyond her twenties. She had always wanted to marry and to raise a family, but she didn't want to settle for anything less than the right person. And now, here was Toby Pearson, and his two daughters. She didn't overanalyze the connection, but when she spoke with him she was immediately relaxed and drawn in.

Things moved quickly. During the fourth date they agreed, over dessert at a Mexican restaurant, they both wanted a long-term relationship. Toby felt reassured, and considered how to introduce Katy to his girls. Of course they would have to proceed carefully. He was nervous that if Grace and Lily became attached to Katy, seeing her as their new mommy, and the relationship didn't work out, they would face heartache all over again. That would be emotionally devastating. He even checked in with Dr. Connie multiple times about what to do. She warned him of the dangers of introducing a potential new partner too early. "Just don't," she said.

Still, there was something about Katy that felt right. Toby came up with a plan. He engineered an informal meeting on Saint Patrick's Day, something that wouldn't be intimidating. Katy was already out with a friend and her baby at a ceili—a traditional Gaelic social gathering, with folk music and dancing. Toby was with Grace and Lily. They all met up fairly casually, a chance encounter in a crowd of high-spirited revelers, watching colorful Irish dance groups performing steps to jigs, reels, and hornpipes. Within this swirl of distraction, Grace and Lily met Daddy's new friend.

That evening Katy came around to the house for dinner, bringing a large box of monster cookies frosted with big eyeballs, much to the girls' delight. At the dinner table, Katy noticed the girls seemed relaxed and polite and, also, a bit silly. Lily was still in her pressure garments, still required to wear her mask, her healing skin still compressed. Toby was very aware that it wouldn't necessarily be easy for Katy to come into this household, this private space, where he tended to the girls' burn injuries so patiently. He knew it would take a strong person to deal with this, and he worried it might be overwhelming for anyone.

If it was, Katy didn't let on. She understood this meeting was a big deal, and she knew he would never have introduced her to Grace and Lily if he weren't serious about their relationship. Soon she would graduate from being "Daddy's friend," to being "Daddy's good friend." By then, Grace, Lily, and Katy had started to bond.

At first Toby kept his relationship with Katy fairly discreet. But one Sunday, Carolyn and her friend Karen dropped by Toby's house to visit Grace and Lily. Carolyn maintained a regular presence in the lives of the girls, who were always excited to see their aunt. She'd also been vigilant about keeping the girls in touch with their grandparents on Kathryn's side of the family, taking them for visits to Duluth around Thanksgiving and Christmas, as well as planning a fun trip in the summer. During this house call, Carolyn and Karen walked through the living room, half noticing a dark-haired woman busy in the kitchen. They assumed she was a babysitter. Later, on their way out, Toby said, "Oh, by the way, this is Katy."

Back in the car, it suddenly dawned on the two women. Why did Toby have a babysitter on a Sunday?

"Oh, he's on a date!" said Karen.

"Damn it, why does Toby get to date first?" said Carolyn, joking with her friend.

"He's almost a model character from a Danielle Steele novel," said Karen. "A good-looking widower, with two little kids who survived an accident. It's classic!"

They laughed at Karen's cheeky observation. Of course, Carolyn and her friends had discussed the possibility of her dating again, but it had stayed a hypothetical idea at first. They even had a list of ideal men—George Clooney, Anderson Cooper, and, more realistically, a doctor at the hospital where Carolyn worked. But Carolyn had yet to feel ready. Karen wondered if this encounter with Katy might open her friend to the possibility of meeting someone new.

In the late spring, Grace and Lily faced another important event—their first flight since the plane crash. This was obviously something else that had to be carefully managed by Toby, in collaboration with Dr. Connie. Toby's plan was to fly down to Denver, Colorado, with them to see his brother and their cousins. It was a short flight—no more than two hours—but conceptually it loomed large. Whatever hidden phobias the girls had about flying would have to be confronted, but Toby determined the sooner the better. If they waited too long, who knew if they'd ever have the nerve to fly again? He envisioned Grace and Lily, when they became young women, traveling to Europe—London, Paris, Berlin—and beyond. So, he thought, let's start with Denver.

Grace's initial response to the idea was not positive. She flat-out refused ever to board a plane again. She'd once made a statement that everyone in the family liked to repeat: "It's not the flying I mind, it's the crashing." It had seemed funny, wry, and perceptive at the time—echoing Amelia Earhart's oft-quoted line, "Trouble in the air is very rare. It is hitting the ground that causes it." In fact, it was typical of a five-year-old's response to the two separate experiences. Having matured now, at the age of seven, Grace was suspicious of the connections between the flying and the crashing.

Lily still believed they were two separate phenomena not related at all. According to Dr. Connie, she was in preschool thinking mode, and the thought of a plane ride held no fear. However, Dr. Connie knew that sensory reminders—for example, turbulence or a vision of clouds—could activate hormones and panic similar to the feelings of the original trauma—in other words, a flashback. That was the worst-case scenario.

To preempt this, Dr. Connie created playful scenarios where Lily and the doctor pretended to be flight attendants, using the dolls and teddy bears as the passengers. Together they prepared a snack for everyone on the flight, then told everyone to fasten their seat belts. They imagined the noise level was loud because of the big engines, and talked about the G-force that could be felt on takeoff. They talked about the noise of the pilot "putting the tires in the trunk," and reminded the passengers of the bumps as the plane moved through the clouds. Lily enthusiastically immersed herself in this game, which she played several times before the flight.

Simulated play wasn't going to cut it for Grace. Instead she put together paper airplanes and talked about things that could help her feel safe. Then she remembered the good-luck charms she'd made, which had worked before against the monsters. She made one for the trip—a very detailed paper airplane with writing and decorations on it. She believed this would help her manage her emotional reactions. Her plan was to give it to the pilot before takeoff.

In the lead-up to the Denver trip, Toby also worked carefully with Grace and Lily to complement Dr. Connie's work. He bought a book about planes and talked about the difference between the big plane and the small plane. They talked about the day of the flight, imagining the sequence of events—checking their bags, going through security, fastening their seat belts, and then, once in the air, getting a free soda and pretzels. Toby explained gently that by the time they were done with that, they'd be almost landing and coming down, and their ears would pop. He went through it religiously, a week before and then again on the day before the trip.

He'd called Dr. Connie to ask, "Are they ready to go on a plane ride?"

She said yes, but added a recommendation: Buy a portable DVD player from Target just in case the psychological prep didn't take. "When all else fails I know there is always distraction!" Toby took her advice.

On the day of the flight, Toby and the girls arrived at the airport without too much anxiety, passing through security and arriving at the gate. Before boarding, Toby spoke quietly with the attendant at the gate: "Just to warn you, my two daughters were in a plane crash. So there's a chance they might start to freak out." As he did so, Lily ran down the passage toward the plane, full of excitement, and in a loud voice said, "Free pretzels, here we come!"

The flight attendant looked back at Toby. "Looks like she's doing okay."

Once on board, Grace insisted on handing her good-luck charm to a member of the flight crew—at least he looked like a pilot—who was standing by the door. "I made this for the pilot," she said.

The plane eventually took off, and the journey to Denver began with no sign of nerves. The three sat in their own row— Toby in the middle, with Grace and Lily switching in and out of the window seat, from which they could see the vast geometry of Nebraska's fields; sometimes the girls would guess the name of a big river winding far below. They even talked about how cool it felt to be above the clouds. Did they make the connection? Toby couldn't detect any anxiety from them, though he felt relieved there was no turbulence. At the end of the flight, the girls each got a special pin from the flight crew—their wings—a small but significant moment. All that preparation with their dad and Dr. Connie had paid off. Or was it the good-luck charm, Grace's artful talisman, that had kept everyone safe?

Over the July 4 weekend, the Pearsons headed up to Big Elbow Lake, near Park Rapids, where Toby's parents owned a cabin. It had been a family tradition to gather for the national holiday, with the families of Toby's brothers and sister converging on the place for the long weekend. Among them were nine children, including Grace and Lily, all around a similar age. The previous year, the carefree nature of summer on the lake had been inevitably compromised by the harsh legacy of the accident, but a year later, the situation had improved slightly. Toby had met Katy; in fact, she'd already met Tom and Maureen in May, when Toby had taken her and the girls up to the cabin to open the fishing season. During that first trip, she and Lily and Grace had their first solo trip to Itasca State Park, home of the headwaters of the Mississippi River. One of the chief thrills of the visit was a chance to cross the river near its point of origin, stepping across boulders to reach the other side. Katy had led Grace and Lily across, though Lily briefly lost her footing on a boulder and became upset when her leg, still clad in compression garments, got wet. Katy's concern quickly dissipated when she saw Lily was okay, and they would certainly have a story to tell when they returned to the cabin. Now, though, on this summer trip, Katy met the wider family. Any anxiety she had was immediately swept away in the maelstrom of cousins, uncles, aunts, and grandparents. Because she adored life on the lake, and the great outdoors, Katy was right in her element.

Meanwhile, after more than eighteen months, Lily no longer had to wear her plastic mask during the day. She still had to use it at night, but that didn't matter half as much. At least during the day, she could join her cousins splashing around in the water, unencumbered by the constant clutch of the mask. It took time, though, for Lily to get used to this little step back toward normality.

When Dr. Mohr gave Lily and her dad the good news, Lily's reaction surprised Toby. At first she refused to remove the mask, walking pensively back to the car. Perhaps Toby had imagined his daughter whooping for joy at this moment of liberation, but no. After talking to Lily in the car, Toby surmised that she now considered the mask a form of protection, a way of hiding her scars. Without it, she would be vulnerable. They talked some more as Toby drove her to Snuffy's Malt Shop—a famous Minnesota diner—to celebrate with a cheeseburger, French fries, and a malt. After this feast, Lily was ready to concede she no longer needed the mask. When Grace asked her, "Aren't you happy that you don't have to wear your mask anymore?" Lily said, "Yes!" Come the July Fourth weekend, she'd happily ditched it. Her little cousins would hardly notice the difference. They were all too busy having fun together.

That was the gift of the cabin on Big Elbow Lake. It was a sanctuary away from the constant stares that Lily felt and endured. Without the mask, there was some visible scarring, but her aesthetic results, as Dr. Mohr had anticipated, were looking good. In one snapshot Lily is clearly in her element, an excited five-year-old in the glorious July sunshine, dressed in a pink dress and blue sunhat but still wearing the black compression garments on her body, arms, and legs.

There were some lingering health concerns for Lily. Because of scarring on her windpipe, she still had difficulty breathing. It wasn't life threatening, but as Toby put it, it was life impacting. Maureen noticed it, too, especially after Lily ran around; it was an audible rasp, vaguely asthmatic. Lily had had surgery the year before to remove scar tissue in her throat, but it hadn't fully solved the problem; she was often short of breath and she flushed easily. Toby suspected another procedure would have to be scheduled soon enough. Doctors also kept a careful eye on

Lily's legs, which had been broken in the crash and remained undiagnosed for weeks. Periodic X-rays now made sure the bones continued to grow properly so she could happily dispense with the orthopedic boot, though there was still some lingering weakness in her foot flexion. By now, Grace's physical health was much improved, the skin grafts on her hands and legs having attained what doctors called a good cosmetic outcome. On these summer days, it filled everyone with hope to see the sisters once again dive back into their childhood as they splashed into Big Elbow Lake.

For Toby and his siblings, the weekend was also an opportunity to reconnect. Tony, the physician from Colorado, took a vigilant interest in the girls' health, asking Toby for medical updates. For the brothers and their dad, one of the great pleasures of the lake cabin was the fishing. Once the kids were tucked up in bed, as the sun disappeared behind the dark boreal pine forest, the Pearson boys would take a boat out onto the lake after dinner. Night fishing afforded one of the best opportunities to catch the walleyes, the Minnesota state fish, that populated its lakes. The Pearson crew chugged out across the darkening water and let the peacefulness engulf them as they trolled for fish. During one of their sotto voce conversations, Toby updated his father and his brothers about his financial situation, and especially about the lawsuit with Old Republic. Dornik's remarkable discovery—the possible paper trail—now offered a ghost of a chance they could survive summary judgment. Toby didn't dwell on it for a long time. Out on the twilight lake, with the loons calling to and fro, the lawsuit seemed like a distant thunderstorm.

11

THIS ISN'T GOING AWAY QUIETLY

So what. That was a response Dornik heard often from aviation attorneys who did not share his excitement about his deposition breakthrough. That response poured cold water on his argument that Old Republic had a responsibility to do a minimal background check before insuring someone. If there was no obligation for an insurance company to check, any application could potentially be a fraud, but "so what."

Then Dornik stumbled upon another idea to advance this argument. He contacted the Department of Commerce—the agency that regulates insurers in Minnesota—to examine the language of the statute on canceling policies of commercial liability. He explained the Pearsons' predicament to the department chief, as well as outlining Old Republic's unyielding position on the issue of the material misrepresentation. He pointed out that, without much effort, even he had been able to verify Erickson's accident history with the FAA. Was Old Republic justified in denying coverage more than a year after the policy was issued? What remedy would the state suggest?

The Commerce enforcement investigator, Steven Klebba, sent out two letters to Old Republic explaining his department's position. "While we agree that the facts seemingly show that a misrepresentation was made on the policy application, we are of the opinion that with regard to the third-party liability coverage . . . the company in this case cannot unilaterally refuse coverage," he wrote. "Given the time between the initial application, issuance of the policy and date of loss, it appears your company had ample time to properly verify the underwriting information that was presented, such as verifying listed pilot licensing information and accident history. Unfortunately, this does not appear to have been done."

Klebba reiterated his department's position in a second letter in June, following correspondence from the insurance company. However, in anticipation of the summary judgment hearing on the issue, the department decided to wait on the court's decision before taking the matter any further.

Despite this argument from the state, Old Republic would not be pressured to settle. They believed the court would side with them, granting them summary judgment to back up their position. The "so what" consensus in Dornik's legal circle prevailed: "It doesn't matter what you say or do; the company is never going to offer you any money." Dornik wanted to believe otherwise. The estate could argue that Old Republic was acting in bad faith, knowing that argument could lead to a much bigger claim against them down the road. Letters between attorneys flew back and forth, but to no avail. By late summer, they had a date for the hearing—October 24, 2005. If they prevailed before a judge, that would be the gateway to a trial. Dornik, and Old Republic, understood all too well how that would look: a multibillion-dollar-insurance company versus two injured little girls.

Dornik knew better than most how much power, how much emotional sway an injured child could have with a sympathetic jury. It was part of the personal injury business—part rational, part sentimental. During April and May, Dornik found himself arguing a case in Le Mars, a small town in Iowa famous for its dairy farms. It was a medical malpractice suit on behalf of the parents of a four-year-old boy whose meningitis was misdiagnosed, resulting in massive brain damage. The case pitted Dornik against the only doctor in town, or so it seemed to Dornik, and that meant the odds weren't favorable for a win. Of those medical malpractice suits that got to a jury, almost 80 percent of the verdicts favor the physician. Plaintiffs' attorneys have found that since most people don't have a deep knowledge of medical topics, they usually trust the doctor's evaluation during a trial.

During jury selection, Dornik faced a row of potential jurors who viewed him with skepticism, if not downright hostility. They were dairy farmers who evidently disliked big-city lawyers. Dornik did something that turned this around. He unhooked the little boy from his feeding tube, lifted him from his wheelchair, and carried him over to the jurors, introducing him to each person individually: "This is Kelly," he said. When he'd finished, two-thirds of the jury pool was in tears.

Once a jury was selected, he had to keep their trust. Would they still view him as a city slicker from Minneapolis come to cash in on a tragedy? To counter this, Dornik had long learned to abide by a simple dress code in the courtroom. He always wore a dark two-button suit, a plain white shirt with a tie, and a simple black-faced watch. He always wore his wedding ring. He had other habits that he faithfully observed on trial days. He abstained from drinking coffee (to avoid too-frequent bathroom breaks), ate only an apple for lunch, carried Life Saver mints to stop his mouth from getting dry when called on to expostulate in front of the judge and jury, and, most important, he placed an old pocket watch in his briefcase—his lucky charm. It had belonged to his dad, who'd died when he was two years old.

The trial in Le Mars continued for nearly five weeks. In time, everybody in the town was pulling for the family, and for Mr. Dornik, to win his malpractice case. By the end of the trial, Dornik felt like a celebrity in town. Cheered on, he won the case, securing millions in damages for Kelly's family. Afterward he got a card from Kelly's mom with a photo of her boy. The greeting read: "John, if you are ever having a down day, just look at my picture and remember when you kicked ass at my trial and about what a difference you made in my life, love, Kelly."

Messages like these validated Dornik's decision to become a trial lawyer. He chose a career defending plaintiffs whom he felt had been wronged. Yet he knew that some lawyers in his field gained a bad rap as unscrupulous, self-serving ambulance chasers. He'd faced down aggressive people in his professional and private life who tried to challenge his motives, especially during the nineties when lawyer bashing went hand in hand with corporate efforts to curb lawsuits. He'd been tagged as a parasite, the scum of the earth, a bloodsucker. Dornik, however, consoled himself with an amusing adage: "Personal injury lawyers are like cats. You hate them until you get one of your own."

As Dornik saw it, there was nothing frivolous about being defrauded, ripped off, or injured due to malfeasance or negligence. He was always sympathetic to clients who arrived at his office, upset and apologetic, often introducing themselves as "not the suing type." Dornik knew from experience the confusion and loss felt by patients and family members after tragedy changed their mind. It was Dornik's job to transmute this suffering into tangible compensation. If that meant eliciting sympathy from a jury using emotional courtroom tactics, then so be it.

Dornik felt strongly that if he could get Toby's case to go to trial, he'd be able to work his magic on a jury. Grace and Lily would surely capture a jury's heart. They were the most sympathetic clients he'd ever had—sweet, young, and heroic. Of course, Toby hated the idea of subjecting his girls to such exposure but—publicly at least—he had to indicate a willingness to let this happen. When Toby sat down with Dornik to talk about tactics for the hearing, they even discussed bringing Grace and Lily to court. Eventually they thought better of it, deciding that a conservative federal judge might perceive this as overt emotional pressure. This wasn't a trial yet.

Dornik had already upped his PR campaign in favor of the Pearson girls. With the hearing approaching, there was already an uptick in media interest both on a local and a national level. Dornik insisted that he would be the aggressor in combative interviews—the bad cop to Toby's good cop—allowing Toby to sidestep any legal mudslinging. Then they reviewed how they would argue the case.

In Minnesota—and indeed in almost every state—all automobile owners are required to carry liability insurance that covers third parties in the event of an accident. Under Minnesota law, there is a specific statute that spells out the conditions of this mandatory coverage, including the provision that protects innocent third parties who are injured in an accident. Under one section of the statute, the language makes it clear that even if an insurance policy were later found to be invalid, the third-party coverage would still be honored. The language states: "Such liability may not be canceled or annulled by any agreement between the reparation obligor and the insured after the occurrence of the injury or damage; no statement made by the insured or on the insured's behalf and no violation of said policy shall defeat or void said policy." However, there was no such law that covered aviation liability insurance for private plane accidents, so in this regard Toby and his girls were vulnerable because they had no defined right to compensation since Old Republic had rescinded the entire policy. They were victims twice, first as injured survivors and again as innocents in a system that provided them inadequate protection.

Dornik planned to use Minnesota's auto insurance statute as an analogy, arguing that, although the language wasn't explicit, it implied that the state supported third-party claims in the event of an accident. After all, thought Dornik, wasn't tort law intended for just such a scenario as this one—to protect and compensate the innocent members of society? This point of view was backed by the Minnesota Department of Commerce, which had published a manual, "Aviation Insurance Private and Commercial," that included guidelines for coverage, stating, "Any 'voidance for fraud' provision MUST make an exception so as NOT to apply to liability coverage." Strictly speaking, though, this was a guideline and not a statute, so Old Republic could argue that the department was trying to enforce laws that weren't on the books. From Dornik's perspective, it made no sense for the state to mandate liability insurance for aircraft—which it did—and not extend the same compulsory coverage to protect third-party passengers from the negligence of the aircraft operator. Surely public policy would support this argument. Still, nothing was guaranteed. They needed backup.

Dornik called the second most powerful politician in the state, Mike Hatch, the attorney general and a Democrat who was considering a run for governor against the Republican incumbent Tim Pawlenty. In explaining Toby's situation, Dornik hardly needed to remind Hatch of the political capital to be gained by supporting such a case. "Why don't you join us and argue that this policy should be enforced?" suggested Dornik.

Hatch had followed the Pearson case with interest—it was still big news, and he knew Toby as a fellow lawyer. If at first he demurred, a personal visit by Toby to his office in Saint Paul helped secure his involvement. Toby knew Hatch had a reputation as a champion of the underdog. He also felt pretty convinced that having the state in court would send a powerful message. After the meeting, Toby and the attorney general shook hands. Hatch was officially on board.

On September 21, 2005, Hatch filed an amicus curiae—a legal brief presented to the court—asserting the broad public interest at stake: "The State will argue that Old Republic's position is contradicted by Minnesota Statute, case law and public policy, and that adopting that position would not only leave the Pearson girls with serious, uncompensated injuries, but would also set a harmful precedent for any Minnesotan relying on coverage from an insurance policy that they did not personally apply for."

The day of the hearing finally arrived. Dornik and Toby had done as much as they could to prepare for this critical moment in court. The idea to involve the attorney general in the case proved to be a good one. That morning Hatch made it official—he would be running for governor. It was perhaps the worst-kept secret in Minnesota politics, but the timing was perfect from Dornik's point of view. Hatch announced his candidacy at a statewide convention of the Minnesota Nurses Association in Saint Paul. "I believe health care is a right, not a privilege," he declared, making his number one priority clear. He received a table-pounding ovation from the gathering of several hundred nurses who endorsed him.

Dornik met Toby at his office on Fifth Street. When he walked in, Dornik noticed that Toby had dressed in a sharp suit and tie. He was undoubtedly nervous, but his expression was one of grim determination.

"You know, you never want your client to look better than

you in court," Dornik said with a smile. "But today I'll make an exception."

Toby threw back his head and laughed his big laugh that was now familiar to Dornik. Dornik was skilled at putting people at ease, but both men knew that everything turned on today's hearing. Dornik tried to lighten the mood by cracking jokes as they walked through the skyways of Minneapolis—a network of climate-controlled pedestrian walkways that link city blocks together—until they arrived at the nearby federal courthouse in the modernist high-rise called the Minneapolis Building. Before they entered, Dornik stopped and said, "No matter how this comes out, it's my honor to do this."

As Dornik might have predicted, thanks to his prehearing publicity and the imminent arrival of Hatch, the courtroom was packed with more than a hundred people, which was highly unusual for a hearing. They strode in ready to do battle. Dornik and Toby greeted Rick Snyder, the attorney for the Erickson estate who would be arguing the case alongside them. Protocol required them to greet the opposing counsel, led by Michael Lindberg, who was representing Old Republic Insurance Company. Toby eyed him warily, as if he were a personal enemy, though he said nothing to betray his feelings, which were at odds with the realization that the attorney was simply doing his job to defend his client. The judge on the case, Joan Ericksen, was known to be fair but pro-business, or, as Dornik put it, "not exactly a screaming liberal." She entered, and the hearing began.

Lindberg walked over to the podium in the center of the courtroom and began the argument on behalf of his client, Old Republic. The fact is, he said, the company had been led to believe that it was insuring a pilot who had no accident history.

Charles Erickson had made a material misrepresentation on his application form, which in the eyes of Old Republic increased the risk of loss. Had the company known he'd had a previous accident—the year before the fatal 2003 crash—it would never have insured him.

"If in fact the insurance company had actual knowledge that the applicant was a liar, there is no logical explanation as to why they issued the policy," said Lindberg. "The only reason the policy could possibly have been issued under these facts is if the folks who made the decision, namely the underwriters, acted in good faith relying upon the written submissions. And if they relied on other facts such as the fact that this gentleman had an accident earlier, then there's no reason to write this policy."

Then he tried to engage with what he called the "big defense," attacking Dornik's point that the void for fraud provisions in aviation insurance policies were not enforceable when it came to injured passengers or other third parties. Lindberg rambled on at some length in an effort to dismiss this argument. "You can't start from this utopian idea that all injured people should have an insured defendant to sue."

It was uncomfortable listening for Toby and Dornik because Lindberg did have the facts on his side, unfriendly though they seemed. By contrast, at the heart of Dornik's defense was an appeal to common sense, emotion, and the right thing to do, implied in the language of the statutes and state policy. He knew that a conservative judge could easily dismiss this argument and favor the black and white of contract law.

Lindberg went on to give an example of different scenarios where an insurance company had the right to deny coverage if a pilot violated the terms of his policy. For example, if a single-engine pilot flies a twin-engine plane, there is no coverage for that. "Or another qualification would be a non-instrument rated pilot flying in instrument flight conditions, flying in the clouds," he continued. "The statute allows that claim to be denied. Those injured plaintiffs, innocent victims that they may be, don't get coverage."

The judge interrupted, asking Lindberg whether people injured in a car accident could sue the insurance company for damages, even in the event of a violated policy. Lindberg had to concede that this was true, even citing the statute upon which Dornik based his argument. "And that, of course, is the great difference between the world of auto insurance and the world of aviation insurance," he said. "We don't have a statute like that in Minnesota that explicitly says what the legislature says about cars."

Lindberg finished his argument and sat back down. It was the defense's turn to make its case. Dornik and the counsel for the Erickson estate, Rick Snyder, had agreed to split the argument between them, with Snyder going first. He argued that the insurance company had no right, under the law, to rescind the policy retroactively. The law only allowed an insurer to terminate a policy in advance, by giving ten days' notice. It couldn't just come along and treat the policy "as if it never existed" by rescinding it. The only option for Old Republic would have been cancelation, not rescission. By the time an accident happens, he insisted, it's too late to cancel. "Allowing retroactive rescission would defeat the very purposes of the statute. It would mean that planes would be flying without insurance," said Snyder.

The judge questioned Snyder about this key point, before the attorney general got up to argue for the State of Minnesota in Toby's defense. Earlier, there'd been a tense moment at the defense table when Hatch had yet to appear. He'd been stuck in traffic after announcing his candidacy, but had rolled in with his entourage at the last minute. Hatch, still throwing off sparks from his earlier adrenaline-pumping performance, took the floor. Reporters, who'd inevitably drifted off during the dry, legal complexities of the previous arguments, suddenly perked up at the dapper politician's appearance.

He went straight to the heart of Dornik's point that the state's insurance statutes implicitly guaranteed protection to third-party victims. "As public policy, we want to make sure that before an airplane takes off, that the owner of that airplane has coverage—not to protect the airplane, pilot or the owner. We don't care about the owner. What we care about are innocent people, about the passengers, or homes that are hit."

The judge again pointed out that the legislature guaranteed this protection for cars, but not for planes. Hatch blustered a little in his argument but essentially insisted that in principle it did guarantee protection, that the laws made no provision for an insurance company to rescind the policy after the fact. Now he gestured toward Toby. "Here we've got little Gracie and Elizabeth getting in an airplane. Are they able to ask the pilot how many hours they're flying?" asked Hatch, referring to the number of hours a pilot has logged in the air, a measure of experience. No, he argued. Their safety is only guaranteed because the state insists that the pilot carry aviation insurance. By issuing the policy the company is "warranting that it's going to protect the public," said Hatch. "And those two little girls are part of the public."

Perhaps it wasn't the most elegant performance, thought Dornik, but he was pleased that Hatch had weighed in. Now it was his turn. Dornik rose and stepped over to the podium. With the polish of a practiced trial lawyer, he outlined his evidence that Old Republic was the insurer for both aircraft that Erickson crashed, and that the policy's underwriter, Steve Knowle—whose deposition Dornik had submitted to the court as evidence—had prior knowledge of the other accident. It was obvious, he said, the company could have or should have known about the prior accident and failed to take action, as it was all too happy to be receiving the premiums from the new policy.

"I think the bottom line is they really didn't care. They wanted to extend this coverage," said Dornik, hitting his stride. "Then the accident occurred, and the injuries in this case, Your Honor, Thomas Pearson's wife Kathryn died, and his two little girls are injured horrifically. It's an awful, awful accident. Coincidentally, within days of the accident, the insurance company found out, wow, about Mr. Erickson's [previous] accident.

"Now, suddenly when there's a big loss, suddenly information is available to them that wasn't available for the 11 months prior to that, I don't know. But they denied the claim right away. And, of course, then sued Mr. Pearson, and that's what brings us before you."

Dornik then pushed further, casting doubt on the presumption that Charles Erickson had actually lied on his form; the facts were "ambiguous." When it came to the pilot's so-called misrepresentation, the burden of proof fell on the insurance company to show there was "an intent to deceive, or in the alternative, that it increased the insurer's risk of loss.

"I believe, Your Honor, that there's been no misrepresentation proven," declared Dornik. "It would be unlikely that a jury would conclude that Mr. Erickson intended to deceive and defraud [the insurance company and the underwriting company] about his prior aviation accident when it was precisely those same entities that investigated the prior accident, handled the insurance claim, determined that the accident resulted in a total loss, and paid for the loss. Whether Mr. Erickson intended to deceive and defraud the Plaintiff is an issue for a jury."

That was Dornik's goal: to get the whole case before a jury, knowing he'd be able to defeat Old Republic's unpopular stance.

In closing, he returned to the argument made by Hatch that "the wrongful acts of the insured should not deny liability coverage for the Pearsons." He concluded by reminding the court that Toby wasn't in court by choice, as a plaintiff, but as a defendant who was "sued by a multi-billion dollar insurance company."

Judge Ericksen brought the hearing to an end, thanking the lawyers for their arguments. She wasn't going to make a judgment that day. The order would have to wait for a few more weeks. Dornik greeted Toby with a smile. He looked drained by the proceedings, which Dornik knew had been emotionally difficult for him. For two years, he'd been waiting for this day in court. Still, they agreed it had gone well, and now they had to wait for the judge to rule. As they headed out, Dornik encountered Lindberg hurrying out, perhaps eager to escape his opponents and the inevitable gauntlet of reporters and television cameras that awaited them.

"You're screwing with the wrong people," said Dornik, a sly smile on his face. He was half-serious, half-joking. "This isn't going away quietly."

Dornik didn't mean to sound like a macho lawyer. It just seemed self-evident to him, in the context of the court, and with the inevitable media interest, that the Pearsons would command the greater share of sympathy. His thought was borne out as they left the building. As expected, a posse of journalists and camera crews jostled for interviews at the bottom of the courthouse steps. Dornik wanted everyone, including Hatch, to make a statement, picturing it all on the five o'clock news.

"We're grateful to have had our day in court, and glad that we could make our arguments and tell our story," said Toby. "I can only put so much energy in the games and stuff that are being played by the insurance company. I am trying to focus on other things, such as making the best life that I can for my little girls."

Dornik stepped forward and summed it up more bluntly, questioning how "a multibillion-dollar insurance company whose insured causes the death of a woman and terrible, horrific injuries to two little girls can then turn around and sue their father because they don't want to provide coverage."

Suddenly there was a flurry of activity, as Lindberg was spotted trying to leave the courthouse unnoticed. Reporters started to chase him for a comment, but he hurried off with his head down. Later that day, the image of Old Republic's lawyer apparently running away was all over the evening news. It had been a good day for the defense.

After the hearing, the Pearsons remained in the media spotlight. This was a national story now. The calls kept coming in, including one from the *Dr. Phil* talk show, which was eager to put the Pearsons on the couch with the celebrity psychologist. Dornik thought the request a hoax, gleefully mocking the caller, but it turned out to be a legitimate producer. Although grateful for the offer, Toby turned down the request. He was reluctant to expose Grace and Lily to too much media scrutiny, although before the hearing he had agreed to let a reporter from *People* magazine write a high-profile feature on his family's plight. He thought of it as a Hail Mary in case the court ruled against him. If he didn't have the law on his side, Toby figured, only public opinion could influence the case in the long run. The weeks rolled by, and now the story appeared just before Thanksgiving 2005, titled "Who's to Blame?"

"People approach me, shocked and dumbfounded by what the insurance company is doing," Toby told the magazine. "Without that support it would have been a lot more difficult."

The insurance company's behavior drew the scorn of many across the state, and nationwide, as evidenced by the outpouring of news reports. Local radio stations followed the hearing, and even a conservative talk show host expressed sympathy for the Pearsons' "battle to get their medical bills paid." It was rumored that thousands of people flooded the insurance company's headquarters with e-mails expressing outrage and disgust, so many, in fact, that the deluge crashed the company's server.

At Thanksgiving, Toby drove with Grace and Lily to his parents' house in Mankato. Both Toby's brother Andy and his sister, Beth, were there with their families, and the girls could hardly wait to jump out of the car to play with their cousins again. Later on, everyone gathered around the table for the traditional Thanksgiving dinner—turkey with ham stuffing, and for dessert Toby's favorite, pumpkin pie. As was the custom in the Pearson family, before the meal everyone took their turn to give thanks for something or someone in their life. When it got to Grace's turn, she said, "I'm thankful for my daddy." Lily, ever attentive to her older sister, followed her example. "I'm thankful for my daddy, too!"

After Thanksgiving, Auntie Carolyn and Grandma Mar took the girls out for a holiday treat to see *The Nutcracker* at the Duluth Auditorium. The girls were excited about seeing real live ballerinas in tutus, though having to sit still for a couple of hours was a challenge for Lily, who preferred to stand in the aisle and wiggle around to the music. The girls loved dancing. Over the last year, Grace had started to attend the Just for Kix program, which had dance classes for young children. Now that her burns were healing, Grace was excited by the prospect of wearing ballet shoes again; Lily and Toby would watch as Miss Marnie tried to drill the girls. It built self-esteem and required strenuous physical movement, which, Toby had been told, promoted elasticity in damaged skin. So it was with wide-eyed wonderment that Grace and Lily watched the Sugar Plum Fairy and her cavalier perform their dance, just as Carolyn watched her nieces get lost in the magic (for a few precious minutes anyway). It was a bittersweet image for Carolyn. She wished that Kathryn were there with her girls; she wished there wasn't that startling juxtaposition between Lily's beautiful dress and the dark compression garments underneath; she wished people wouldn't stare.

A few days before Christmas, on December 21, the phone rang at the Pearson home. Toby answered. It was Dornik.

"Well, Toby, we got our decision," he said. "We won."

According to the judge's ruling, the constructive notice argument—that the insurance company surely knew about the prior accident—seemed to have won the day: "Viewing the record in the light most favorable to Defendants, a reasonable fact finder could conclude that Old Republic knew of the true facts regarding Erickson's accident history. Accordingly, a reasonable fact finder could conclude that Old Republic did not rely on Erickson's alleged misrepresentations and that the misrepresentations therefore were not material. As a result, the Court denies Old Republic's motion for summary judgment. Having denied Old Republic's motion . . . the Court need not address Defendants' alternative arguments in opposition to Old Republic's motion."

When Dornik hung up, Toby was so overwhelmed with relief he cried for ten minutes. It had been a long journey to this point and, despite all the potential pitfalls, he'd made it past the summary judgment, the looming threat that had dragged him into the strange world of aviation liability law. He called family members to tell them the good news. That night Toby and a group of close friends went to a local restaurant, Champs, to celebrate the victory, raising a toast to friendship, support, and clearing another hurdle. But Toby knew it wasn't over. Now he had to prepare himself and the girls for a possible trial.

December turned to January. Toby kept running.

The slow burn on the insurance case had frustrated everyone, but with the hearing decided in his favor, Toby could breathe a little easier. Ever since those uncertain days at Regions Hospital, running had saved his sanity. It had relieved his stress, allowing him to cultivate patience and perspective on the family's well-being. Plus, he now had a running partner in Katy. Together they discovered new places to explore around Minneapolis. They often ran down by the banks of the Mississippi River and then headed west toward Lake Nokomis—one of the many beautiful lakes in Minneapolis. Steeped in the mythology of Hiawatha, the Native American leader immortalized by Henry Wadsworth Longfellow in his epic nineteenth-century poem, *Hiawatha*, Lake Nokomis took its name from Hiawatha's grandmother:

> Downward through the evening twilight,
> In the days that are forgotten,
> In the unremembered ages,
> From the full moon fell Nokomis,
> Fell the beautiful Nokomis

This was where Toby had started running, years before, in a familiar landscape still imbued with memories. Running here—around Nokomis, by the Mississippi, and along a tributary of the river called Minnehaha Creek—freed up Toby to talk with Katy about the case, allowing the two to grow ever closer. It was a tremendous relief for him to have a partner in whom he could confide and now share the burden of planning ahead. They also decided something else during these restorative runs: They would run a marathon together—not just any marathon, but the well-known Grandma's Marathon in Duluth. The marathon date was less than six months away, June 17, 2006, which gave Toby time to set some important plans in motion. It was a goal. In reality, there was a lot to do before then. He was still bound up in aviation liability law and its inadequacies, and another confrontation with the insurance company was imminent. Would there be a trial, or would Old Republic agree to settle? His resiliency had paid off so far, as the process had dragged on for years, and the company was even now denying every entreaty for settlement. At least that's how it seemed to everyone. Perhaps now, or soon, the company would realize it was dealing with a long-distance runner.

Leading up to the hearing, Old Republic had evidently refused to settle for the policy limit, believing the court would back up its position. Now, however, having rolled the dice and lost in court, the advantage shifted to the defendants. Having failed to defend and indemnify the Erickson estate by resolving the case within the policy limits when it had the chance, Old Republic could now be held liable for damages beyond that amount. The estate could argue it had been abandoned and, as such, was now exposed to a third-party claim. Such a third-party claim would be significantly more than the $1 million policy limit. How much more?

As was typical in personal injury cases, Dornik calculated the full cost of the damages that could be used in a wrongful death claim. He employed Dr. Jenny Wahl, the chair of the economics department at Carleton College in Northfield, Minnesota, to assess the economic loss for the Pearson family. These calculations took into account several factors, including the net loss of income to the family because of Kathryn's death, as well as the loss of the estimated value of Kathryn's relationship with Toby and the girls. This took into consideration the fact that Toby had to employ numerous babysitters so that he could work, as well as the more subjective assessment of his family's loss of advice, comfort, assistance, protection, counsel, and companionship.

The damages calculated for Lily were extensive, factoring the already staggering costs of her health care to date, as well as projecting future costs of medical and psychological care. Having met both girls on several occasions, Dornik knew the extent of their injuries, in particular Lily's facial scarring that, he asserted, would be an impediment in her pursuit of a job, friends, and even a life partner. This unsettling fact carried a financial value.

Grace's injuries, both medical and psychological, were also assessed. Dornik spoke with Toby to get a deeper insight into the lingering effects of the plane crash on Grace. He heard that Grace's heroism—protecting her sister—came at a heavy cost. Since the crash, Dornik noted, "Grace went from being a carefree little girl to acting as if she were a 40-year-old woman with the weight of the world on her shoulders." As Dornik saw it, she'd watched her uncle and mother burn to death and witnessed her sister terribly burned while in the middle of nowhere. All the while, she stoically suffered with her own excruciating burns and broken bones, so it was hardly surprising—Dornik would assert—that she suffered with traumatic memories.

In addition to Grace and Lily's staggering medical costs, both past and future, the economist would also attempt this impossible calculus of "pain and suffering."

It was obvious to any lawyer that the sum total of all these damages would easily exceed the maximum liability of the insurance policy. Dornik "estimated that the medical bills and survivor benefits of the case could run between $10 million and $16 million," according to an article in the *Star Tribune* published on the day of the summary judgment hearing.

With the stark reality of this figure, the stakes had changed for all parties. In such a scenario, an insurance company that had breached its contract to cover losses could potentially face a multimillion-dollar bad-faith claim. It could, according to legal precedents, be held financially liable for putting its own interest ahead of the interest of its insureds. It could argue back, slinging bits and pieces of case law to justify its reluctance to pay this new, higher demand. Who was really to blame for such a predicament?

Nothing happened. Time passed. Dornik looked at his calendar.

He called Toby. "I'm going to push for the earliest trial date that Judge Ericksen will give us. Okay?"

Toby agreed, though reluctantly.

For the first time, a trial seemed like a reality. A courtroom image coalesced in Dornik's imagination—an archetypal tale: Two little girls in summer dresses bravely trooping in, holding hands with their stoic father, a widower who would recount the story of the crash. Clouds. Woods. Fire. A jury forced to weep. Enter the big, bad wolf. It wouldn't look good.

For a while Dornik didn't take any further calls or engage in correspondence with the insurance company. It was a strategy of sorts, but he felt worn down by the process. But this silence must have sent a message because then, suddenly, from one phone call to the next, the impasse was over. The prospect of a mediation between all the parties was floated. In Dornik's experience, this was a positive sign. Although he was still cautious, Dornik picked up the phone and called Toby to break the news. Soon a date was set: May 23, 2006.

As the day approached, Toby found himself waking up in the early hours again, his mind running around and around the arguments. It was as though he were stuck in a loop. More than this, he loathed the notion of putting price tags on everything from his daughters' catastrophic injuries to the value of Kathryn's life. Yet his legal mind understood this was part of the process to leverage a fair settlement. As much as he needed the money, the concept of settlement was now tied in to his own cultivated sense of social justice. He would do much more with this thought later.

The mediation was scheduled to take place in the offices of Fredrikson and Byron on South Sixth Street, where Rick Snyder worked. At the beginning of the day the three parties gathered, sitting around the large conference room table. There was Lindberg and a representative from Old Republic's headquarters in Atlanta, as well as Rick Snyder and Tom Erickson (Charlie's brother) for the estate, and of course Dornik and his client, Toby. Retired judge the Honorable Robert G. Schiefelbein presided over the proceedings, setting the ground rules with a long introductory talk. He seemed motivated to find a solution, although the atmosphere remained tense in the room. Then the individual parties went off to separate rooms, with Dornik and Toby staying in the conference room.

From Toby's point of view, the whole endeavor was based on a risk-reward calculation. If the settlement figure he and Dornik wanted was too high for the insurance company, then they would walk away; but if Old Republic pitched too low, they risked losing this chance to settle. They'd presented their first figure to the parties and now there was nothing to do but wait for a response. It seemed a tortuous game of calling each other's bluff, a silent auction in a high-stakes game. Who would give ground first? Toby felt nervous and, to break the tension, he and Dornik talked about what was going on with the Minnesota Timberwolves, the local basketball team who'd just missed the NBA playoffs for the second straight season.

In preparation for the day, Dornik had cautioned Toby about what to expect during a typical mediation. On the face of it, a mediation was supposed to be a civilized dance in which both parties—reluctant to go to trial—would take steps toward resolution and a dollar amount acceptable to plaintiff and defense alike. However, Dornik explained, in reality sometimes that dance could mask a deeper war, less seen than felt, one that pitted power against emotion. Dornik knew that a mediation was usually more difficult for a plaintiff, the aggrieved party, already emotionally worn down by their feelings of loss, anger, and resentment. The fact that Toby was a defendant in this case would hardly mitigate such emotions. Of course, a mediation was yet another occasion for the plaintiff to be reminded of his predicament, and perhaps his relative impotence in the face of corporate power. In addition to this emotional toll, there was the psychological one of being that much closer to the goal, "the optimistic figure," only to be denied the closure of a settlement. Finally, there was the ongoing financial burden, of bearing half the costs of the mediation day, all the more grating when the other side had billions of dollars at its disposal.

Dornik knew from experience that a powerful corporation could exploit a vulnerable plaintiff with the specter of a settlement, only to make it disappear at the last minute. It was hardly a fair fight. A case in point: A few years prior to Toby's case, Dornik had represented one of a number of plaintiffs, who'd sustained significant injuries in a major plane crash in the Far East. Several people had died in that accident, and others had been badly hurt. Inevitably, the case ended up in mediation with various interested parties flying to Minnesota from all over the world, including representatives of a major European insurance company. Then to everyone's astonishment, even as the participants gathered under one roof, the insurance company made an aggressive declaration: "We're never going to give you a single penny." And that was that. It stunned Dornik that the company would spend tens of thousands of dollars merely to deliver this killer message. It was a psychological hammer blow to the plaintiffs, but even this case eventually ended in settlement. Despite this baleful memory, Dornik approached Toby's mediation day with a degree of equanimity. He certainly made sure Toby understood the potential pitfalls of bringing hope and emotion and power into the same room.

It was a slow grind. Then it was lunchtime. The afternoon brought more of the same. The mediator shuttled back and forth with offers and counteroffers. As much as Toby wanted to move toward a solution, he felt confounded by the process. While he understood these were standard negotiating tactics in play, for him the issue was high voltage. He didn't want to go to trial, but even now, the lawsuit was still alive. Toby felt his anger, which had long been bottled up, rise. It provided a bolt of sudden energy. They were clearly getting nowhere, and he let his frustrations be known. Toby thought of the babysitter and Grace and Lily back at home. He wanted to leave.

"I don't think we're going to get there today," said Dornik, sensing Toby's agitation.

"I agree," said Toby. "Not today."

They got up and started to leave. The mediator came back in and started to remonstrate with them. "Wait! Wait!"

"We're done for today," said Dornik firmly. "They can call us."

Dornik and Toby walked toward the exit. On the way, they encountered Rick Snyder, who was also taken aback by this decision, but he seemed to understand.

As they returned to Dornik's office, Toby felt rattled and frustrated by the wasted day. Dornik offered a slightly more reassuring take. "It's another step," he said. "If that mediator is worth his salt, he'll call us. They know we mean business."

In the following weeks, Dornik carried on conversations with Schiefelbein, who conveyed the messages to Old Republic. He had a feeling that he was making inroads. As far as the insurance company knew, Dornik was gunning for a trial, and Snyder was trying to position for a potential bad-faith claim against it. Old Republic probably didn't need reminding of its potential seven-figure exposure. By the early summer, Dornik realized that the company would soon make a business calculation, determine a number, and finally stop fighting the Pearson claim. More litigation would be a waste of money. It wasn't official yet, but there was reason to hope.

Old Highway 61 runs along the edge of Lake Superior for a twenty-mile stretch, between Two Harbors and Duluth. With its course along this distance, Grandma's Marathon offers sublime views of the lake for runners in need of inspiration. The road also has another claim to fame, as part of the original Highway 61, which stretched seventeen hundred miles from the Canadian border all the way to New Orleans, subsequently mythologized by Bob Dylan on his album *Highway 61 Revisited*. Typically the cool breezes off the lake would make the 26.2-mile run more bearable than usual, but June 17, 2006, was uncommonly hot and muggy. As runners approached the starting line at 7:30 A.M., most were already sweating.

This wasn't good news for Toby on his first marathon. Aside from his personal pride, running next to Katy, he had another compelling reason to finish the race. He planned—unbeknownst to her—to propose once they had crossed the finish line. Toby had told Katy's family about his intentions—her mother, sister, and brother (who was also running the marathon) gathered—as well as his own friends, who were excited by the prospect of seeing Toby and Katy happy. Many were there to cheer them on. Toby had asked his friend Jim Metry to carry the ring and hand it to him after the race. Of course, he'd also told Grace and Lily about the plan, too. He was running the race—had always intended to run the race—for them. The words on his T-shirt affirmed that promise; it read GRACE AND LILY.

They set a moderate to slow pace from the start, carried along on a flow of good feeling and excitement shared by the thousands of runners. They had originally planned on taking drinks at every other station along the route, but because of the heat, they went to every one. It was clear no one would be setting personal bests on this day. As the pace settled down, Toby pointed out familiar landmarks to Katy. They passed the Lakeview Castle, where Toby had talked with Father Graham to share his grief, and chuckled again at the priest's admonition to watch out for overzealous women. Farther on, they passed a little resort where Toby's grandparents had stayed every summer with their two black Labradors, and where the dogs would be put through their paces in field trials designed for hunting dogs. Toby's grandparents had given him and Kathryn a young black lab called Star who became a faithful running partner, padding alongside Toby back when he'd run with Lily in a jogging stroller.

Closer to Duluth—about mile eighteen of the marathon—they approached Toby and Kathryn's old home on London

Road. Out front, the woman who'd bought the house from Toby was waiting with a friend. He and Katy stopped briefly to greet them, before carrying on. Now things started to get a lot tougher. Katy and Toby saw many runners falling by the wayside, suffering from heatstroke. By the time they hit Lemon Drop Hill at mile twenty-two, a difficult uphill stretch along the mostly flat course, Katy was starting to feel the pain. "I just want this to be over," she said. Because of the layout of the course, the finish line was tantalizingly in view, but several more miles intervened. Toby urged Katy on, an unusual feeling since Katy was the more experienced runner. Runners around them were in all sorts of discomfort, cramping up, hobbling, and collapsing by the roadside from the heat. They persisted through the interminably long last few miles, determined to make a good show at the end as they approached the finish line. Here, on the final stretch of Canal Park, the crowds congregated, dense and raucous, cheering everyone on. It was enough to carry Toby and Katy past the finish line, with a time of four hours and forty minutes. It was a long way from the four hours they had anticipated but, given the extreme conditions, it was still a victory.

The emotions of finishing a difficult marathon surfaced through Katy as they crossed the finish line. Her mother, who was standing nearby, mistook this emotional reaction for something else. She wondered if Toby had already proposed. This wasn't true. Fortunately, Katy's mother didn't reveal anything, asking cautiously, "Why are you crying?" Katy responded, "Because I feel so awful!" After replenishing her energy levels with bananas and water, Katy felt better, though she was still none the wiser about the impending proposal. Now her family had to maneuver her back to Toby, who'd slipped away, on the pretext he was looking for Grace and Lily, to collect the ring from his friend. By now the clouds had rolled in and the atmosphere was heavy with moisture. The rain was ready to unleash, so there was some urgency.

Toby appeared, with an enigmatic smile. Katy made her way over to him, suspecting something. Then he proposed.

"Will you marry me?" he said, opening the case to show the ring. "I'd get down on one knee, but if I do, I'll never get up again."

The answer was yes. Katy also realized now why Toby had insisted on a slow pace during the marathon. It made sense. It would hardly have made for a good story if Toby had collapsed from heatstroke. With that, Katy's family came around the corner with big smiles on their faces, letting her know they'd been in on the secret all along. Just then the sky opened, and a torrential rain poured down. Everyone started running down the street to a local Dairy Queen, where Grace and Lily awaited with Jim and Teri Metry. The group came in, flushed from the run and its romantic coda, and Toby made the announcement that he and Katy were engaged. Katy held out her hand to show the ring. Cheers came from the gathered group, but Grace was instantly mad. She had wanted to be there, and Lily had, too. When Carolyn arrived, Grace took it upon herself to tell her auntie that her dad and Katy were getting married. Carolyn was surprised, and yet as difficult as it was to imagine Toby with someone new, someone who wasn't Kathryn, she felt a sense of relief at his new prospect of happiness. It was a restoration of balance to his life. Besides, the girls seemed to really like Katy.

A little while before the race, Toby had talked to the girls about his plan to marry Katy. When he told them, they first expressed excitement, but then they wondered—what should they call Katy? Toby asked what they wanted to call her, and they both thought "Mom." Sensing some uneasiness, Toby asked if they felt weird about this because "Mommy Kathryn" was their mom; they said yes, it was weird. Toby explained gently that there'd always be a special place for Mommy Kathryn; it was just that now they'd have another mom, which would also be special. Lily thought about it and decided it would be a good deal to have two moms, adding, "And besides, you won't have to be both a mommy and daddy anymore." Grace smiled at her little sister's wisdom.

That summer, Grace wrote Katy a letter that expressed her feelings:

> *Dear Katy,*
>
> *You are similar to me. You like the outdoors. You are really active. You respect other people. You are really wise. You're fun to go on trips with. You make me feel good when you laugh. You are silly and cheer me up easily. I like your smile. You understand when I miss my mom. You are adventurous.*

According to Dr. Connie, the letter represented a significant psychological step for Grace and one that she wanted to put into writing. It indicated that she was approaching her father and Katy's future without guilt. Now they knew for sure there would be a wedding soon. That was a big deal. Grace also knew that her dad was involved in a "big fight" with some people.

"You can't get married until this case is settled," Dornik had told Toby. Toby had laughed about the joke at the time, but there was an element of truth to Dornik's warning. The case, and the prospect of the settlement, had built up in his mind as an obstacle to his moving forward—not only because the settlement money was crucial to the security of the family, but also because he didn't want Katy entangled in the case. So when Toby finally got the call from Dornik, in late July, saying the insurance company had made a fair offer, he accepted with a huge sense of relief. He felt especially happy that Grace and Lily would not have to take the stand in court.

Letters of agreement between the parties were drafted. In settling the case, Old Republic made no admission of liability. Although the actual amount agreed upon would be sealed by court order, the matter was resolved to the satisfaction of all parties. In many ways Toby's resilience had been vindicated. The long road that had started with few believing they stood a chance ended with an agreement.

Suddenly, before the checks were even signed, Toby's health insurance company, Wellmark Blue Cross and Blue Shield, sent a letter threatening a suit, insisting *it* had the first claim on any recovered proceeds for Lily's medical care. In the insurance world, such a claim is known as subrogation. Toby didn't know the fine details of this arcane piece of insurance law, but once again he was forced into a defensive posture. He faced an aggressive insurance company determined to claw back a large portion of what he'd struggled to win. Toby had believed his family insurance plan would protect him from further costs. After all, he'd had a contract with the company and paid his premiums for years so that the family would be covered. This was the deal, wasn't it? Now the insurer wanted its money back.

Originally, under common law, subrogation was permitted for property claims but not for personal injury claims. Then, in the 1960s, under pressure from car insurers who wanted to limit medical payouts on their policies, a few states started to permit it. Subrogation moved into the personal injury realm. Health insurance companies, too, feeling squeezed by rising health-care costs, realized there was considerable bounty to be found by targeting accident settlements. They started to become more aggressive about being reimbursed from personal-injury suits, sniffing around accident-related diagnosis codes to find possible tort claims. Then they'd pounce with a subrogation demand. Insurance companies defended this practice by insisting that in a personal-injury suit, victims seek compensation beyond the costs of health care, for pain and suffering and lost income. Surely they had a right to the money they'd spent. The concept is grounded in a civil policy that an injured person should not be allowed "double recovery."

In reality, accident settlements are often ambiguous. Plaintiffs don't always receive the imagined large pots of settlement money, so that once the insurer seizes its share, there's little left over for the victim. Further, in cases where injuries and medical costs are catastrophic and ongoing (such as Lily's third-degree burns), such a money grab can feel like pillage to the families of victims struggling to plan ahead.

In fact, the month before Toby faced this threat of subrogation, a vivid illustration of this contentious practice made the headlines. It involved the case of a fifty-two-year-old woman from Missouri, Deborah Shank, permanently brain-damaged and confined to a wheelchair after a truck slammed into her minivan. She'd received a $700,000 accident settlement from the trucking company. Legal fees and other expenses left a balance of $417,000 to be put into a special trust for the round-the-clock care she now required. However, as time passed, the health plan managed by her former employer, Walmart Stores Inc., sued the Shanks for the $470,000 it said it had spent on her health care. The case shocked her beleaguered husband and the nation. Many people were not aware of the boilerplate language hidden in the small print of their health insurance plans, allowing some insurers to do this. Neither was Deborah Shank. Nevertheless, in August 2006, a U.S. district judge sided with Walmart, ruling that Shank must abide by the terms of her health insurance contract. The decision devastated the family. (Bombarded with bad publicity, Walmart agreed to reverse its demand two years later.)

Toby's initial inclination was to say no. "Tell them zero," he told Dornik.

Under the contractual terms of Toby's insurance, it appeared that he would have to pay off Wellmark from Grace and Lily's damages. Because the health plan was issued in Iowa (Toby's employer, National Catholic Rural Life Conference, based its head office in Des Moines), the state law gave it the right to potential subrogation money from the Pearson accident settlement. It insisted it should be the first payee. Grace and Lily's medical bills had already far exceeded half a million dollars, and Wellmark staked its subrogation claim for a substantial portion of this money. At first Dornik thought he'd have to negotiate yet another settlement, but he quickly discovered that Wellmark's claim was actually in conflict with Minnesota state law. Certain insurance-related clauses protected Minnesota residents from these grim subrogation terms. It could apply, according to the statute, only after a covered person received a "full recovery from another source."

Since full recovery hadn't happened—with the Pearson claim against the estate still outstanding—Dornik asked Wellmark to "walk away" from its demands. He asked nicely, but then added, "In order to recover its subrogation interest, Wellmark Blue Cross and Blue Shield will be forced to sue Thomas, Grace and Elizabeth Pearson in Minnesota as it will not be able to get jurisdiction over the Pearsons in Iowa." Wellmark pushed back, but Dornik insisted the company could not enforce this provision on his client. It would be illegal, he warned, and surely something that would interest the Minnesota state insurance commissioner.

Wellmark backed off and voluntarily agreed to waive its subrogation interest, though it hardly relished the idea of suing the Pearsons. Dornik informed the company that he'd be presenting his petition to the court on October 16, 2006, finalizing the allocation of the Old Republic settlement. It provided a last opportunity for Wellmark to challenge. On the day of the hearing, no one from the health insurer showed up. The judge was satisfied. Finally, the settlement money could be distributed to Grace and Lily, to be put into annuities for their future.

The "big fight" was over. It wouldn't be long before Toby started another one.

13

THE WRONG DAVID

Grace and Lily knew they were going to be flower girls at their dad's wedding. The girls felt excited about the day but also worried about the details, about their dresses, their hair, about where they would be sitting. They knew a lot about weddings, especially with all the bride and groom play they'd done over the years, which had been a natural part of their therapy with Dr. Connie. In the lead-up to the big day, Grace and Lily told Dr. Connie that they did not want their dad and Katy to go alone on a honeymoon before "they do the family honeymoon." However, Grace finally conceded: "Well, I will tell them that I guess I expect them to go, but I won't tell them that I want them to." Nobody was more aware of the girls' underlying need to feel included than Toby. He explained to them, Daddy and Katy are getting married, but this is also the start of our new family.

The wedding took place on a warm, late autumn day—November 4, 2006—in the chapel on the campus of the University of St. Thomas. With a chamber ensemble playing an arrangement of the bluegrass melody "The Lover's Waltz," Grace and Lily slowly escorted their dad up the aisle of the church, one on either side. The girls wore burgundy dresses, which matched the gowns worn by Katy's sister, Molly, and Toby's sister, Beth.

They each clutched a floral bouquet. For many of Katy's friends, this was the first opportunity to see Grace and Lily, and it was a touching sight, this man and his daughters who had suffered, fallen through clouds, but who now seemed radiant.

Members of the wedding party from both sides of the family gathered at the foot of the altar. Each placed a flower stem into a crystal vase, a symbol of the union of the two families. Carolyn and her parents had been invited, too, made to feel welcome on a day that would inevitably evoke memories of Kathryn. Toby's dad had ushered them up to front pews, to sit near the girls.

When the bride entered, the guests rose to their feet. Katy beamed as she walked down the aisle in a white bridal gown, escorted by her mother, and soon joined Toby at the altar. Toby's longtime friend, the gregarious and hearty Monsignor James Habiger, led the wedding mass.

Habiger had long been a champion for social justice as the executive director of the Minnesota Catholic Conference, and represented the faith on political, legal, and social matters in the Minnesota House and Senate, where he was familiar as an ebullient lobbyist in priestly black. For Toby, this man who'd once declared, "We're not interested in legislating morality, but we're interested in the morality of legislation," was an inspiration. Moreover, Habiger had helped Toby land his first job as a lobbyist, and had baptized both Grace and Lily. Having comforted Toby in his grief after the plane crash, Habiger now delighted in seeing Toby looking happy once again. As Toby and Katy prepared to make their wedding vows, hands reaching out to each other, Habiger's voice cracked with emotion as he hailed them as "Dear friends."

After the vows were exchanged, Habiger leaned into Toby and Katy with his sincere congratulations. Then he asked, "Now do you want to call the little ones up?" With that, Toby beckoned to Grace and Lily, who were sitting in a front pew with their grandparents. They came up to the altar to stand with Katy. She knelt down between the girls and said the vows she'd written for them.

"Grace and Lily, I promise to take care of you, to guide you, to love you forever, and to be your mom," Katy said.

The entire congregation seemed to hold its breath.

Toby handed Katy two rings, which she then placed on Grace's finger, and on Lily's. Grace and Lily shyly kissed their dad and Katy, obviously feeling a little bashful in the moment. The girls then placed a flower stem in the vase with the others, and together as a new family, they proceeded to the statue of the Virgin Mary, where they presented the bouquet as an offering to the spiritual symbol of motherhood.

After the wedding, the celebration moved to the historic Town and Country Club, a Saint Paul landmark, which boasted views over the Mississippi River. Following an elegant brunch, many friends and family toasted the happy couple. Spontaneously, Carolyn stood up to offer her heartfelt wishes. She introduced herself as Kathryn's sister and welcomed Katy to the family. On a wave of emotion, she praised Toby as a wonderful father, saying she was happy to know that Grace and Lily would thrive and be loved even more, now that they had a mom again. The toast moved everyone, especially the Wall family. The moment was a gentle but important acknowledgment of Kathryn's life and legacy. While no one wanted to take away from the celebration of Katy and Toby's wedding, Carolyn sensed that some in both families found the day tinged with sadness. It couldn't be helped. Katy felt very moved by the toast and later thanked Carolyn for her gracious and beautiful words of welcome.

After the reception, Katy and Toby escaped on their own for a walk down to the Mississippi, with the bride still dressed in white. It was a moment of quiet reflection after an emotional day, watching the mighty river gather strength as it meandered its way south. It was at that moment, Toby told Katy, he realized he was "no longer in emergency mode." When she looked into his eyes, she could see it was true.

Just before Christmas, Toby attended a political fund-raiser in the grand ballroom at the Radisson Hotel in Saint Paul. It was an important annual event, scheduled in advance of the next legislative session, which allowed lobbyists to mingle with the newly elected members of the House of Representatives in Minnesota. On his way into the hotel, he bumped into an old school friend, Margaret Anderson Kelliher, heading to the same event. She told Toby she'd just been elected by her caucus to be Speaker of the House, starting in January 2007. The Democrats had won control of the House in the 2006 election. Toby expressed his delight and gave her a hug.

She asked about Grace and Lily. She told Toby a story about one of her own children, who'd been playing at a park in Minneapolis with a little girl wearing a face mask. It had been a while ago, but Kelliher now realized that the unknown girl must have been Lily. Toby nodded. She must have been out with her aunt Carolyn, who often took the girls to the playground. As they walked in, Kelliher said to Toby, if there was anything she could do, especially in her new capacity, to let her know. That's when the idea struck—his moment of awakening.

He would change the law. What happened to his family would not happen to anyone else, and he was uniquely positioned to do something about it. He could speak with the weight of experience.

As he schmoozed the politicians in the ballroom, Toby saw Michael Paymar, the representative from his district. They'd encountered each other working together at the Capitol build-ing. Toby presented his idea: What would you think about chang-ing the law for airplane liability insurance? Paymar had heard about the man who'd lost his wife in a plane crash and whose daughters survived against all the odds. He hadn't realized it was Toby's family. He was intrigued by the idea.

"Come visit me," he told Toby, who recognized a standard line when he heard it. Still, he thought he detected something in that response that seemed sincere, so he vowed to follow up on Paymar's invitation.

Because he'd been dragged into the world of aviation liability insurance, Toby found he already possessed a working knowl-edge of insurance statutes in the state. He got in touch with Dornik to discuss the finer points of what was missing. Together, they decided that the language written in the Department of Commerce's manual, "Aviation Insurance Private and Commer-cial," should be put into statute: "Any voidance for fraud provision must make an exception so as not to apply to liability coverage." This would bring the law in line with the policy for auto insur-ance, thus protecting innocent third parties from being left high and dry after an accident. How controversial could that possibly be?

Toby drafted some language he wanted to become law, which looked entirely reasonable. He also discovered that the manda-tory minimums on damages hadn't been updated since 1976; in fact they seemed positively anemic at $25,000 for "passenger bodily injury or death." Toby thought, Why not add a zero? Bringing the minimum up to $250,000—a number that would certainly start the conversation. The next step involved taking the draft language to the grandly named Office of the Revisor of Statutes, on the sixth floor of the State Office Building. The office comprises attorneys, editors, and other specialists whose job is to help put new ideas into legal language. Here Toby met up with Tom Pender, responsible for Department of Commerce legal issues, as insurance fell under his jurisdiction. It gradually took shape. After a few more revisions, the first pass of what would become H.F. 772 began as follows: "A bill for an act relating to insurance; increasing the required minimum liability limits on aircraft insurance; providing that aircraft liability insurance is not voidable retroactively after a claim; amending Minnesota Statutes 2006, section 360.59, subdivision 10."

Significantly, it included the following language, which would have saved the Pearsons a lot of heartache had it existed in 2003: "No statement made by the insured or on the insured's behalf and no violation of the policy defeats or voids the policy."

Toby understood—as a lobbyist, as a defendant once bereaved, and as a father—that God was in the details of this fairly dry, statutory language.

Now he needed a legislator to sponsor the bill in order to introduce it into the legislative session. He would need at least one for the House and another for the Senate. Toby followed up on Michael Paymar's invitation and made an appointment to see the fifty-three-year-old lawmaker, who'd proved himself a passionate advocate on public safety issues. As Paymar listened, Toby explained his plan to change the law for the good of others. As heartrending as Toby's story was—and it certainly would help move things along—Paymar had to decide whether the law stood any chance of passing. Hundreds of potential bills came his way every year, but being worthy didn't necessarily make them viable.

"Give me three downsides to what you're proposing," said Paymar. He needed to know from the beginning what he was up against. While he would do his best to carry a bill to the floor, Paymar was the first to admit he wasn't an expert on aviation insurance law.

"This is going to be fought vigorously by the insurance companies, and probably the pilots' association," said Toby, referring to the Aircraft Owners and Pilots Association (AOPA), a politically powerful lobby group for general aviation pilots.

Paymar knew that any good lobbyist would tell the truth, and here it was from the lips of someone who'd been raked over the coals by the insurance industry. Taking on the insurance lobby, Toby and the lawmaker knew, was no easy task. It was organized and potentially aggressive. However, Paymar read conviction in Toby's eyes and voice. He shared his belief that this should be the law of the state, asserting that people would understand that potential injustice could strike anyone if things remained unchanged. He agreed to sign on.

Toby gathered other names, too, and significantly, his friend Margaret Anderson Kelliher. Once the Speaker signed on, Toby knew this would send a strong message that the Democratic leadership was behind it. He also sought Republican signatures and secured Representative Jim Abeler and others. The ball was definitely rolling.

On the Senate side, Toby approached a lawmaker from Duluth, Senator Yvonne Prettner Solon. She had a vivid memory of the two girls who'd survived alone in the woods after the plane crash. Toby made his case to the senator, who expressed dismay that the public policy protecting third parties wasn't in statute. She found it upsetting that insurance companies weren't doing their due diligence to decide whether a person should be insured but nonetheless were happy to collect fees all along. She thought Toby's argument was "plain common sense" and that his proposal would help clarify the law consistent with people's values. Prettner Solon agreed to sign on as the chief author on the Senate side, initially thinking the bill would not prove controversial. She would quickly be surprised by the vehemence of the opposition.

Toby collected more signatures, and the bill was introduced on February 8, 2007.

Opponents rapidly appeared, determined to kill the bill. As many knew, the insurance industry was allergic to change. Any whiff of a threat, especially if it hurt profits, meant lobbyists were dispatched to eliminate the problem. But the figure of Toby complicated the problem, not only because he was a colleague, a fellow lobbyist, but also because everyone knew his story, the arc of tragedy and recovery he'd experienced. He was a man who'd suffered, who now offered a rational solution to a gap in the law. Opposing him would be a delicate matter. Certainly no one wanted to be seen as heartless, but the lobbyists were paid to do the bidding of their clients. So Toby had to be treated tenderly, nipped in the bud early before anything flowered into law.

On the Senate side, opponents had already managed to "bottle up the bill," which meant it wouldn't get introduced into any of the all-important committees. This meant it was going nowhere.

Meanwhile, Toby tried to circumvent this opposition. On the House side, he approached Joe Atkins, the chair of the Commerce Committee, which had jurisdiction over insurance issues in Minnesota. In fact, members in the legislative body looked to the committee for guidance on the complex issue of insurance. There was a saying in the Minnesota State Capitol: "If it passes in the Commerce Committee, it passes on the House floor." For this reason, lobbyists wanted to prevent Atkins from giving the bill a reading in committee. A phalanx of insurance industry people had already streamed into his office before Toby had even approached him. Their request: put this bill in a drawer and let it die.

Atkins had a wry sense of humor about all of this. It was par for the course. Of course he was a regular target for lobbyists. He was even tracked at lunchtime by a certain bank lobbyist who knew his regular route to the cafeteria. He'd intercept Atkins apparently out of nowhere and set about trying to schedule a meeting. Atkins might roll his eyes while eating his sandwich, but it was a strategy that worked for this particular bank lobbyist. The insurance lobbyists certainly had no qualms about interrupting his lunch.

Atkins now listened to Toby make his case. He thought Toby's story was not only compelling, but also that it demanded a change in the law. Atkins considered the proposal of major importance because, as he put it, "any time you're talking about life and death it's major. And when aviation insurance is concerned, it's always major because there's no such thing as a minor plane crash." Still, he wondered if this apparently straightforward solution might be fraught with unintended consequences. There was not only the insurance lobby to contend with, but also the more loosely affiliated pilots' lobby, which would most likely prove a challenge. Atkins urged the various parties to meet informally to discuss the plan.

The insurance lobby did not respond. Atkins suspected it was trying to run the clock out on the bill. If it didn't get a hearing and a positive committee vote by the end of the legislative session, it was as good as dead. Atkins observed that in a David-and-Goliath scenario like this one, Goliath never thought it had to deal with David.

At Toby's request, he therefore did something unusual. He decided to schedule the bill for a hearing, although nothing had been worked out. Atkins knew it would be alarming to many, but he went ahead and did it. Toby discussed this strategy with Paymar, and they agreed it was a gamble but the only way to have the lobbyists take him seriously. As far as the insurance lobby was concerned, it was the "shot heard around the world." Within fifteen minutes of posting the news, Atkins was being chased down the hall by lobbyists.

"What are your intentions?" was the refrain.

"To pass the bill," replied Atkins, brushing them off. He told them they had to work things out with Toby. All things being equal, he said, Toby had a better idea than they had reasons for opposition.

That broke the dam. The lobbyists started to pay attention.

On the day of the hearing, the members of the Commerce Committee gathered in the Basement Hearing Room of the State Office Building. A quorum was present, along with representatives from the insurance industry, as well as Toby and Dornik. Atkins opened the meeting with a recap of the Pearsons' ordeal, and then gave the floor to Toby.

Toby started by addressing the mandatory minimums. He had since agreed to lower the limit from his original $250,000 suggestion to $100,000. The insurance companies had contested the original figure, as expected, and this was a compromise that was still an improvement on the 1976 limits. Then Toby addressed the reason for the second part of the bill.

"In trying to recover I experienced the highs and lows of three years of litigation, hearings, mediation before finally arriving at a settlement. In that time I had to relocate my family, change jobs, pay all the medical bills, change the schools that Grace and Lily attended and leave the very supportive community of family and friends in the city of Duluth. Generally I had to change every aspect of my life and the lives of my children."

Then he got to the point of the clause.

"By assuming that there is no voidance for fraud, as it pertains to liability insurance and putting the Commerce Department procedures into statute, no other family will have to experience what I experienced over three years of negotiation and litigation. It's for this reason that I urge you to support this bill."

Dornik backed up Toby's statements with a reminder that the provision mirrored the same language that applied to automobile insurance.

The representative from the insurance industry, Bev Turner, a senior executive from Travelers Insurance, took the floor. She pointed out that although her company did not sell aviation insurance in Minnesota, it was a carrier poised to enter into this potential market. Still, she insisted, the bill now presented a barrier. "It may preclude us from coming into the Minnesota market because it takes away our defenses."

How would it do this? She provided a list of scenarios whereby the insurance company would be exposed. What if the pilot let his ten-year-old girl pilot the plane, and it crashed? What if the plane was used to haul illegal drugs? What if the aircraft certificate was pulled from the plane and the pilot flew and crashed it anyway? Turner used these examples to demonstrate the unintended consequences of the bill, which she said would take away the company's "coverage defense."

Turner addressed the other clause on the bill: "No statement made by the insured or on the insured's behalf and no fraud or violation of the policy defeats or voids the policy." Turner countered this with the argument that it was impossible for an insurance company to do due diligence on a pilot. Although the FAA licensed and regulated pilots, as well as maintaining an accident database, Turner insisted there was no way to cross-reference a pilot with an accident. That left an insurance company with only one option to assess risk: to rely on the pilot's application when certifying their history, where they're going to use the plane, their medical history, and their accident history. In short, if the bill passed with such a clause, it would take away the insurance company's ability to accurately underwrite the policy. The strong implication was that aviation insurers would flee the state in droves, a threat that members took seriously.

"I want to say we have worked with Mr. Pearson, the proponent of the bill and can't even understand the loss and tragedy that his family underwent, but we want to make sure on the other side that the pilots have affordable insurance and that they have access to an insurance market, so this product can still be made available. I know Mr. Pearson had no interest in shutting that down in the state and neither do we, so we have a common interest in trying to figure where we can go from here."

Members of the committee questioned Turner on her argument, including Representative Dean Simpson, a Republican, who worried that changing policy might deter Minnesota pilots from registering in the state.

Turner agreed. "It's breaking new ground here in the state."

Toby countered that he had no intention of changing the relationship between the insurance company and the insured person. He said they could still argue over whether there should be coverage; they could still sue each other over whether somebody was paying out for something they shouldn't have been. "But as for an innocent third party who has no way of knowing, no way of finding out, and has absolutely no way of controlling whether or not the plane hits them, crash lands on their house, anything in that nature, I mean we can come up with all the absurd categories that we want—and I've lived one of them—we're simply looking at addressing the relationship with the injured third party who is completely innocent. In my case it was my three- and four-year-old girls, my daughters."

"The question before you is, should the three- and four-year-old girls have to fight against the insurance company to get money? Or should that be a relationship between the insured and the insurance company? Who should be fighting that fight?"

Atkins moved that the bill be passed out of the committee. It received strong support from the members, though Toby heard a couple of voices saying "Nay." The insurance lobbyists were disconcerted by the rapid progress of the bill, which many had believed was going nowhere, or at the very least would never get the votes in the committee. Still, Toby's strategy had paid off so far. Together with his powerful and influential chief author, Paymar, they'd worked aggressively behind the scenes to gather support for the bill, skirting the propaganda of the insurance lobby. The hearing helped focus the issue, and the pilots' lobby started to consider the proposal more seriously, given the fact that it would protect their own families. Maybe this was good for them?

Then, Yvonne Prettner Solon got Senate Chair Linda Scheid to schedule a hearing on the Senate side in the Commerce Committee. As the bill gained momentum, the insurance lobbyists realized they needed to engage Toby directly to see if he was persuadable. Most began to understand that if they didn't deal with Toby the bill would pass with exactly the language Toby originally drafted. Fortunately for the lobbyists, they had an ally in Christine Zimmer, a fellow insurance lobbyist who also happened to be a friend of Toby's from college. The two positions weren't mutually exclusive, for which the insurance lobby was very grateful. Zimmer became the unofficial go-between, shuttling between the insurance crowd and Toby. Nobody, it seemed, wanted to be in a position to go up against Toby, stare into his eyes, and declare his bill no good, despite the business imperatives under threat.

For her part, Zimmer felt moved by Toby's story. Her daughter Josie, who regularly coached a gymnastics class for young girls, had recently told her mom a story about one particular gymnast. One day during class, as Josie stood there talking to a friend, she felt a little hand slip into hers. Without looking down, she knew it belonged to Lily Pearson because of the tactile sensation of the scarred skin. For Zimmer, this small detail reminded her that this bill wasn't academic for Toby, but flesh and blood.

Toby would argue back and forth via his friend about the issue, until the time came for all the lobbyists to meet. Zimmer set up a meeting in the cafeteria at the Department of Transportation, close to the Capitol building. Arrayed around him at the table, Toby counted about fifteen lobbyists, all representing different clients, some of whom were fervently against the bill. The stumbling block for the lobbyists was still what Toby called "the deniability part." No one liked the idea that the insurance company should be on the hook for damages no matter what the pilot said or did. Toby returned to his argument, countering the comments coming in from every side, but it was clear the insurance lobby demanded a compromise.

Meanwhile, on the Senate side, Prettner Solon was having trouble convincing a couple of senators to support the bill. Toby went to appeal to them, but they insisted they wouldn't vote for a controversial bill, with one pressing Toby to "just work something out." The bill could have died there, but Paymar and Prettner Solon suggested they press on by passing the first part of the bill—on the minimums—while holding off on the second part of the bill. As a compromise, the bill would require a so-called meet-and-confer group consisting of pilots, insurance representatives, and Toby to discuss relevant issues and submit a written report to the House and Senate by mid-November. Once the shortened bill passed, the meet-and-confer group would meet four times between June and November. The bill's chances of passing depended on whether a compromise could be forged.

On the grounds of the Minnesota State Capitol, there stands a bronze sculpture depicting two images of the aviator Charles Lindbergh—as a small boy, arms outstretched, pretending to fly, and as the intrepid young man who made the first nonstop solo flight across the Atlantic. Although he was born in Detroit, Lindbergh grew up in Little Falls, Minnesota, by all accounts a childhood experience that inspired his imagination and determination to fly. Several of Lindbergh's inspirational quotations surround the statues. "The accumulation of knowledge, the discoveries of science, the products of technology, our ideas, our art, our social structures, all the achievements of mankind have value only to the extent that they preserve and improve the quality of life," reads one.

As members of the insurance and aviation community gathered at the State Capitol to discuss Toby Pearson's aviation liability bill, perhaps they lingered in front of the sculpture and read the inspiring words, making a connection to their current endeavors. Participants, some of whom had flown in from out of state, could hardly fail to be impressed as they approached the mighty State Capitol, a Beaux-Arts-style building with a distinctive dome modeled after the Basilica of Saint Peter's in Rome. This landmark, made of white Georgia marble, shone brightly in the summer sun.

The meetings took place in the cool, dark interior of Capitol Room 125. By now, everyone took Toby's bill seriously, perturbed that anyone would have the audacity to change the status quo. The roster of attendees made it obvious that even major insurance companies wanted to engage with this formal process. It included representatives from American International Group,

Wings Insurance, and Travelers Insurance, as well as national aviation insurance trade groups that had a vested interest in liability insurance. There were also representatives from the pilots' groups, including AOPA, and lobby groups that helped promote the business interests of pilots. Finally, a Republican member of the House, Mike Beard, led the meetings.

Beard's presence was significant. A private pilot, he'd initially resisted Toby's bill. In fact, when it was first introduced, he thought to himself, Holy cow! Who is this Toby Pearson, and why does he want to kill the aviation industry? Then Toby met him, told his story, and explained his perspective: It was surely in the interests of pilots to demand protection from their insurance company without fear that it could be easily voided after an accident. Erickson, whatever his faults, was left high and dry. Beard found Toby to be passionate, realistic, and very fair. Thus won over, Beard went back to the pilots' groups and reassured them that Toby Pearson was not waging a war on general aviation but instead sought to strengthen liability protections for third-parties *and* pilots.

The fact that a Republican (the party was then in the minority) with a pilot's license chaired the meetings sent a strong message to skeptics: This was to be a bipartisan effort. With Beard at the helm, the powerful pilots' lobby AOPA—"the big kahuna," joked Beard—felt comfortable being a part of the process. Confrontation was kept to a minimum, although Toby thought certain blowhards from out of state initially wanted to lord it over this upstart gathering. However, even they got into the spirit of the discussions, which focused on the extent to which coverage for injured third parties could be mandated. Would it raise premiums? How would third-party passengers know if a plane had adequate coverage? Should a pilot be required to display a certificate of insurance?

The group also discussed the possibility of establishing a state or federal pilot registry, allowing insurers to cross-reference the NTSB's aviation accident data with the FAA's database of pilots. It seemed logical for aviation underwriters to be able to track pilots when reviewing aviation insurance applications—basic due diligence. Furthermore, this would enable pilots with good flying records to obtain more favorable premiums, which would be offset by the higher premiums of pilots with "accident-ridden records." While many in the group thought this a generally good idea, some worried about the legality of allowing private companies to track pilots nationally. Still, many believed this idea deserved further discussion at a federal level.

In terms of the specific language of the bill, things began to evolve. Insurers wanted to limit its scope by requiring a direct-cause relationship between the breach of a policy and an accident; only then could an insurance company step in and deny coverage. The researchers found that this law applied only in some states, known in insurance parlance as causal states, such as Montana or Texas, where it was allegedly harder for an insurance company to deny coverage. Tom Pender drafted some proposed statutory language that would modify Toby's draft:

Compliance exclusions permitted; exception. Provides that an insured's action or failure to act is not a basis for refusing to pay a claim, unless the action or failure to act had a "direct causal connection" to the event that led to the claim. (For instance, the pilot's failure to keep a certification current or report a health problem to the insurance company cannot be used to deny a claim unless it had a direct causal connection to the accident. The claim could be made, for instance, by a passenger or a person whose home is damaged by the plane, etc.)

The pilots—who generally had a love-hate relationship with their insurers—liked this new language. Typically after an accident, an insurance investigator might go through the plane, sniffing out violations. If a pilot accidently hit a deer on the runway—as one of Beard's colleagues had done with considerable damage to the aircraft, with the unlucky deer being sliced into four pieces—surely he shouldn't be denied coverage if an insurer then discovered an out-of-date medical certificate. That was an FAA violation, but what did one have to do with the other? The new language, the pilots began to realize, would give them more protection.

Toby disliked the compromise and thought the "direct cause" solution weakened his favored language. With respect to coverage of liability for bodily injury, death, or property damage suffered by a third party, Toby had always insisted on liability insurance being guaranteed—neither canceled nor annulled after the fact of an accident, for whatever reason. The compromise language seemed less robust and handed an insurance company another opportunity to hesitate before paying out. Toby sent the language to Dornik, who agreed it would not prevent an insurer from denying coverage, but it could limit a company's ability to act in bad faith. In Toby's case, this language would probably have spared him the torment of the big fight. Still, Toby was realistic enough to understand that his early draft of the bill was unlikely to remain intact. After all, Tim Pawlenty, the Republican governor of Minnesota, would have to sign any bill that passed. Since Pawlenty was already hinting at running for president, he was hardly likely to aggravate the insurance lobby.

By the time the Aviation Insurance Meet and Confer Group wrapped up its last meeting on November 15, 2007, there was enough support to send a favorable report back to the Commerce Committees in both the House and the Senate, with some reservations: Travelers Insurance "remained neutral," while AIG still objected to the language. Perhaps the pilots were the happiest. Beard thought the language of the final bill "helped solidify confidence between pilots and their insurance company."

From Toby's perspective, it was an imperfect result, but it was a step forward. After the initial disappointment of not getting what he wanted, Toby ended up with a bill that reclaimed some of the vast advantage from the insurance industry for the unknown innocent hurt in a future plane crash. That had been his focus all along.

With the agreed compromise, the big showdown was over. Now that the controversial elements had been neutralized to the satisfaction of the holdout senators, the bill went through the Senate Commerce Committee without any trouble. One senior member shook Toby's hand and congratulated him on the compromise language. It was a lesson in democracy, and what many called the sausage-making process of lawmaking. It was surprising, infuriating, and in the end an education, even for a lobbyist like Toby, who'd walked the hallowed halls of the Capitol for years.

On the day of the vote on the House floor, Toby brought Grace and Lily into the Capitol building, to the spectator gallery to watch their dad's bill being voted on. They were excited to see where their dad worked and wide-eyed at the huge crystal chandelier in the rotunda, as well as the many statues and the flags inside the grand old building. Sitting in the front row of the gallery, they could peer down onto the floor. What were all those people doing? Then Toby pointed out his representative, Michael Paymar, who stood to present the bill that he'd put his name on a year and a half earlier: "A bill for an act relating to insurance; regulating denials under aviation liability coverage." Any legislator could ask him a question at this stage, but he had to field very few. Then, one by one, the representatives voted "Yay." After the bill passed, Paymar looked up to the gallery at Toby, Grace, and Lily and smiled. In the formal context of the House, it felt like a big victory, and a reminder that government can intervene to help people fight against injustice.

Of course, presiding over the House members was Toby's friend, Margaret Anderson Kelliher, who gaveled the proceedings in and out. After the passage of the bill, but while the House was still doing its business, the Speaker took the unusual step of inviting Grace and Lily down to the floor. They padded down the staircase, where they met Kelliher. Toby, as a lobbyist, was not permitted to enter the chamber, but now he watched Grace and Lily walk over the moss green carpet to the Speaker's chair, where Kelliher handed them the gavel. Lily held it up, standing next to her sister, as she and Grace smiled for a snapshot, an image that would always serve as a reminder of the resilience of the family, and in particular their dad. In the retiring room, an emotional Michael Paymar gave the girls a big hug, and more pictures were taken. It was a historic moment for the Pearson family, but Lily had eyes only for a large and delicious-looking cake on the table behind them. On her way out, she wondered out loud why she hadn't been allowed a slice.

Later that week, the law passed unanimously in the Minnesota Senate, much to the delight of the senator who'd sponsored it, Yvonne Prettner Solon. For her, it was a bill about fairness and living up to a promise, which even the most powerful should be obliged to keep. Soon after, on April 10, 2008, Governor Tim Pawlenty signed the bill into law; it would go into effect on January 1, 2009.

It was a remarkable achievement for Toby, who'd been on the brink of ruin. He'd wrestled a degree of order out of chaos, turning whatever dark emotions that had roiled him into the light of a legislative victory, justice. This was his answer to the oppressive nature of loss, grief, and anger, a way of fighting back.

Toby recalled an encounter he'd had with Joe Atkins outside the elevator bank in the State Office Building soon after he'd survived the skirmish with the relentless insurance lobby. He could laugh about it now. At the time, Atkins was both impressed and startled by Toby's determination to tackle an industry that could spiritually crush him.

"Boy, when you decide to take somebody on, you really take 'em on! Why pick a fight with this Goliath?" said Atkins.

"They picked the fight," said Toby, with almost a shrug. "They just picked the wrong David."

14

AN ANOMALY OF HISTORY

On May 24, 2005, a pilot and his wife flew the Mitsubishi MU-2 twin-engine turboprop they had recently purchased to Hillsboro, Oregon. The couple had invited some new friends, Art and Jean Pogrell, to accompany them on a short flight to have dinner in Salem, Oregon. The pilot, Michael McCartney, had owned a number of airplanes over the years and logged thousands of hours, although he had little recent flight experience. After exchanging greetings, the two couples boarded the high-performance plane. Since it was a warm, clear evening, the flight promised to be quite an adventure. The plane taxied to the runway and took off, but seconds after becoming airborne the plane rolled, nosed down, and crashed just off the end of the runway. Everyone on board was killed.

Enter the Pogrell family's lawyer, Ladd Sanger, who found that the pilot carried no liability insurance. In the case of compensation for Art and Jean Pogrell's four children, Sanger tried to proceed against the pilot's estate, but McCartney had put the bulk of his assets in a trust, which made it very difficult for Sanger to obtain a recovery for his orphaned clients. He could therefore cover only a small percentage of the judgment against McCartney.

For lawyers like Sanger, this story illustrates a stark truth—unknown to many—about general aviation: There is no federal law that obliges the owner or pilot of a private plane to carry any type of insurance to cover injuries to passengers or a third party on the ground. "There is so little insurance required in the general aviation context, it's frightening," said Sanger, a leading aviation attorney in Dallas, Texas. While aviation is regulated at a federal level, when it comes to insurance for private aircraft it's left up to the individual states. According to the FAA, there's a reason for this. "We don't require aircraft that are operating under Part 91 to have liability insurance because we have the statutory authority only to regulate airlines that are engaging in interstate or foreign air transportation. This authority does not extend to general aviation operations."

With no federal requirement, only a few states mandate that private pilots carry insurance—Minnesota, of course, is one—but it's a patchwork quilt. Sanger, who has labored for years to focus attention on this gap in regulation, pointed out that any private operator of an airplane can "haul people around over a crowded city, and doesn't have to have a stitch of insurance."

Federal aviation insurance for private planes may not loom large on the national agenda, but a lack of liability insurance can have disastrous consequences for innocent victims and families like the Pogrells. From a plaintiff lawyer's perspective, with no liability insurance guaranteed, recovery is a crapshoot.

"A person who is injured as a result of an airplane crash can only seek recovery from a person and/or entity who is liable, in negligence, strict liability, or warranty. If it is 100 percent pilot error, and that pilot is uninsured, the only thing that an injured party can do is seek to recover a judgment against the pilot's personal assets—most often a very difficult proposition," said Stuart Fraenkel of Kreindler and Kreindler. Fraenkel is another prominent aviation accident attorney and an experienced pilot who's seen his fair share of plaintiffs flounder against judgment-proof estates.

Even when a pilot does have liability insurance, the mandatory minimums are often low, typically limited to $100,000 per seat. This doesn't go very far for plaintiffs who have lost a major wage earner in the family, who find themselves plunged into difficult financial circumstances. In many states, those minimums haven't changed in decades and are hardly adequate.

"In contrast to most of the rest of the developed world, the United States has not taken the lack of liability insurance on the aviation context seriously." That's the central argument of a 2008 study conducted by Sanger. It points out that the European Union and Canada have mandatory aircraft insurance requirements for all aircraft operators. The coverage requirements for small general aviation aircraft in the EU are significant. A Cessna 172, operating noncommercially, flying with a pilot and three passengers as in the Pearson case, must carry approximately $5.2 million in insurance with $158,000 per seat minimum for the passengers. An EU member state may refuse to allow a plane to land if it fails to comply with the mandatory insurance requirement. The study finds that Canada has perhaps the world's "most comprehensive and equitable mandatory insurance system." Any air operator in Canada is required to have liability insurance for death or bodily injury in an amount not less than $300,000 multiplied by the number of passengers on board, with a sliding scale depending on the size of the aircraft.

Many general aviation pilots bristle at the thought of yet more regulation for their pursuit. There's a strong libertarian streak in pilots, perhaps best summed up by another quotation by Charles Lindbergh: "I believe the risks I take are justified by the sheer love of the life I lead." Many don't want politicians encroaching upon the thrilling paradise of sky and clouds, the very essence of freedom. The hinterland looks pretty good from the cockpit at ten thousand feet, and pilots don't want more regulation set by Washington. That's how the argument against runs. While many pilots elect to carry insurance, some choose to risk it and do without despite the best advice of their colleagues, or the urging of AOPA, which offers its members a range of insurance options. One pilot (in an online forum) justified his decision not to carry liability insurance as follows: "I have no wife and kids, only take up a few close friends and family, so I'm not too worried about being sued. Odds are anything that would set off a lawsuit would also kill me, so not a big risk to me." When pushed for his reason, he said he refused to pay the $4,700 premiums he was quoted by the insurance company.

Fellow pilots were swift in their condemnation:

"Please carry liability."

"Having no insurance can wipe out a retirement nest egg in no time. If it is a younger scofflaw, having one's wages garnished for the next twenty or thirty years can be significantly life altering."

"I believe such an attitude is both selfish and unfair. What you're basically saying is that you expect others to cover the cost of any damage or injury you cause."

"If it's too expensive, it simply means you shouldn't be doing the activity in the first place."

As well as it being a public safety issue, most pilots consider taking out liability insurance to be common sense, but just how common is it for general aviation pilots to risk it and forgo insurance? FAA inspectors—effectively the aviation police—keep a stern eye on pilots who might fly without a license, which they admit does happen. Sometimes it's just a lapse, and other times something more fraudulent. However, since there is no federal law covering insurance, it's beyond the FAA's purview to investigate this area. Pilots beyond the thirty-mile veil of a big city might be more inclined to take a risk and go without coverage. Still, according to Marlan Perhus, an FAA official based in the Twin Cities, someone who flies without liability insurance is playing Russian roulette.

The Pogrells' ill-fated dinner date in Portland perfectly illustrated this danger. Sanger brought the story to the attention of the American Association for Justice, the leading organization for trial lawyers representing plaintiffs in the United States. If anyone was bristling with indignation about the consequences of not carrying liability insurance, it was the AAJ's Aviation Task Force, which included some of the most influential and knowledgeable aviation lawyers in the country, among them Mike Slack and Ladd Sanger (of Slack and Davis) and Stuart Fraenkel and Justin Green (of Kreindler and Kreindler). Over time the lawyers had compiled a lengthy list of stories of accidents that resulted in severe hardship to passengers and their families.

The lawyers wanted to use these stories to advocate a change at a federal level. Together they had drafted some language mandating that the FAA "engage in rulemaking to require mandatory minimum insurance" for owners and operators of aircraft flying in the United States. This referred not only to private planes but also to aircraft flying passengers for hire, such as charter flights with no set schedule. They argued that it was in the public interest to impose such a change, which would prevent "callous owners and operators [from] shirking their personal and financial responsibility."

Sometime in late summer 2008, the AAJ received a call from Toby Pearson, who also had a compelling story. He explained that he'd successfully changed the liability laws in Minnesota, faced down big insurance, and now he wanted to try something on a federal level. Did it help that he knew Jim Oberstar, the chairman of the Committee on Transportation and Infrastructure—Mr. Aviation himself—who had taken a personal interest and offered to help?

By changing the law in Minnesota, Toby opened the door to a wider world of aviation accidents and their aftermath. He might have tightened the bolts on aviation insurers in his state, making it more difficult for them to wriggle out of a contractual obligation, but when he zoomed out for a bird's-eye view he could see a problem. A pilot from another state, a neighbor even, could simply fly in—over the cornfields surrounding Mankato, over Duluth, over Grand Marais, or Saint Paul—without any insurance whatsoever. If he were registered out of state, he wouldn't be subject to the laws of Minnesota. How would anyone know the pilot's status until catastrophe struck?

Toby had hoped to transfer what he'd done in Minnesota and apply it on a federal level, but he, too, was startled to learn that there was no mandatory liability law in the United States for general aviation. He'd have to take several steps back to get an all-encompassing federal regulation in place before getting anywhere near a "no void for fraud" clause. As it stood, a pilot could shop around for a place to license his plane, and therefore opt out of any state requirement to carry liability coverage.

Now Toby called Oberstar's office in Washington and spoke with the congressman's chief of staff, Bill Richard, whom Toby had encountered when he'd worked with the National Catholic Rural Life Conference, and even before that during his previous job. Toby reintroduced himself, explaining his story, his recent success in Minnesota, and the fact that early on Congressman Oberstar had offered his help. Richard responded positively, asking for copies of the recently passed legislation, saying that he would "run it up the flagpole," by which he meant have the Aviation Subcommittee staff look into it. Toby felt encouraged. Maybe his victory in Minnesota could grow into something of national importance.

That's when he called Mike Slack at the AAJ. It interested Toby to hear that the lawyers had drafted a bill proposing changes that aligned with his own legislative efforts. Now that Oberstar's office was engaged with the issue, the aviation lawyers arranged a meeting with the congressman in Philadelphia in November. As the lawyers outlined their concerns, Oberstar made a comment that illustrated he understood the incongruity of the situation: An uninsured pilot could potentially fly his own private Boeing 737 aircraft over a city, while a person with a $500 car was required to have automobile liability insurance. It was a succinct summary of the situation. "The fact that a person is required to have insurance to drive to the airport, but is not required to have insurance to fly an airplane is unconscionable," the lawyers responded in a follow-up letter to Oberstar.

The lawyers attached their proposed "Mandatory Minimum Insurance Requirement" language to the letter, which they said would complement the existing law, FAR Part 205, which required commercial airline carriers to have liability insurance. This, they argued, would be effected through a rule-making process, which, they hoped, would circumvent the cumbersome process of passing a new law through an act of Congress. Rule making is typically used by state and federal agencies—having already been granted authority to regulate a particular activity by Congress—to fill in the gaps in legislation.

With regard to general aviation, the lawyers proposed the following:

For aircraft which are not flying passengers for hire, the owner and operator shall maintain third-party aircraft liability coverage for bodily injury or death of persons, and for damage to property, within limits of $300,000 for any one person in any one occurrence, and a total of $1,000,000 per involved aircraft for each occurrence, except that for aircraft with more than 60 seats or 18,000 pounds maximum payload capacity, the owner or operator shall maintain coverage of $5,000,000 per aircraft for each occurrence.

The lawyers also included other elements to their proposal to prevent aircraft manufacturers and airlines from seeking immunity from lawsuits by citing the Federal Aviation Act, which required an aircraft be certified as airworthy. Just because the FAA had signed off on the certificate, the lawyers insisted, did not allow manufacturers and operators to evade responsibility for negligent conduct. Of course, when equipment failed on an aircraft, it could have tragic consequences.

During a trip to Washington, D.C., in mid-September, Toby met with Oberstar in his office. It was terrible timing: The financial markets were in meltdown and the members on Capitol Hill were in crisis mode, running from one meeting to another to try to save the financial markets. It was the beginning of the most important week in American financial history since the Great Depression. Despite the financial red alert, Oberstar made time for his fellow Minnesotan, inquiring about Grace and Lily, and congratulating Toby on his breakthrough with the legislation. Then he had to run.

Later that autumn, Toby followed up again with Bill Richard on the liability issues raised by his Minnesota statute, and the proposal drafted by the AAJ lawyers that they'd sent to Oberstar. Toby also spoke to Stacie Soumbeniotis, who was the deputy chief counsel on the House Aviation Subcommittee, and who listened as Toby outlined his thinking on the subject. With the economy still the primary focus, it was a tough time to engage lawmakers on the topic.

In time, Toby would have his answer. Staff on both the House and Senate Transportation Committees felt that the proposals would meet "very serious resistance," and would "scare up a hornet's nest . . . the committee wasn't going to pick up such an issue." The Republican staff felt that there would be a "jurisdictional problem" if the Transportation Committee attempted to tamper with insurance laws, which fell under the purview of the Banking and Housing Committee.

From Oberstar's perspective, Toby's predicament was a symptom of a much larger problem with insurance regulation in the United States, one that went to the issue of state versus federal control. Oberstar had been mulling this since the initial brunch with Toby at Black Woods in 2004. The congressman saw the roots of the problem as going back to an arcane but significant Supreme Court ruling in 1868, *Paul v. Virginia*. This decision held that the sale of an insurance policy was not an act of commerce and thus not subject to regulation by the federal government. That was the precedent for the next seventy-five years, when it was overturned by another Supreme Court decision in 1944, *U.S. v. South-Eastern Underwriters Association*, which determined that selling insurance across state lines was an act of interstate commerce and therefore should be regulated by the federal government (a power granted by the Commerce Clause of the U.S. Constitution).

The decision was anything but an insignificant event, even though it happened on June 5, 1944, on the eve of the D-Day Normandy landings. It even made the front page of *The New*

York Times the next day, June 6, though it was eclipsed by the booming news from Europe: "Allied Armies Land in France in the Le Havre-Cherbourg Area; Great Invasion is Under Way." Still, a small column underneath saw fit to carry the Supreme Court news, with the headline "Federal Law Held Ruling Insurance." The story continued: "The Supreme Court by a four-to-three decision today held that the insurance companies of the country with assets of $27,000,000,000 and annual premium collections in excess of $6,000,000,000 are in interstate commerce and thus subject to the Sherman Antitrust law. The decision upset precedents which began with a contrary decision by the court more than seventy-five years ago and have been reaffirmed repeatedly since the adoption of the anti-trust law in 1890."

A few weeks after his first meeting with Toby, Oberstar had spotted this "remarkable juxtaposition" in June 2004, during the sixtieth anniversary of the D-day landings, when he traveled to Normandy with members of Congress. He was given a souvenir edition of *The New York Times* from the historic day. "I looked at the front page and saw the headline and my eye flicked over to the left, and sure enough there it was, this insurance issue that is an anomaly of history. It makes no sense that the Congress cannot regulate insurance, which is by definition sold across state lines."

In fact, so unsettling was this 1944 Supreme Court decision, ruffling the feathers of state regulators and insurance industry leaders, that Congress overturned it in 1945 with the passage of the McCarran-Ferguson Act, which preserved the authority of the states and exempted the insurance industry from most federal regulation, including antitrust laws.

That's where the law stood when Oberstar pondered the insurance issues raised by Toby and the AAJ. In his estimation, it wasn't a stretch to say that if this question of federal oversight of insurance had been fixed after World War II, there might have been more options for innocent third parties like the Pearson family.

As 2009 began, with President Barack Obama in the White House and the Democrats with majorities in both chambers, Oberstar considered revisiting the idea. He and his staff reasoned that the FAA could, in its exercise of licensing and certification, impose a general aviation insurance requirement, but that it would have to be in the state in which the pilot or aircraft owner operated, or in the home state where the pilot and aircraft were based. However, they would still bump up against the McCarran-Ferguson Act, which would not permit them to impose insurance requirements beyond those required by the individual states. Trial lawyers, though, continued to argue that since the FAA has exclusive authority for licensing and registration of pilots and aircraft, it could rule that proof of insurance is required for any aircraft registration to be valid.

The Aviation Subcommittee mulled this over informally for a while but decided to wait until the second half of the Obama administration to push further, thinking it would stir up controversy before then. Oberstar believed that the rule change would be challenged by the insurance industry, and probably by AOPA, as they would see it as an additional cost. "However," he added, "I don't think they'd have success at that because it's in their own best interest to have insurance."

Then, in 2010, one of the greatest political upsets in Minnesota history occurred—the eighteen-term Oberstar, the longest-serving member of Congress in Minnesota history, lost his seat to an upstart Republican politician (and an ex-navy pilot), Chip Cravaack. It stunned everyone, not least Toby. It also meant that he'd lost his powerful ally on Capitol Hill. For now, those federal changes would have to wait.

15

RESILIENCY

Carolyn always knew that one day she'd have to return to the cabin on Shady Rest—it wouldn't be a fun trip, but it was a necessary one. And so it was, six summers after the accident, she found herself back on Gunflint Trail, sitting next to her dad, who was behind the wheel. Carolyn didn't say much, moving through a familiar landscape that was now colored with memories and thoughts of that day. Much had happened since then. Her friend Cindy sat quietly in the back. Another two friends, Karen and Carrie (the other two legs of "the three-legged stool" that was their friendship), and Carrie's husband Mark, followed in a second car.

At the trailhead, Carolyn parked the car, and she and Jack took the boat out into the international boundary waters toward the cabin. The others would follow. The last time she'd crossed this water, the day of the accident, her worst fears had yet to be realized. No matter the bright sun, the fact of the crash cast a shadow over this crossing, a sad and reflective voyage for both Carolyn and Jack. It was surely a relief to reach Shady Rest, meet up with their friends, and unwind after such a difficult journey. Six hours. Six years. That night, the group dragged chairs out onto the deck to watch a meteor shower. It was both beautiful and bittersweet, a reminder of the old days at Shady Rest when life was carefree. The endless days of youth, unmarked by tragedy. Things had changed.

"How am I supposed to get through this?" Carolyn had once asked Karen, back in the dark days when grief was strange and stupendous. "If Charlie had died, I could've counted on Kathryn. If Kathryn had died, I could've counted on Charlie. But to lose both of them? How do I get through that?"

Still, Carolyn had come through, had survived this double blow. The second Thanksgiving after the accident, Carolyn had heard a radio show about grief and how the holiday season magnifies its power. For the first and only time in her life, she phoned in to the radio station, feeling compelled to reassure those silently suffering. On the air she said, "For those of you out there going through this, I want you to know, it does get easier. It does turn around. You realize that you still miss the people who aren't with you at the holiday table, but you'll be thankful for the people who are."

Carolyn did find this strength and support in her friends, and especially her nieces, becoming more devoted to Grace and Lily. As Lily recovered, she bonded closely with her auntie Carolyn, often wanting to sit by her, sleep by her, and snuggle with her. (Lily was Carolyn's "snuggle bud.") After all, her aunt was the last familiar face looking down at her as she was sedated at the little hospital in Grand Marais. Early on, Grace seemed to attach herself to Grandma Mar, who, bereft at having lost a daughter, perhaps found her again in her miraculous granddaughters. After Toby and the girls moved away to Saint Paul, Carolyn made sure to take the girls back up to Duluth to see Marilyn and Jack in the summer and during the holidays. Pictures of Kathryn adorned the walls of Marilyn's house. The girls could ask questions, and Grandma Mar could tell them stories of their mom.

Once, after the girls stayed with her, Carolyn noticed that some of her jewelry was missing. She called Toby. "Can you ask the girls if they know where's my jewelry?" she said. Toby checked their room, and sure enough, found a pouch full of bracelets, earrings, and necklaces belonging to Auntie Carolyn. "It's up here!" said Toby. The girls must have packed it into their overnight bag. Although it was never stated, it seemed to Carolyn the purloined purse was a way for Grace and Lily to possess a little piece of their mother. Perhaps the girls had a lingering memory of Mommy putting on her own jewelry, smiling back at them as she fixed her earrings.

In the years after the crash, Carolyn had wanted to make sure the girls knew who their mother was and how much she loved them, and also to impart some of Kathryn's creative passion. It was important for the girls, just as it was important for Carolyn. Their survival had, from everyone's point of view, blessed the family, fending off greater desolation. Even as Marilyn and Jack struggled with the loss of their daughter, their granddaughters provided a constant reminder that life and love would survive. "I think that the fact that the little girls survived transferred all our energies into their welfare instead of mourning our own loss," said Jack Wall. And John, too, Carolyn's brother—the first person to share the news with his mother and with Toby on that summer's day—who'd reeled in the aftermath, found comfort and solace in his memories of taking Grace and Lily fishing on the early-morning lake. For this, he would always be their uncle Walleye.

Sadness would never be fully redeemed, but life would go on. Carolyn of all people understood this well. Her work as a nurse in radiation oncology brought her into contact with cancer patients, including children, which required her to demonstrate not only empathy but also the clinical focus necessary to face the facts. She'd seen firsthand what a cancer diagnosis—the disorientation of such news—could do to a patient, to their family. They would never look at life the same way again. Having lived through a personal crisis, Carolyn understood this all too well. Yet in her work, Carolyn was able to compartmentalize, keeping her life separate from the work at hand, even as she faced people struggling with sickness, sadness, and loss. Although she did it rarely, she once felt compelled to invoke her own story to help a woman who was inconsolable after the death of her husband. Carolyn shared her own loss, of Charlie and Kathryn, and reassured the grief-stricken woman: "It does get easier."

In 2005, Carolyn sold the big house on Mount Curve, where she and Charlie had lived, and moved to a new, smaller home in a leafy neighborhood in southwest Minneapolis, with Kalli, her trusty spaniel, as a companion. Carolyn received no inheritance from the death of her husband. (Because the Erickson estate remains liable for damages, any liquid assets made available after the sale of UltiMed, Charlie's company, would first be used to pay a variety of people, including the Pearsons. Only then would Carolyn be eligible to receive anything for the loss of her husband.) For a long time after the crash, Carolyn never felt she needed to be with anyone else, even as her friends encouraged her to start dating.

Then, in 2008, a friend of a friend introduced her to Chris Farrell, a freelance journalist in his midfifties who'd made his career writing and broadcasting about personal finance for national news organizations. On their first date, Carolyn noticed that Chris was handsome, tall, and intelligent. He was very articulate, with a great speaking voice. It made sense: He was an economics correspondent for shows on National Public Radio, as well as the author of two books on personal finance, with a third in the works. After a cautious start, the two began spending more time together and enjoyed biking, or going to movies and concerts, or just the simple pleasures of cooking at home.

Sometimes Carolyn thought about the life she used to lead— her sailing adventures with Charlie, the thrill and intensity of racing the boat across Lake Superior. She didn't miss that aspect of sailing but still fondly recalled the more gentle moments— dropping anchor off a little island, buzzing ashore in the little dinghy, picking wild raspberries, or just lazing around the cockpit, feeling the soft sway of the boat on the water, looking up at the stars. The lake still called. Yet even as Carolyn felt tempted to sail, nowadays she was less inclined to make it a priority, especially if it looked like rain. She joked that she'd become a fair-weather sailor, but life in her corner of Minneapolis was good. She felt content.

One day, Carolyn decided to drink that bottle of red wine, the Brunello from Tuscany that she'd saved since her fortieth birthday. She invited Karen to join her; together they raised their glasses. The wine had spent more than enough time in the cupboard. As for the other bottle, the one destined for Shady Rest, the Côtes de Rhône that survived the crash, Carolyn has considered drinking it on a special occasion—an anniversary— but is yet unable to find the right moment. "Perhaps it will stay unbroken, unopened forever," said Carolyn. "It made it through the crash. Perhaps it's better to leave it intact. A sort of symbol of our memories or something like that."

In May 2013, Carolyn attended Grace's confirmation and found her niece's rite of passage to be a deeply moving experience. Looking at Grace in her white dress, Carolyn could hardly believe "what a beautiful, strong young woman" she'd become. She thought of Kathryn, and felt her presence at the ceremony. Afterward, back at home, Carolyn found a book she'd once given

Grace and Lily sometime after the crash. It was called *Angel Catcher for Kids: A Journal to Help You Remember the Person You Love Who Died.* The book, designed to help a young person deal with the loss of a loved one, invites a child to record precious memories of the person who died, in pictures and words. It provides certain cues. Carolyn recalled Grace filling it out, with Lily sitting next to her, watching her write.

Weird

Everyone seems to be acting weird. I'm not sure what is going on. Here is what happened . . . *My Mommy died in a plane crash.*

I feel . . . *Confused.*

To make myself feel better I will . . . *remember her.*

Fly

When you died, the real you left your body. I guess that is what some people call the soul of a person. I know the body you left behind isn't all of you.

This is what we are going to do with your body . . . *burn it up.*

Here is where I think your soul is now . . . *in my heart and heaven.*

Last time I saw you I wanted to say . . . *I love you so much.*

I wanted you to say . . . *I love you too.*

I felt . . . *good.*

Now I feel . . . *sad.*

Remembering

These are some of the last memories we shared. (Grace drew a
picture of Kathryn and herself planting flowers.)

One last thing

Before you died, I wish I had told you . . . *the plane was going to
crash.*

Before you died, I wish you told me . . . *how much you loved me.*

Going nuts

I am so mad! I want to scream. To get all these mad feelings
out, I am going to . . . *punch my pillow and then I will hug my Daddy.*

In the years that followed the wedding, Toby, Katy, Grace, and
Lily settled into a new house in the Highland Park section of
Saint Paul. Once the girls started going to local schools, Toby
could finally go back to work full-time. Katy, too, having graduated from the University of Minnesota, began working as a
middle school counselor, where she dealt with the trials and
tribulations of fifth, sixth, seventh, and eighth graders. Toby
continued his work as a lobbyist for the Catholic Health Association of Minnesota in his role as executive director. As such,
he represented the public policy priorities for many different
Catholic health organizations in Minnesota, including hospitals
and long-term care facilities. In 2008, he added another contract to his lobbying with Care Providers of Minnesota, whose
main clients are nursing homes. Obviously, the experience and
skills Toby used to engage the legislature over health care helped
him in his quest to change the aviation liability laws in Minnesota.
The law that Toby changed—defined in Minnesota Statutes
2006, section 60A.081, subdivision 1; Minnesota Statutes 2007

Supplement, section 360.59, subdivision 10—went into effect on January 1, 2009.

In recent years, Toby reflected on the odyssey that had brought him to this point, from the first news of a little plane lost in the fog to the curlicues of the Minnesota governor's signature on a piece of hard-fought legislation, bookends of a life-changing few years. He wrote down a headline for his story—"Resiliency"— characterizing it as a journey of struggle and ultimate triumph. He started it with a quotation from a book, *Strategies for Survival: The Psychology of Cultural Resilience in Ethnic Minorities,* an extract that channeled the words of Dante: "One travels through an underworld of horrors and torments, slowly descending through good and evil, harmony and chaos, ending in the dark woods. Eventually one reaches paradise, but first one must touch bottom and ride the back of a wild, primitive being."

As he wrote about it, Toby defined his achievement in psychological terms as one of resiliency and love. The question of blame, of who was responsible, of liability, he answered by pointing a finger at the inadequate insurance laws, with a goal of effecting change on a federal level, "so that nobody in the nation has to go through what I had to go through."

For John Dornik, the case of *Old Republic Insurance Company v. Erickson et al.* was, he said, "one of the most satisfying accomplishments of my career." When he agreed to take the case, he knew his chances of succeeding were slim to none. Still, he took a chance because he believed it was the right thing to do and, despite the odds, he prevailed on behalf of his client. This experience, he said, forever changed his approach to work. Now, when a case comes along, he's more inclined to ask, "Is this a good person being wronged?," trusting that his fee will take care of itself, as it did in this instance. Toby's example as a dedicated father also inspired Dornik to give greater consideration to his own family, "to work a little less and spend more time with them." At his wife's urging, he sold his vintage Honda motorbike after being knocked down by a car, an accident that left him in the hospital for a few days. Thankfully his injuries were covered by the car driver's mandatory liability insurance.

In June 2011, the U.S. Government Accountability Office began an investigation into the characteristics and trends of general aviation accidents and what the FAA can do to improve general aviation safety. Conducted at the request of the Senate Committee on Commerce, the House Committee on Transportation, and the Aviation Subcommittee, the GAO published its report, "General Aviation Safety," in October 2012. It noted that the FAA had set the goal to reduce the general aviation accident rate per 100,000 flight hours by 10 percent from 2009 to 2018. However, the report added, "given the diversity of the industry and shortcomings in the flight activity data, this goal is not sufficient for achieving reductions in fatality rates among the riskier segments of general aviation." While the report did not explore liability or insurance issues, it did raise the question of how best to assess risk on a national level, noting: "Without more information about the training of general aviation pilots—and not just those who are in accidents—FAA's efforts to identify and target risk areas and population is impeded."

EPILOGUE: BACK TO THE FOREST

The children sit by the fire sharing their stories. They are no longer lost in the million-acre forest. The trees that surround them—sentinels of white birch and pine—stand guard against the circling world. Here, no mishap will overtake them. The fire casts a warm glow, draws the circle of friendship ever closer, warms hands and faces, toasts marshmallows, keeps secrets.

These children have stories to tell. For many here, fire has another legacy beyond the benign snap and hiss of dry wood, shifting and crackling in the orange glow. The firelight flickers in the eyes of the children, who remember the pain, etched into their memories, into their skin, the legacy of burns. They are survivors who gather every summer to share their stories, safely.

Some of the stories are hard to hear. A boy scalded with boiling water. A little girl who fell into a fire pit. Another scorched her palms on the wood stove. The stories are definitely hard to hear, gut-wrenching, but the children tell them as a matter of course, if they want to. A house fire; a car accident; a plane crash that set the trees ablaze.

Grace and Lily come to burn camp every summer with their dad and Katy. It's become an important rite of passage, a retreat from the outside world, a place where cosmetic differences don't matter. The children sit around the fire, away from their parents, smaller kids in one group, older kids in another. Grace and Lily have nearly always been together, but soon Grace will join the older kids. Their stories are intertwined and yet uniquely felt. This must be acknowledged.

This is Camp du Nord, a remote summer camp in the Minnesota Northwoods, on the shores of Burntside Lake. The Pearsons first came here at the urging of Chris Gilyard, whose wise counsel comforted Toby and the girls in the early days at Regions Hospital, when everyone was raw and vulnerable. As Chris anticipated, she met resistance at first about the concept of burn camp. This typically happens with parents of children who've been badly burned.

"I don't want my kids to form their identity around their burn injuries," Toby had told Chris. That was the beginning. However, Chris knew, better than most, the importance of community when it comes to dealing with a lifetime of being scarred by fire. Now they're here. Toby, Katy, Grace, and Lily are veterans of the camp, coming every summer. They are a reassuring presence for other families, new arrivals who may be timid, unsure of how to tell their story, of how to share their trauma with others, describing it for the first time.

It's important. When a child is burned, the whole family suffers. A terrible burn can burden parents and siblings, who experience higher levels of stress when people stare at a disfigured son or daughter. A family worries about isolation and teasing—society's biases and prejudices toward disfigurement. What does it mean to survive something, physical and psychological, like this?

Toby tells his story to a small gathering of parents. He has the five-cent version and the five-dollar version. He's learned how to calibrate the story over the years. He tells the five-dollar version: The plane crash, how Kathryn died, how Uncle Charlie died, and the fairy tale of the children's survival and discovery. When he's finished, moms and dads in the little support group—six or seven families—are crying. But Toby isn't finished yet. He wants to talk about recovery, resilience, finding love again, and forming a new family. He's holding Katy's hand, as if to say to the fearful and the heartbroken, See, don't give up.

Faces are flushed. Maybe Toby has validated someone else's reality, someone else who is still waking up in the predawn gloom, wondering how to make it. As if to say—as poet Louise Glück put it—"At the end of my suffering there was a door."

"I have found that people go to the wilderness for many things, but the most important of these is perspective. They may think they go for the fishing or the scenery or companionship, but in reality it is something far deeper. They go to the wilderness for the good of their souls." So said Sigurd Olson, the American nature writer and environmentalist who fought to protect the wild beauty of northern Minnesota. His words sum up the philosophy of Camp du Nord.

Minnesotans understand this sentiment. The wilderness is a redemptive force, the pine trees, the light, the lakes, and the hundred little islands out there beyond the shore—Beach, Bear, Blueberry, Spirit, Gem, Good Dog, Loon, Lost Girl, and Honeymoon. Grace and Lily love it here. They especially love the water. They are strong swimmers. In this way, they take after their mom, Kathryn, the founder of the Midnight Membership, her secret swimming club. Her daughters are surely one with this piece of family folklore.

One day toward the end of the camp, after the workshops and the counseling are done, parents and children take part in a family triathlon. It's the tradition at Camp du Nord. Lily swims the fifty yards; Toby, of course, runs the half mile, and then

Grace and Katy paddle another half mile in the canoe. During the final stage of the race, a throng of people gathers on the shore—swimmers, runners, counselors—a crush of color and energy urging teammates onward. The wind kicks up, ruffling the surface of the clear, cool lake. Grace and Katy dig deeper, their bright paddles flashing in the sunlight. They're almost there. From the dock, Lily and Toby cheer them on, watching their canoe move toward an invisible finish line on the water.

NOTES AND SOURCES

I was first inspired to write this book after reading Toby Pearson's striking five-page account of his experiences, which he titled "Resiliency." His story clearly had all the elements of a great narrative—a family's journey from tragedy to triumph. This book would not exist without the extraordinary cooperation of Toby, who shared his life story with me in great detail and with great patience. I traveled to Minnesota on two occasions, in 2010 and 2012, where I met Toby, Katy, Grace, and Lily at their home in Saint Paul. I also traveled with Toby up to Grand Marais, where we spent several hours trying to identify the location of the crash site. Over the last three or four years we have spoken on the phone regularly and for many hours. Toby also encouraged many of his family, friends, and colleagues to participate in interviews with me.

Toby was remarkably candid with me about all aspects of his experience, with one exception. He could not and would not discuss the details and terms of his settlement with Old Republic Insurance Company, which is subject to a confidentiality agreement. As Toby's attorney, John Dornik was likewise bound by this agreement. Subject to the agreement, neither Dornik nor Pearson could make any derogatory statements about any of the parties in the lawsuit, including the insurance company. For information pertaining to the case and its settlement, I relied on the extensive court documents, press reports, and also legal precedents to provide context where appropriate.

Like Toby, Carolyn Wall spent many hours talking to me about her recollections of her life before and after the crash. She provided a remarkably detailed account of the day of the accident. In many subsequent scenes also, her recall of the telling detail has made this story all the richer. I met and interviewed Carolyn in New York and at her home in Minneapolis. We also had numerous long telephone conversations. In addition, Carolyn provided me with written recollections in e-mails, and shared with me excerpts from Kathryn's diaries. She, too, facilitated my contact with other members of her family.

John Dornik similarly spent many hours on the phone with me. We also met at his offices during one of my trips to Minnesota. In addition to his recollections of the case and his interactions with Toby Pearson, he explained many of the legal elements that pertained to this case. In particular, Dornik provided legal context to many different aspects of personal injury law, as well as the concepts of material misrepresentation, constructive notice, and subrogation law. He also helped me navigate through the complexities of Minnesota insurance statutes.

Christine Gilyard provided me with great insight into the physical and psychological challenges of being a burn survivor. She took the time to give me a guided tour of the Burn Center at Regions Hospital, which included the visit to the room where I saw the cabinet with the white plaster casts of burn survivors' faces.

Attempts to contact the attorney who represented Old Republic Insurance Company during this case received no response.

Nearly all the interviews in this book were on the record, with the exception of several legal sources I interviewed on a not-for-attribution basis. All the dialogue in this book has been carefully reported. I have endeavored to render remembered conversations accurately, cross-referencing where possible with both interlocutors and/or other participants. While no one's memory is perfect, there have been no material differences between individual recollections. Where I have attributed a state of mind or a feeling to someone, usually that person expressed it directly in an interview. In the rare instance where this didn't happen, the person typically revealed it indirectly to someone else who has vouched for its validity.

I also consulted *The Year of Magical Thinking* by Joan Didion (New York: Alfred A. Knopf, 2005), and *Introduction to Aviation Insurance and Risk Management* by Alexander T. Wells and Bruce D. Chadbourne (Malabar, Fla.: Krieger Publishing Company, 1992).

1. WE FELL OUT OF THE SKY

For the narrative of the crash and its aftermath, I relied on interviews with Dan Anderson, Chief Deputy Sheriff Mark Falk, Rev. William Graham, Patrice Menor, Toby Pearson, Rodney Roy, Carolyn Wall, and Jack Wall.

For background on the Mars encounter: Associated Press, "Mars Makes Closest Pass to Earth in 60,000 Years," August 27, 2003, http://www.nytimes.com/2003/08/27/science/27CND-Mars.html (accessed September 13, 2013).

Sky Dan: Shawn Perich, "Flying with Sky Dan," *Northern Wilds*, www.northernwilds.com/pages/Explore/faces/flying-with-sky-dan.shtml (accessed September 1, 2013).

1971 plane crash: Cessna N9881X, October 26, 1971, in Hovland, Minn., NTSB Identification: CHI83FA225.

Article and book on National Superior Forest: Miron L. Heinselman, *The Boundary Waters Wilderness Ecosystem* (Minneapolis: University of Minnesota Press, 1996); United States Department of Agriculture, Forest Service, "About the Forest," www.fs.usda.gov /main/superior/about-forest (accessed September 1, 2013).

2. TOBY AND KATHRYN

The account of Toby's and Kathryn's early years is from interviews with Rev. William Graham, Rachel Hovland, Greg McGee, Rev. Rene McGraw, Maureen Pearson, Toby Pearson, Beth Peterson, Todd Richter, Carolyn Wall, Jack Wall, and Marilyn Wall. I also relied on Kathryn Wall's diary entries.

For background on Duluth: Anita Zager, *Duluth: Gem of the Freshwater Sea* (Cambridge, Minn.: Adventure Publications, 2004).

For background on Mankato: Greg Breining, "A Sense of Place: The Legacy of Names," *Minnesota Conservation Volunteer Magazine* (January–February 2001), www.dnr.state.mn.us/volunteer/janfeb01 /legacyofnames_sop.html (accessed September 2, 2013).

For Toby's intellectual interests: Paulo Freire, *Pedagogy of the Oppressed* (New York: Continuum International, 1970, revised 2000); Gene Sharp, *The Politics of Nonviolent Action, Part Two: The Methods of Nonviolent Action* (Boston: Porter Sargent Publishers, 1973).

For Reagan's speech: Gerald M. Boyd, "Raze Berlin Wall, Reagan Urges Soviet," *The New York Times*, June 13, 1987, www.nytimes .com/1987/06/13/world/raze-berlin-wall-reagan-urges-soviet.html (accessed September 2, 2013).

For Chris Gueffroy: "Death Strip: Berlin Pays Tribute to Last Person Shot Crossing Wall," *Spiegel Online International*, February 6, 2009, www.spiegel.de/international/germany/death-strip-berlin -pays-tribute-to-last-person-shot-crossing-wall-a-605967.html (accessed September 2, 2013).

Federal Farm Bill: Public Health Law Center, William Mitchell College of Law, www.publichealthlawcenter.org/topics/healthy -eating/federal-form-bill, 2010.

Paul Wellstone: David E. Rosenbaum, "A Death in the Senate: The Senator; Paul Wellstone, 58, Icon of Liberalism in Senate," *The New York Times*, October 26, 2002, www.nytimes.com/2002/10 /26/us/a-death-in-the-senate-the-senator-paul-wellstone-58-icon -of-liberalism-in-senate.html (accessed September 2, 2013).

3. NOT ENTIRELY PLEASED WITH GOD

For the account of the two funerals, I relied on interviews with Karen Allison, Lynn Grano, Greg McGee, Toby Pearson, Todd Richter, Carolyn Wall, Jack Wall, and Marilyn Wall.

Report on ABC News: Sandy Drag, "A Tragedy and a Miracle," ABC Eyewitness News, September 1, 2003.

Jacob Brackman and Carly Simon, "Never Been Gone," C'est Music (ASCAP 59594236) /Maya Productions Ltd (ASCAP 35205711), June 1979.

Why did Kathryn die?: William C. Graham, "Not entirely pleased with God," eulogy, funeral of Kathryn Wall Pearson, September 6, 2003.

Sam McBratney and Anita Jeram, *Guess How Much I Love You* (Somerville, Mass.: Candlewick Press, 2002).

4. CRASH PHYSICS

On the consequences of surviving a plane crash, I relied on interviews with Ben Cauley, Todd Curtis, Ph.D., Stuart Fraenkel, Bill Hansult, Shuronda Oliver, Toby Pearson, and Ladd Sanger.

"Down to the sea": Ovid, *Metamorphoses*, Book VIII, by Sir Samuel Garth, translated by John Dryden, et al. (Charleston, S.C.: Nabu Press, 2011).

Panama plane crash: Deposition of Francesca Lewis, Superior Court, State of California, October 1, 2008; Juan Zamorano, "Rescuer Describes Finding Sole Survivor of Panama Plane Crash," Associated Press, December 27, 2007, http://legacy.utsandiego.com/news/world/20071227-1516-panama-missingplane.html (accessed September 13, 2013); Howie Masters and Myrna Toledo, "Panama Plane Crash: Inside the Amazing Rescue Mission," ABC News, February 15, 2008, abcnews.go.com/2020/story?id=4256875&page=1 (accessed September 2, 2013).

Mammoth Lakes plane crash: Rob Kuznia, "Two Killed in Cherokee Crash Near Mammoth Lakes Airport," *Santa Barbara News-Press*, January 12, 2006; http://www.airtalk.org/two-killed-in-cherokee-crash-near-mammoth-lakes-airport-vt43033.html (accessed September 13, 2013); NTSB report LAX06FA082, August 30, 2007, http://www.ntsb.gov/aviationquery/brief.aspx?ev_id-20060120X00101&key-1, (accessed January 14, 2014).

NTSB regulations: AOPA, 22nd Joseph T. Nall Report: *General Aviation Accidents in 2010*, www.aopa.org/-/media/Files/AOPA/

Home/News/All%20News/2012/December/Ambushed%20by
%20Ice/11nall.pdf (accessed September 2, 2013).

Accident figures reported by the NTSB: National Transportation
Safety Board, Aviation Statistics, Table 1, http://www.ntsb.gov/
data/aviation_stats_2012.html.

FAA figures on general aviation: United States Government Ac-
countability Office, *Report to Congressional Committees: General Aviation
Safety, Additional FAA Efforts Could Help Identify and Mitigate Safety Risks*,
October 2012, http://www.gao.gov/assets/650/649219.pdf (accessed
September 13, 2013).

Caffeine-swilling pilots: Jeff Wieand, "The Whole Truth About Two
Parts," *Business Jet Traveler*, October 1, 2011, http://bjtonline.com/business
-jet-news/whole-truth-about-two-parts (accessed September 2, 2013).

"Crash physics" excerpt: AOPA, *1999 Joseph T. Nall Report: Accident Trends and Factors in 1998*, http://www.aopa.org/Pilot-Resources
/Safety-and-Technique/Accident-Analysis/Joseph-T-Nall-Report
/1999-Nall-Report-Accident-Trends-and-Factors-for-1998 (accessed
September 17, 2013).

Buddy Holly crash: Claire Suddath, "The Day the Music Died,"
Time, February 3, 2009, http://content.time.com/time/arts/article
/0,8599,1876542,00.html (accessed September 2, 2013); Pamela
Huey, "Buddy Holly: The Tour from Hell," *Star Tribune*, February 3,
2009, www.startribune.com/entertainment/music/38282249.html
(accessed September 2, 2013).

Ben Cauley/Otis Redding crash: Chester Higgins, "Eyewitness
Tells of Redding's Violent Death," *Jet Magazine*, December 28, 1967;

Bob Mehr, "Bar-Kays Hornman Ben Cauley Is a Survivor," *The Commercial Appeal*, December 9, 2007, www.commercialappeal.com /news/2007/Dec/09/otis-redding-40-years-later-life-legacy -bar-kays (accessed September 2013).

"People tell me there's a reason": Nick Coleman, "Anguished Father Begins New Life," *St. Paul Pioneer Press*, September 17, 2003.

I also referenced Jane Briggs-Bunting and George Howe Colt, "Anatomy of a Plane Crash," *Life* magazine, April 1988; Juliane Koepcke, *When I Fell from the Sky: The True Story of One Woman's Miraculous Survival* (Green Bay, Wis.: Title Town Publishing, 2011).

5. ONE STEP AT A TIME

For events at Regions Hospital, I relied on interviews with Mark Falk, Chris Gilyard, William J. Mohr, Toby Pearson, and Beth Peterson.

History of burns: George T. Pack, *Burns: Types, Pathology, and Management* (Philadelphia: J. B. Lippincott Company, 1930); Rong Xiang Xu, Xia Sun, Bradford S. Weeks, *Burns: Regenerative Medicine and Therapy*, 1st edition (Basel, Switzerland: Karger Medical and Scientific Publishers, January 2004); I. L. Naylor, B. Curtis, and J. J. R. Kirkpatrick, "Treatment of Burn Scars and Contractures in the Early Seventeenth Century: Wilhelm Fabry's Approach," *Medical History* 40 (1996): 472–86.

Gilyard poem: Chris Gilyard, *Walking Through the Ashes*, copyright © 2002.

Toby in Regions: Nick Coleman, "Anguished Father Begins New Life," *St. Paul Pioneer Press*, September 17, 2003; Mary Lynn Smith, "Amazing Grace," *Star Tribune*, September 17, 2003; "Girl, 4, Shields

Sister in Plane Wreck," ABC News, September 18, 2003, http://abcnews.go.com/GMA/story?id=124760&page=1? (accessed September 17, 2013).

6. A PERIOD OF WILD SUSPENSE AND UTTER BEWILDERMENT
For the investigation into the causes of the crash, I relied on interviews with John Dornik, Mitchell Gallo, Lynn Grano, Dr. Fred Patterson, and Ladd Sanger.

Wentworth Aircraft: Paul Merrill, "South Twelfth," stuffabout minneapolis.tumblr.com, page 233, November 19, 2009, http://stuffaboutminneapolis.tumblr.com/post/250029580/southtwelfth-things-i-learned-about-from-mike (accessed September 2, 2013).

General aviation accidents: NTSB, "Risk Factors Associated with Weather-Related General Aviation Accidents," NTSB Report, September 7, 2005, www.ntsb.gov/doclib/safetystudies/SS0501.pdf (accessed September 13, 2013).

Spatial disorientation explanation: William J. Bramble Jr., "Spatial Disorientation in Large Commercial Airplanes: Case Studies and Countermeasures," 61st Annual International Air Safety Seminar (IASS), Flight Safety Foundation, October 2008; Scott McCredie, *Balance: In Search of the Lost Sense* (New York: Little, Brown and Company, 2007).

Wild suspense: Quoted in B. Melvill Jones, "Flying over Clouds in Relation to Commercial Aeronautics," *Aeronautical Journal*, May 1920. Cited by William J. Bramble Jr.

Spatial disorientation in birds: Hanneke Poot, Bruno J. Ens, Han de Vries, Maurice A. H. Donners, Marcel R. Wernand, and Joop M.

262 NOTES AND SOURCES

Marquenie, "Green Light for Nocturnally Migrating Birds," *Ecology and Society* 13, no. 2 (2008): 47, www.ecologyandsociety.org/vol13/iss2/art47 (accessed September 2, 2013); A. D. Herbert, "Spatial Disorientation in Birds," *The Wilson Bulletin* 82, no. 4 (December 1970): 400–19, Wilson Ornithological Society, http://sora.unm.edu/sites/default/files/journals/wilson/v082n04/p0400-p0419.pdf (accessed September 2, 2013).

Buddy Holly crash: Civil Aeronautics Board/NTSB Accident Aircraft Report, released September 23, 1959, http://www.fiftiesweb.com/cab.htm (accessed September 17, 2013).

Graveyard spiral: Leslie Aulis Bryan and Jesse W. Stonecipher, *180-Degree Turn Experiment* (Urbana: University of Illinois Institute of Aviation, 1954); Melchor J. Antunano, "FAA Pilot Safety Brochure: Spatial Disorientation," FAA Civil Aerospace Medical Institute, www.faa.gov/pilots/safety/pilotsafetybrochures/media/SpatialD.pdf (accessed September 2, 2013); "Graveyard Spiral," cockpitintelligence.blogspot.com, May 17, 2010 (accessed September 2, 2013).

JFK Jr. crash: Mike Allen and Carey Goldberg, "Kennedy's Plane Lost: The Overview," *The New York Times*, July 20, 1999, www.nytimes.com/1999/07/20/us/kennedy-s-plane-lost-the-overview-kennedy-flight-ended-in-a-plunge-radar-shows.html (accessed September 2, 2013).

Missed approach procedure for Grand Marais Airport: NTSB Report CHI03FA296.

Paul Wellstone crash: NTSB, "NTSB Cites Flight Crew Failures in Crash of Airplane Carrying Senator Wellstone, 7 Others," NTSB

Press release, November 18, 2003, www.ntsb.gov/news/2003/031118a.htm (accessed September 2, 2013).

7. THE SECOND LUCKIEST PERSON OF THE YEAR

For the domestic scenes featuring Toby and Carolyn, I relied on interviews with Karen Allison, Dan Anderson, Lynn Grano, Toby Pearson, and Carolyn Wall.

NTSB Report on the Wellstone crash: NTSB, "NTSB Cites Flight Crew Failures in Crash of Airplane Carrying Senator Wellstone, 7 Others," NTSB press release, November 18, 2003; NTSB Factual Report DCA03MA008, http://www.ntsb.gov/aviationquery/brief.aspx? ev_id-20021025X05384&key-1; Bob Collins and Mark Zdechlik, "NTSB Blames Pilots for Crash That Killed Wellstone, 7 Others," Minnesota Public Radio, November 18, 2003, http://news.minnesota.publicradio.org/features/2003/11/18_zdechlikm_ntsbreport/ (accessed September 2, 2013); Jodi Wilgoren, "A Lifetime Together, Serving the People," *The New York Times*, October 26, 2002, www.nytimes.com/2002/10/26/politics/campaigns/26FAMI.html (accessed September 2, 2013).

Gibson interview: ABC News, *Good Morning America* with Charlie Gibson, November 17, 2003.

Anderson meeting: *Inside Edition*, CBS, November 26, 2003.

"Father and Daughter": © 2006 Words and Music by Paul Simon, from *The Wild Thornberrys*, Music Sales America, 2003.

Second luckiest person: Kay Harvey, "The Lucky Ones," *St. Paul Pioneer Press*, December 28, 2003.

8. THE RISK OF LOSS

For the legal issues pertaining to liability insurance, I relied on interviews with John Dornik, Lynn Grano, James Oberstar, and Toby Pearson.

Legal documents: *Old Republic Insurance Company vs. Erickson et al.,* Court file no. 04-1398 (JNE/RLE).

Financial facts on Old Republic: Old Republic International Corporation, United States Securities and Exchange Commission Form 10-K, filed March 11, 2004, http://services.corporate-ir.net /SEC.Enhanced/SecCapsule.aspx?c=80148&fid=2664015 (accessed September 17, 2013); Old Republic International Corporation, "2004 Annual Report to the Shareholders," http://ir.oldrepublic .com/phoenix.zhtml?c=80148&p=irol-reportsAnnualRep (accessed September 17, 2013).

"The accident could ruin him": David U. Himmelstein, Deborah Thorne, Elizabeth Warren, and Steffie Woolhandler, "Medical Bankruptcy in the United States, 2007," *The American Journal of Medicine* 122, no. 8 (August 2009). According to the report: "62.1% of all bankruptcies in 2007 were medical . . . Most medical debtors were well educated, owned homes, and had middle-class occupations."

Most knowledgeable lawmaker: Chad Trautvetter, "GOP House Victory Costs GA Some Allies," *Aviation International News,* November 29, 2010, www.ainonline.com/aviation-news/aviation-interna tional-news/2010-11-29/gop-house-victory-costs-ga-some-allies (accessed September 2, 2013).

Hibbing accident: David Field, "Air Crash Blamed on Pilots, FAA Failures," *The Washington Times,* May 25, 1994.

Lorilei Valeri: Jean Christensen and John J. Oslund, "She's Taking on the Commuter Airline Industry," *Star Tribune*, May 22, 1994.

Safety bill passed: "Rep. Oberstar Airline Safety Bill Passes House 16 Years After Hibbing Plane Crash," *Federal News Service*, July 31, 2010, http://www.fednews.com.

"If it was blind luck": George Lamson Jr., as quoted in the trailer to *Sole Survivor*, a documentary by Ky Dickens, 2012, www.solisurvivorfilm.com.

Galaxy investigation: David Phelps, "Probe Blames Galaxy Crew," *Star Tribune*, January 15, 1986; John J. Oslund and David Phelps, "Passengers Were Victims of FAA's Flaws, Study Finds," *Star Tribune*, January 20, 1986; David Phelps, "Oberstar Cites Indictment, Urges Grounding of Galaxy," *Star Tribune*, September 10, 1986; David Phelps, "U.S. Orders Hearing on Galaxy's Fitness," *Star Tribune*, September 13, 1986; Dan Oberdorfer, "Lone Survivor of Galaxy Crash Settles with Airline," *Star Tribune*, January 15, 1987; David Phelps, "Galaxy Case Brings Airline-Oversight Reforms," *Star Tribune*, November 20, 1987.

9. FALLING THROUGH CLOUDS

For the accounts of Grace, Lily, and Toby's emotional progress, I relied on interviews with William C. Graham, Molly Hans (formerly Molly Stein), Constance McLeod-Hvass, Teri Metry, Toby Pearson, Beth Peterson, and Marilyn Wall. I also relied heavily on the excellent, detailed notes taken by Molly Stein during the sequence of interviews she conducted with the Pearson family in the spring of 2004, which allowed me to re-create the scene inside the house.

Molly Stein's impression of Grace and Lily: Jacob and Wilhelm Grimm, "Snow-White and Rose-Red," *Household Tales* (New York: P. F. Collier and Son, 1909–14).

"The brain never forgets": Bessel A. van der Kolk, Alexander C. McFarlane, and Lars Weisaeth, eds., *Traumatic Stress: The Effects of Overwhelming Experience on the Mind, Body and Society* (New York: The Guilford Press, 1996).

Moving from Duluth/kite festival: Steve Kuchera, "Cities Help Soothe Accident's Wounds," *Duluth News Tribune,* September 3, 2004; Steve Kuchera, "Girls Still Recovering from Plane Crash," *Duluth News Tribune,* September 26, 2004.

10. DISCOVERY
For revelations about the crash, insurance policy, and emotional progress, I relied on interviews with John Dornik, Constance McLeod-Hvass, Teri Metry, Katy Pearson, Toby Pearson, and Rodney Roy.

Erickson crash: NTSB Reports CHI03FA296: Factual Report, Probable Cause (http://www.ntsb.gov/aviationquery/brief.aspx? ev_id-20036903X01453&key-1), Full Narrative; Steve Kuchera, "Investigation Finds Pilot Flew Too Low on Airport Approach," *Duluth News Tribune,* September 3, 2004.

Transcript of deposition: *Old Republic Insurance Company vs.Erickson et al.,* exhibits court file no. 04-1398 (JNE/RLE).

11. THIS ISN'T GOING AWAY QUIETLY
For the hearing, I relied on interviews with John Dornik, Toby Pearson, and Richard Snyder.

Letters from Steven Klebba: *Old Republic Insurance Company vs. Erickson et al.*, court file no. 04-1398 (JNE/RLE). Exhibit 6.

Malpractice lawsuits: Anupam B. Jena, M.D., Ph.D., Amitabh Chandra, Ph.D., Darius Lakdonvalla, Ph.D., and Seth Seabury, Ph.D., "Outcomes of Medical Malpractice Litigation Against U.S. Physicians," Archives of Internal Medicine, June 11, 2012. archinte .jamanetwork.com/article.aspx?articleid-1151587 (accessed January 14, 2014).

Automobile statute: 2012 *Minnesota Statutes*, 65B.49 subd.3(3)(a); Minnesota Department of Commerce, "Aviation Insurance Private and Commercial," Court file no. 04-1398 (JNE/RLE) Exhibit 7.

Hatch announcement: Conrad deFiebre, "It's Official: Hatch Is in the Race for Governor," *Star Tribune*, October 25, 2005.

Court hearing: Certified transcript from the record of proceedings, *Old Republic Insurance Company vs. Erickson et al.*, Court file no. 04-1398 (JNE/RLE), October 24, 2005.

"Our day in court": Glenn Howatt, "2 Years After Plane Crash, Insurer Takes Family to Court," *Star Tribune*, October 25, 2005.

"Multibillion dollar insurance company": Greg Vandegrift, "Father of Injured Girl Still Fighting Insurance Company," KARE 11, October 25, 2005, www.kare11.com/news/news_article.aspx?storyid=109822 (accessed September 2, 2013).

Bill Hewitt, "Who's to Blame?" *People*, November 21, 2005.

Judge's ruling: *Old Republic Insurance Company vs. Erickson et al.*, Court file no. 04-1398 (JNE/RLE).

12. OLD HIGHWAY 61

For the background on the mediation and the marathan, I relied on interviews with John Dornik, Constance McLeod-Hvass, Katy Pearson, Toby Pearson, and Richard Snyder.

Henry Wadsworth Longfellow, *Hiawatha: A Poem*, Electronic Text Center, University of Virginia Library, http://etext.lib.virginia.edu /etcbin/toccer-new2?id=LonHiaw.sgm&images=images/modeng& data=/texts/english/modeng/parsed&tag=public&part=all (accessed September 2, 2013).

Leading up to the hearing: Joseph R. Simone, "Liability Insurance—A Move to Limit the Excess Judgment Damages Award," *Fordham Law Review* 42, issue 2 (1973): 440, http://ir.lawnet.fordham.edu/ cgi/viewcontent.cgi?article=4576&context=flr (accessed September 2, 2013); *Short vs. Dairyland Insurance Company*, 334 N.W.2d 384 (Minn. 1983).

Wrongful death damages for Kathryn's lost relationship: *2012 Minnesota Statutes*, 573.02.

Settlement estimate/seven-figure exposure: Glenn Howatt, "2 Years After Plane Crash, Insurer Takes Family to Court," *Star Tribune*, October 25, 2005.

The mediation: William L. Ury, Roger Fisher, Bruce M. Patton, *Getting to Yes: Negotiation Agreement Without Giving In* (Boston: Houghton Mifflin Harcourt, 1992); Therese L. White and Bill White, "Managing Client Emotions: How a Mediator Can Help," Chapter

45, *AAA Handbook on Mediation*, American Arbitration Association, JurisNet, L.L.C. 2010; Jeff Kichaven, "'Is That All?' Attorneys Need to Prepare Their Clients for Mediated Settlements," *Los Angeles Daily Journal*, March 8, 2000.

Subrogation: Michelle Andrews, "Adding Insult to Injury," *Smart Money*, July 1, 2000; Vanessa Fuhrmans, "Accident Victims Face Grab for Legal Winnings," *The Wall Street Journal*, November 20, 2007, http://online.wsj.com/article/SB119551952474798582.html (accessed September 2, 2013); Paul Halpern, "Law Professor Roger Baron on Subrogation and Erisa Reform," *Lawyers and Settlements*, April 6, 2008, www.lawyersandsettlements.com/articles/employ ment/roger-baron-interview-10364.html# (accessed September 2, 2013).

13. THE WRONG DAVID

For the account of Toby's efforts to change the law, I relied on in- terviews with Joe Atkins, Mike Beard, Michael Paymar, Toby Pear- son, Yvonne Prettner Solon, and Christine Zimmer.

Msgr. Habiger: Pamela Miller, "Obituary: Rev. James Habiger Was a Voice of Wisdom and Compassion," *Star Tribune*, October 22, 2012, www.startribune.com/local/175334711.html (accessed Sep- tember 2, 2013); Doug Hennes, "Monsignor James Habiger, Social Justice Champion, Dies," University of St. Thomas *Newsroom*, October 9, 2012, www.stthomas.edu/news/2012/10/09/monsignor -james-habiger-social-justice-champion-dies/ (accessed September 2, 2013).

History of Bill H.F. No. 772: Minnesota State Legislature, https:// www.revisor.mn.gov/bills/bill.php?b=House&f=HF0772&ssn=0 &y=2007 (accessed September 17, 2013); Final bill that passed,

Chapter 182—H.F. No. 2898: An act relating to insurance; regulating claim denials under aviation liability coverage amending Minnesota Statutes 2006, section 60A.081, subdivision 1; *Minnesota Statutes 2007 Supplement*, section 360.59, subdivision 10.

"That broke the dam": Transcript of the Minnesota House of Representatives, Commerce Committee Hearing, H.F. 772, March 6, 2007.

Meetings in the State Capital: Aviation Insurance Meet and Confer Group, Report to Legislature, January 7, 2008, http://www.leg.state.mn.us/docs/2008/mandated/080023.pdf (accessed September 17, 2013).

14. AN ANOMALY OF HISTORY
For the federal context of aviation liability law, I relied on interview with Stuart Fraenkel, James Oberstar, Toby Pearson, and Ladd Sanger.

McCartney crash: American Association of Justice, letter to James L. Oberstar, Attachment III; NTSB Accident Report SEA05FA105.

Ladd Sanger, "Mandatory Aviation Insurance: A Domestic and International Perspective," Slack and Davis, LLP, Dallas, Tex., www.slackdavis.com/wp-content/uploads/2009/05/mandatory_aviation_insurance08.pdf (accessed September 2, 2013).

Lindbergh quotation: Richard L. Collins, "Risk? You Bet," *Flying Magazine*, October 2001.

Pilot's Online Forum: www.pilotsofamerica.com/forum/archive/index.php/t-39057.html (accessed September 2, 2013).

AAJ proposed language: American Association for Justice, letter to James L. Oberstar, Attachment I.

Most important week in American financial history: James B. Stewart, "Eight Days," *The New Yorker*, September 21, 2009.

"In time, Toby would have his answer": Quotations are from James Oberstar.

McCarran-Ferguson Act: Jonathan R. Macey and Geoffrey P. Miller, "The McCarran-Ferguson Act of 1945: Reconceiving the Federal Role in Insurance Regulation" (1993), *Faculty Scholarship Series*, paper 1605, Yale Law School Legal Scholarship Repository, http://digitalcommons.law.yale.edu/fss_papers/1605 (accessed September 2, 2013); Charles D. Weller, "The McCarran-Ferguson Act's Antitrust Exemption for Insurance: Language, History and Policy," *Duke Law Journal* 1978, no. 2, http://scholarship.law.duke.edu/cgi/viewcontent.cgi?article=2664&context=dlj (accessed September 17, 2013).

Oberstar's defeat: Albert Eisele, "Oberstar's Stunning Defeat Makes History," *MinnPost*, November 4, 2010, www.minnpost.com/politics-policy/2010/11/oberstars-stunning-defeat-makes-history (accessed September 2, 2013).

General aviation safety: United States Government Accountability Office, *Report to Congressional Committees: General Aviation Safety*, October 2012.

15. RESILIENCY

For summation, I relied on interviews with Karen Allison, John Dornik, Toby Pearson, and Carolyn Wall.

Dante quote: Quoted in Peter Elsass, *Strategies for Survival: The Psychology of Cultural Resilience in Ethnic Minorities* (New York: New York University Press, 1992).

EPILOGUE: BACK TO THE FOREST

On the burn camp, I relied on interviews with Christine Gilyard, Katy Pearson, and Toby Pearson.

Poem: Louise Glück, "The Wild Iris," *The Wild Iris* (New York: Ecco, 1993).

Sigurd Olson quotation: Quoted in the Camp du Nord, YMCA of Greater Twin Cities handbook, www.ymcatwincities.org/_asset /1bxdbp/dn_Camper-Family-Handbook-2013.pdf (accessed September 2, 2013).

ACKNOWLEDGMENTS

I am grateful to my friend Nathaniel Bellows for bringing this story to my attention. An accomplished writer and poet, he immediately recognized the potential of this compelling tale of one family's journey back from tragedy. Nathaniel encouraged and inspired me to keep going when I wondered whether I could actually write a book. I am indebted to him for all his support. The story first came to Nathaniel's attention via our mutual friend, Sue Shea, a high school friend of Toby Pearson. Without that association, the seeds of this project would never have been planted.

I am fortunate to have a wonderful agent in Cheryl Pientka, at Jill Grinberg Literary Management. I am very grateful for her enthusiasm, belief, and tenacious work on my behalf. It's especially serendipitous that we were classmates at Columbia University's Graduate School of Journalism. Thanks also to Laura Ross, who brought me into the agency, helped steer the book through its proposal stage, and at whose suggestion I benefited from the astute and excellent eye of Rosemary Ahern.

George Witte, my editor at St. Martin's Press, encouraged me from the first and guided this book to completion with great sensitivity. Thanks also to Kate Ottaviano and everyone on the St. Martin's Press team for their diligence.

I am tremendously grateful to James B. Stewart, a writer who sets the standard for contemporary nonfiction narrative. I've been fortunate to serve as his research assistant on two of his books, *Heart of a Soldier* and *Tangled Webs*. These experiences provided me with a front-row seat, privileged view of how a master journalist reports and writes a nonfiction book. I found inspiration in his example, his advice, and his friendship.

Thanks to Charles Kittredge for reviewing the sections of the book dealing with flight; his pilot's eye no doubt saved me from technical slips.

Bruce Dorval listened to me talk about the book. His insights helped deepen my understanding of the psychological dynamics of this story.

My friend Megan Beatie offered her invaluable professional help with marketing and publicity advice. I'm very thankful for her support, encouragement, and her love of books. And to think, our literary association goes back to *Wuthering Heights*!

I'm fortunate to have so many good friends and colleagues whose support and understanding is crucial during such a long-haul endeavor as this. I'm grateful to them all, particularly Louise Barder, Andy Blackman; Evgeny Bogomolov, Susan Buttenwieser, Stephen Coplan, Julien Davoust, Andy Edwards, Ben Finane, Anyo Geddes, Priscilla Gilman, Katina Houvouras, Bruce Kelly, Jane Kittredge, Michael Marray, Dean Olsher, Mary Pender-Coplan, Annie Petrova, Miuda and Chuck Tayman, and Dilyana and Guerguan Tsenov.

Thanks to my family back in England for their love and support: my parents, Judith and Norman Fowler; my sister Abby, her husband, Steven Hartley, and my niece, Tess Florence Hartley; my sister Louise, her husband, Kent Dreadon, and my nephew and niece, Charlie and Nell Dreadon. Also thanks to the Dushkin family—Danail, Nataliya, Kaloyan (in Indianapolis), and Natalia (in Lancaster).

And finally, Magdalena Dushkina, whose emotional support for me never wavered, even when I was otherwise preoccupied with "working on my book." She has my deep love and gratitude. I couldn't have done this without her.